WHEN NICKELS
WERE INDIANS

SMITHSONIAN SERIES OF STUDIES IN NATIVE AMERICAN LITERATURES

Arnold Krupat and Brian Swann, Series Editors

The Smithsonian Series of Studies in Native American Literatures, in recognition of the importance of indigenous literary cultures, represents a long-term commitment to their appreciation and understanding. Envisioning itself as actively shaping and being shaped by the many developments in this growing field, the series will publish books that offer a wide range of perspectives on Native American literatures.

The series is under the general editorship of Arnold Krupat and Brian Swann. Its editorial board members are William Bright, Alfonso Ortiz (Tewa), Kathryn Shanley, Gerald Vizenor (Chippewa), and Ofelia Zepeda (Tohono O'odham). The editorial advisory board is listed below.

All royalties from the series publications will be donated to the Native American Scholarship Fund.

WHEN NICKELS WERE INDIANS

AN URBAN, MIXED-BLOOD STORY

PATRICIA PENN HILDEN

Illustrated by Anne-Marie Hamilton

SMITHSONIAN INSTITUTION PRESS
Washington and London

Grateful acknowledgment is made for permission to reprint excerpts from the following copyrighted works: Louise Erdrich's "Indian Boarding School: The Runaways" reprinted with permission of Holt, Rinehart & Winston, © 1984 by Louise Erdrich. Buffy Sainte-Marie's "Now That the Buffalo's Gone" reprinted with permission of Gypsy Boy Music. Excerpts from *Indian Country Today* reprinted with permission of Native American Publishing, Inc. Excerpts from Paige St. John, "American Indians Hurt by College Admissions Abuses," *Detroit News*, April 12, 1992, reprinted with permission of the *Detroit News*.

COPY EDITOR: Gregory McNamee
PRODUCTION EDITOR: Duke Johns
DESIGNER: Janice Wheeler

Library of Congress Cataloging-in-Publication Data
Hilden, Patricia.
    When nickels were Indians : an urban, mixed-blood story / Patricia Penn Hilden.
        p.   cm. — (Smithsonian series of studies in Native American literatures)
    Includes bibliographical references and index.
    ISBN 1-56098-601-8 (alk. paper)
    1. Hilden, Patricia. 2. Indians of North America—Mixed descent—Biography. 3. Los Angeles (Calif.)—Biography. I. Title. II. Series.
E90.H55A3   1995
979.4'9300497—dc20   94-48466

British Library Cataloguing-in-Publication Data is available

Manufactured in the United States of America
02 01 00 99 98 97 96 95   5 4 3 2 1

∞ The paper used in this publication meets the minimum requirements of the American National Standard for Information Sciences—Permanence of Paper for Printed Library Materials Z39.48-1984.

For permission to reproduce illustrations appearing in this book, please correspond directly with the author. The Smithsonian Institution Press does not retain reproduction rights for these illustrations individually, or maintain a file of addresses for photo sources.

FOR JONATHAN STEINBERG
AND FOR ALL OUR RELATIONS

Grandfather used to say of a thrifty friend: she was so tight she could squeeze a nickel until the Indian sat on the buffalo

CONTENTS

PREFACE

"ANYWAY, THAT'S WHAT I THINK."

This work is what I think, nothing more, nothing less. But I have had inspiration from many people who shared with me the burden of trying to write a "collective autobiography," a story of all of us, mixed bloods, cross bloods, Gerald Vizenor's "Earthdivers." It is a pleasure to name them—some named as well in the notes, some not, but all important.

Timothy Reiss has, again, read, criticized, and caught infelicities and contradictions. More than that, he has accepted with love and generosity what it is to live aside from these things. Without him, nothing could have been written.

Jonathan Steinberg, once again, was a constant, inexhaustible source of tolerance, acceptance, friendship. Thus, the dedication.

Two important groups of friends come next. Those who have stood by me through a difficult time in New York, whose presence is felt all through this text, our informal "talking circle," must come first. They include, first and most important, Harriett Skye. Her story is hers to tell, but with typical generosity, she shared the perspective of one Standing Rock Lakota woman with this mixed-blood writer. She gave us all both her wisdom and friendship as she makes her courageous way through New York University, completing her B.A. and M.A. degrees with considerable distinction, and making a prizewinning film along the way. I am lucky to have such a companion. Chris Eyre, a Cheyenne-Arapaho mixed-blood filmmaker, close to finishing his masters degree in New York University's Tisch School of the Arts, also slips in and out of this text. We have talked a lot. I have intuited more, I hope correctly and inoffensively. The third person whose presence is nearly constant here was introduced to me by my husband, Timothy Reiss. She is Shari Huhndorf, a mixed-blood Yup'ik and native of Alaska, who is writing her dissertation in NYU's Department of Comparative Literature. As is always the case in my experience with Native students, I have learned at least as much from her as she from me. Perhaps the most important thing she has tried to teach me is to recognize the extent to which every single issue, every single mode of under-standing, differs both among cultures (here, European-American and tribal) and among individual inhabitants of those cultures. Each of us, she reminds me, what-ever our blood, speaks for one person only.

And all the others, too, from tribes all across the Americas, live in this work and I thank them: Dean Bear Claw, Waukena Cuyjet-Kapsch, Bill Gossett, Carol Kalafatic, Cathy Paschal, Miryam Yataco, and, occasionally, Moises Pulido and Bob Lancaster. Angela Gonzales, who is supposed to be my "apprentice" (in the Word-craft Circle of Native American Mentors and Apprentices, directed by Lee Fran-cis) has taught me much. Fredy Roncalla, another New York Wordcraft Circle member, has also added his voice here. Last, but not least, is Lloyd Oxendine, one of the first Native people I met in New York. His ideas (though he may not recognize what I have done to them) can be heard all through this text. I hope he likes it.

A second group, no less important to the writing of this work, is the 1992 class of graduate students at Emory University's Graduate Institute of the Liberal Arts. They raised many of the issues explored here, and I hope their intelligence shows through my prose. Some, because they are "my" advisees, or because their work lurks close to mine here, have been more involved than others. These include Ellen Arnold and Janet McAdams (both of whom always came up with citations I had lost as well as many suggestions for the text itself), John Howard, Mthembu Msingatheni, Tina Johnson, and—indefatigable clipper of newspapers, constant friend, stimulating intellectual adversary—Rainier Spencer. Others whose ideas appear here (for better or worse) refracted through the prism of my mind are Makungu Akinyela, Ronald Gordon, Jeffrey Leak, Nancy Koppelman, Heidi Nord-berg, David Pratt, Kerry Soper, Lisa Swanson, and Akinyele Umoja. My co-teacher of that seminar on "Cultural Displacements" shares some blame here: Shigehisa Kuriyama was the first to understand about "crossing." His presence made life at Emory more than just bearable. He taught me a lot and acted as a much-needed brake on my excesses. Irena Grudzinska Gross, too, helped the original formula-tion of this project; she introduced me to Europe's Indians, especially to the Win-netou she had encountered in her Warsaw secondary school. Patricia White Mc-Clanahan, for some time the only other Indian at Emory, also speaks in the ideas contained here, as do several undergraduate students from across the years, most particularly Grant Besser, Dwayne Jefferson, Brendan O'Connell, Allison Shana-han, and Dusty Porter.

Arnold Krupat, good friend, tireless, elegant guide into the world of Native American scholarship, and most recently painstaking and perceptive reader of the raw manuscript, was most immediately responsible for suggesting that I turn a colloquium paper into a book—and that I give it to the series he is editing with Brian Swann. Because the profits (such as they may be) go to a scholarship fund for tribal people, in this case to the "Displaced Homemakers Scholarships" administered by Harriett Skye through the Association on American Indian Affairs, I (in consultation with my sister, who agreed to illustrate the book) decided to submit the work to this series.

While I wrote, many, many people read, corrected, suggested. Of the members of my immediate family, my father, William Penn (who prompted his memory into action whenever I asked), my brother, and my sister, I can say little more than what appears here. Their stories, I believe firmly, are theirs, not mine, to tell or not to tell. To the extent that my sister's story is also mine (we were born only a year apart), she has generously allowed me to use it—and indeed, to expand my own by including her memories and to enrich the text by illustrating it with her drawings. My aunt and uncle, Phyllis and Robert Penn, unearthed old photographs and memories. My father's cousin LaRue Bettis added her efforts, sending me documents and photographs as well as her memories of her aunts and uncles, one of whom was my grandfather. (Memories from the "white side" of the family were shared with me by my warm and hospitable uncle and aunt Robert and Elise Hall and by my cousin Victoria Lindsay Levine, who also generously shared her work on Choctaw music.)

And then there are those who took the time to undertake those critical readings of the rough draft that are essential to every kind of writing. Julio Ramos, whose ideas have long shaped mine (though perhaps not to his satisfaction), read the whole thing. Alfred Arteaga, too, broke into his own work as poet and literary scholar to read the entire manuscript. Our subsequent discussions of childhood years in Los Angeles and of the vexed problems of *mestizaje* go on, building a much-valued friendship. Betty Louise Bell added the perspective of a mixedblood novelist and Native woman. I am grateful for her generous reading, as well as for that of Brian Swann. Joseph Fracchia undertook to add the Socialist Humor Party point of view, reading a substantial part of the book. Maarten van Delden made some important points early on in the project, as did Jane Caplan, still the best reader of manuscripts I know.

There are also those without whose work this kind of book would not be possible. A talk by Kamau Brathwaite—whom I first met when he invited Timothy

Reiss and me to hear him deliver the T. S. Eliot lectures at the University of Canterbury in 1990—on the discovery of the poetic sounds appropriate to a Barbadian voice (captured in his *Barabajan Poems*), first sent me back in time to my own Native world. Since then, nearly every conversation, and certainly every reading of his poetry and prose, have left their marks on my own thinking. Ngũgĩ wa Thiong'o's story of the development of his Kikuyu identity in the face of colonialist Kenya was another valued prompt to my own thinking, as his work, his politics, and his friendship, together with that of Njeeri wa Ngũgĩ, continue to be. The story of Elvira Colorado's discovery of her roots in San Luis Potosí also opened paths into memory, and I thank her for sharing it.

In addition to Arnold Krupat and Brian Swann, my most immediate intellectual inspiration is Gerald Vizenor. As the quantity of citations in this book will suggest, his is the work that to my mind best captures the experiences I am trying to narrate here. There is no imitating him: he is truly sui generis. But he always challenges, always inspires. His willingness to read and comment on a rough draft of the manuscript suggests his grace and generosity to other scholars. I only hope that I have succeeded in using his intelligent and detailed suggestions to good effect, though I suspect he will remain dissatisfied.

Last, let me say what this work is *not:* a trendy theoretical exploration of "identity," a work of "pure" historical scholarship (the world to which I am much more accustomed). It *is* a book addressed to my students and to all those other mixed bloods out there, similarly disconcerted.

.1.
GETTING OUT OF DODGE

 In 1904 the Superintendent of Indian Schools bluntly summarized the difference between the prospects of non-Indian children, supported by both family and community, and those of tribal children, born without what she saw as the necessary social conditions of American experience. "The Indian," declared Miss Estelle Reel, "must make a place for himself in life."[1] With this held firmly in sight, teachers throughout the nation's Indian Schools shouldered their onerous burden, trying to kill the Indian to save the man for his solitary struggle through the life dictated by America's ruling ethos. Miss Reel's teachers' handbook, in prose that blended turn-of-the-century greed with lachrymose sentiment, dictated for Indian children the essential lesson: (white) American life was an optimistic but single-minded pursuit of material wealth.[2]

As Miss Reel's carefully detailed *Course of Study for the Indian Schools* made clear to all her teachers, she shared the assimilationist ideal that shaped progressive era attitudes toward America's indigenous population. Like her most prominent predecessor, Carlisle Indian School founder Richard Henry Pratt, she was convinced that only when every tribal child rejected the dangerous and inhibiting anti-individualism of Native American culture would he or she make "progress" against "inherited weaknesses and tendencies . . . [including] habits of aimless living, unambition, and shiftlessness."[3]

There were but two paths to such assimilation: "early" adoption "into a good white family," or a lengthy period of "outing," when young students from Indian boarding schools were placed with local families, where, in addition to engaging in every kind of domestic or farm work, Indian children would experience "the stir of civilized life" and "compete with wide-awake boys and girls of the white race." Only thus, living in complete isolation from other Indian people, carefully imitating all the habits of host families (except the habit of using Indian children as cheap domestic labor) could Indian children "imbibe the traits of character" which were necessary for success in the capitalist labor market.[4]

Happily, such radical efforts bore less fruit than the reformers hoped. All over America's Indian Country, in cities and towns, on reservations and off, traditions of community continued to link Indian lives. Even those whose blood was mixed, whose connections to tribal communities were sporadic, and who everyday walked the precarious path between antithetical cultural worlds found life-giving support in what soon became "pan-Indian" worlds of Native survival.

This work recounts one such life, that of an urban child of mixed blood. It grows out of what every mixed blood recognizes as a kind of cultural schizophrenia: on the one hand, one lives a "white" life, slipping into the mainstream of habits, expectations, actions, language almost without disguise. Only occasional jarring incidents—when East Coast friends show hurt when one recoils, Indian fashion, from the hugging greeting *de rigueur* in New York, when women friends decide the friendship is unequal because one does not share intimacies—recall the presence of dissimilar inheritance. At the same time, however, the mixed blood is constantly aware of every alien characteristic, every gesture, activity, confidence that offends what one is inside. And that concept, *inside*, is all-important: there, distant from everything around, is where one lives most of the time. Indeed, for urban mixed-blood children, growing up among aliens,[5] the only rest is with other mixed bloods. Only there is there no suspicion: *you* aren't Indian; *you* aren't white.

Writing autobiography, an act that flies in the face of most Native American tradition, pushes this dilemma in one's face. On the white, European side, the heir to modernist self-examination plunges into such inspection of memory with some enthusiasm and fearlessness. On the other, however, the utter reticence of Native America blocks not the remembering, but rather the telling of it to outsiders.

A dilemma.

But once again—and how often this has been the case in my fifty years—Indians ride down the hill to the rescue. From the first moments of this project[6] the work has been a communal one: not only family members but also friends from within and without Indian Country cheerfully—but sometimes testily—joined their efforts to mine. Like other Native American "autobiographical writing," then, this work is written not only by *my* two selves—European-American, Native American—but also by a dozen other individuals, some related by blood, some by race, others by a friendship born from the shared experience of "cultural displacement." In this sense, it is a small fragment of evidence suggesting that efforts to "Americanize" tribal people have failed. In keeping with centuries of tradition, and however mixed their blood, however easily they move in the mainstreams of American life, few Native Americans make either a life, or the story of that life, alone.

For she was the maker of the song she sang.
Wallace Stevens

[A woman is] an eternal dissident in relation to social and political consensus, in exile from power, and therefore always singular, fragmentary, demonic, a witch.[7]
Julia Kristeva

However marginal to the centers of power, both Wallace Stevens's "maker" of order at Key West and Julia Kristeva's fragmented woman bear a clear European identity; whether modernist heir to the Enlightenment faith in reason's mission to "order" the world or more recent denizen of the chaotic world of the postmodern, the subjects here share a certainty in the formal value of telling (or writing) a tale of the self, a conviction and practice passed on through generations of confessors and self-storytellers.

For traditional Native America, on the other hand, both the autobiographical form and its philosophical bases are alien. The unseemly focus on the individual self, her emotions, thoughts, actions sited at the center of the autobiographical universe, defies both Native tradition and much current Native practice. In fact, until the first European interviewers arrived in Indian Country, determined to "record" the lives of individual native people (usually medicine people, leaders, artists, and others deemed worthy of outside attention), the practice of publicly telling the whole of one's own life was virtually unknown.[8]

The tradition may have begun to die rather early on, however. Gerald Vizenor, characteristically reluctant to accept the conventional wisdom, notes that William

Apess's early nineteenth-century work, recently published as *On Our Own Ground*, "could be the first autobiography by a tribal person, and distinct from those 'autobiographies' of Indians written by others." It appears, then, that at least some tribal people quickly joined the rush to record their lives for a literate posterity.[9]

As interest in a vanquished foe became more and more general across an increasingly white, increasingly European America, "Indian autobiographies" began to proliferate. The "told-to" tale was born as "collectors" of Indian lives made their way to Indian Country, seeking authentic Indian experiences with which to titillate an expanding public curiosity. Such tales, moreover, often carried the impress of scholarship. With the spread of "social science" in the second half of the nineteenth century came the belief that studies of human societies—especially those "lower down" the ladder of "civilization"—could yield important information (and profits from its dissemination) about Americans' special claims to world rule.[10]

By 1855 these "told-tos" had achieved sufficient public familiarity to ensure that Henry Wadsworth Longfellow would begin "Hiawatha" with an assurance to his readers that all the information contained in the poem was "authentic":

> Should you ask me whence these stories
> Whence these legends and traditions,
> I repeat them as I heard them
> From the lips of Nawadaha
> The musician, the sweet singer . . .[11]

The epic poem, too, became Native testimony: on the one hand, a Native informant, on the other, a European American author.

> *Mother learned to recite "Hiawatha" during her years at the experimental junior high school for gifted children run by the University of California at Los Angeles. For her, as for many non-Indian Americans, Hiawatha's life represented "Indian Country, eastern USA," and when she recited it to us as a typically eccentric bedtime lullaby, she assumed a teacherly air, suitable for the transmission of information about her Indian children's eastern relations.*

In a rather different sense, any mixed-blood autobiography is similarly hydra-headed. Written by one who, in the words of one recent scholar, "genetically and cognitively straddle[s] two worlds," it becomes a tale described, discussed, debated, and directed by one side of the self to the (sometimes skeptical) other.[12]

This schizophrenia, furthermore, is not exclusive to mixed-blood autobiographers. A curious duality similarly vexes historical accounts of relations between

Europeans, their descendants, and Indians in North America. The soldiers who killed—often slaughtered—Indians, for example, sometimes claimed in later years to have "admired" their victims' "nobility," despite the obvious injustice of their deadly relations with the subjects of their "respect." E. Jane Gay, sent with Alice Fletcher to help "allot" reservation land to Nez Perce people in the 1890s, observed a typically bizarre and schizoid activity at a government school for Nez Perce children. "On Decoration Day," Gay wrote, "we happened to see the procession of school children going out to decorate the graves of the soldiers who slew their fathers in the Joseph war. . . . The procession limped disjointedly along," she added, "the children doing their best to keep step with no fife or drum, but singing 'John Brown's body lies a-mouldering in the grave' and bearing aloft, tied to a fish pole, a diminutive flag, borrowed, for the occasion, from the school Doctor."[13]

The unsettlingly double-sided sensation that accompanies the writing of a mixed-blood autobiography, then, finds still more prompting in virtually every historical or (contemporary) account of the complicated relations between the tribal world of native North America and the universe created by the heirs of the invasion and conquest.

To complicate matters still further, years of feminist politics shape this re-telling as they have shaped the life. At the heart of these politics, moreover, lies one practice of autobiography: the political method of what Italian feminists name *autocoscienza*, self-discovery by tracking, as truthfully as possible, the biographical, historical, and biological details which together constitute and shape the gender of each individual. As I once more practiced a familiar mode of *autocritique* here, however, it became at the same time both a concentration and a dissolution of the mixed "identity" I had carried so long. In other words, it quickly became more than a straightforward narrative produced by the clashing of two cultures, American and European, two classes, *haute bourgeoise* and proletarian, or two genders. It was at the same time a growing realization of the fluidity of the certainties with which most individuals confront life.[14]

I was discovering that like the postmodern universe, I too, am an eternally, multiply divided subject, waking these writing mornings at the top of a city high-rise in the midst of more concrete, steel, and plastic than one can readily imagine, from a sleep filled with dreams of home, echoes of my grandfather, chiding, calling.

In one persistent dream that troubled my nights for many weeks as I worked on this project, I tried to stifle Grandfather's voice, crying with alien New York City aggression and insistence: "I *do* know, I *have* done it, I am *trying!*" But he refused to be banished by daylight. Even as I woke he lingered, reaching across the wide shallow waters of the Clearwater River. I could see him standing on the pebbled ground by his small, incongruously European wood house. Shaded by a tall cottonwood tree, he couldn't hear me, I could not reach him. For many months, I began every New York City morning with the mantra of Louise Erdrich's lines: "Home's the place we head for in our sleep."[15]

Then my friend Harriett Skye banished the dream with a story. I had been reasoning, as I trod my despair through Washington Square Park three times a day with my dog, that it was caused by concrete, fences, and squalor, or perhaps by the madmen crying their paranoia at a studiously blank passing woman. But Harriett instantly knew the real cause: the restless spirits of unmourned dead, six thousand paupers' bodies lost beneath the "park"—buried in an old potter's field, banished from collective memory. Her knowledge ended the dream. And now I, and all our Indian friends in New York, understand.

But as is common in these cases, I remain hesitant to say these things to non-Native people—though I realize that if I couched them in a European language, in the Kristeva manner, in the words and notions of postmodern psychoanalysis, for example—they would accept what I was telling, and smile with understanding. As it is, other than a few embarrassing occupants of the sadly vacuous New Age universe, most of those I know—intellectuals all—would, I fear, react to my telling of these events with their modern version of lines fixed in memory by the New Critical English faculty at Berkeley in the early sixties, Alexander Pope's, "Lo, the poor Indian! whose untutored mind / Sees God in clouds, or hears him in the wind."[16]

This is not to argue, however, that Indian identity—or even a mixed Indian and white identity—is unproblematic, especially, perhaps, in the context of the contemporary United States, where an intense race-consciousness is so completely dependent on locating and defining those "races" which constitute "others" against whom the "white" measures itself. The identity of European North America has from the first moments of conquest depended upon comparisons grounded in race—glimpsed on the other side of a looking glass where skin colors and features (from which "character" is read) represent American "anti-identities."

This is an essay about one of the images seen in those mirrors—the Indian one. But as I have already suggested, it is not a simple, albeit "backwards," reflection.

Rather, it is one quickly mediated by others peering into the same mirrors; all my relations—those related by blood, those adopted over the years—have joined in, sending torn memories and photos, each of which has altered and shifted the once-certain "facts" that structure my life.

Then, too, the mirrors have their own history. From the first hours of the "encounter" between Europeans and Native people, the invaders made and re-made a fun-house hall of mirrors.[17] At various historical moments, an Indian, peering into those glasses, watched her face change into a startling variety of shapes. By the middle of the twentieth century, when my story begins, this process of construction and reconstruction had become so complex, so politically fraught, that the likelihood of discovering which was the "real" mirror, showing a "true" reflection, had become very nearly impossible.

At the same time, this is a simple story, of how two little girls, growing up in Los Angeles after the war, learned to recognize themselves in two mirrors—one reflecting a white self (a less complicated act for the blue-eyed sister), the other showing "Indianness" as it was then transformed and captured in the popular memory of their world, their neighborhood, their family.

L . A .

West beyond Gallup is the endless stretch of highway that runs through Arizona and, blessedly, crosses the Colorado River and the Sierras, whence it descends into paradise. That's where dwell all good things like movie stars and farmers' markets and fresh fruit stands and Disneyland and housing developments by the square mile . . . and the rich white people who aren't Anglos . . . but just people just Americans. . . . You know, like in the surveys and the polls. As in "people do this and that" or "people think such and such." . . . As in almost everything said by Americans and supposed by them to be about the human race.
    Paula Gunn Allen[18]

Los Angeles . . . is not a mere city. On the contrary, it is, and has been since 1888, a commodity, something to be advertised and sold . . . like automobiles, cigarettes, and mouth wash.
    Morrow Mayo[19]

Growing up in Los Angeles from the mid-1940s through the 1950s, our identity was never in question. To be European-American was to be part of my mother's people, "old L.A.," members of the Daughters of the American Revolution who had roundly rejected us—mixed race, working class, definitely not "one of them." To be Indian, on the other hand, however disgraceful to elderly white relations,[20] or indeed, even to some on our Indian side, was to participate in two worlds wonderful to a child of that place and that time: first, we came from America's hereditary nobility—the band of Nez Perces who declined the dishonor of treaties and reservations, Chief Joseph's band.[21] Our father, we learned proudly, is an offspring of a member of that proud Wallowa band. This group's intractability in the face of the "benevolent" efforts by land-stealing settlers to remove them to a reservation preserved them, forever, in the collective historical memories of those who ultimately forced them off their land.

These efforts were recounted in stunningly ambiguous and characteristically schizoid prose by General Nelson A. Miles, who led the final battle against the anti-treaty Nez Perces. The General later recalled, "up to that time it had been their boast that no Nez Perce had ever taken the life of a white man though it could not be said that no white man ever killed a Nez Perce." The surrender, he continued, included "over 400 Nez Perce people," together with their life-giving appaloosas, described neutrally by Miles as "captured stock . . . from the hostile camp." The soldiers were thrilled by their "victory" over the small and starving group of men, women, and children, a victory won by "sacrifices far away in a weird and lonely land, skirting along the base of cold and cheerless mountains."[22] (One cannot help but wonder why those who found Montana so "weird, cold, and cheerless" thought it necessary to kill and capture those who loved that land before they returned to the presumably "unweird" and cheery world of the eastern United States, long since vacant of most of the original inhabitants.)

The Nez Perce band's collective resistance, the outcome of a considered, long-held policy of non-collaboration by members of the Joseph group,[23] doomed them to the punishment of exile to Indian Territory. There, in what is now Oklahoma and Kansas, my relations married other Indians and remained, even after the handful of survivors of Joseph's band were allowed to return to the Northwest—most to the Colville Reservation in Washington State. As if unaware of the devastation wrought by disease and starvation among all the tribes imprisoned in Indian Territory, General Miles remembered the Nez Perces' years of sorrow in highly self-justificatory prose: "They remained there [in Indian Territory] for a few years, and the low malarial district and climate in which they lived caused sad havoc in their ranks. In a short time they had lost nearly fifty per cent of their number by death. I frequently and persistently for seven long years urged that they be sent home to their own country [*sic!*], but not until 1884, when I was in command of the Department of the Columbia, did I succeed in having them returned west of the mountains to near their own country, where they have remained at peace ever since."[24]

Thus the family's tribal identity is not straightforwardly "Nez Perce," but is, more accurately, an experience of "pan-Indian" life, in this case one that began early, among a "rag-bag" of recalcitrant Indians, all paying for their resistance to settlers' encroachment by exile in Indian Territory. For us, descendants of those exiles, tribal identity was stored and shared in stories and ritual practices, not in the daily collective experiences of those who continued to inhabit tribal society, albeit usually on reservation land.[25]

RELOCATION

My father's family moved to Los Angeles in the 1920s, cut off even from the pan-Indian community of Missouri, Oklahoma, Kansas. Thus "relocated" before government-instituted "relocation," the family joined "Indian Country, L.A.," one writer's name for the then-small Indian community in Los Angeles.

There were not many tribal families in Los Angeles in those years, probably never more than about five thousand.[26] But those there were, at least those who acknowledged their Indianness, shared the growing urban culture of "pan-Indian" America. And although one scholar of the phenomenon in Los Angeles has claimed that this culture was primarily "fostered and shaped by the non-Indian stereotype of the High Plains warrior,"[27] and despite the fact that we were growing up amid the very industry whose filmic portrayals of Indians disseminated just this stereotype of the mounted, male, warrior Indian throughout America, this was not our version of "pan-Indianness." Doubtless because of the nature of the L.A. Indian community in those years, our "Indians" were a curious and eclectic combination of off-reservation, mainly Southwestern tribal people. For us—and I think for all our Native friends—the conflicts between Navajos and Hopis, the ways of the Pueblos, and the history of Apache resistance represented what we knew of Indian Country.[28]

In this community, we enjoyed a high status as members of the increasingly legendary Joseph band.[29] At the same time, my father, like many others of his generation, grew up determined to assimilate, to "pass." Even though this determination was softened by pride in his specific identity as a member of the Wallowa group, that pride carried some problems. To some extent, at least, it rested upon some beliefs derived not from history, but rather from romantic stereotypes of "hero" Indians. We children, for example, learned from the words accompanying the photograph of Joseph's 1877 surrender to the United States cavalry at Snake Creek that he, unlike "other Indians" did not speak the "Tonto-talk" of stereotype; instead, he spoke poetry. By age five or six, all of us children could proudly recite Joseph's moving words as he handed his gun to General Howard's representative at the end of a 1,700-mile trek in search of new land for the Wallowa Valley band and their thousands of appaloosas:

Tell General Howard I know his heart. What he told me before I have in my heart. I am tired of fighting. Our chiefs are killed. Looking Glass is dead. Toohoolhoolzote is dead. The old men are all dead. It is the young men who say yes and no. He who led the young men is dead. It is cold and we have no blankets. The little children are freezing to death. My people, some of them, have run away to the hills and have no blankets, no food; no one knows where they are—perhaps freezing to death. I want to have time to look for my children and see how many I can find. Maybe I shall find them among the dead. Hear me, my chiefs. I am tired; my heart is sick and sad. From where the sun now stands, I will fight no more forever.[30]

> Vine Deloria has examined Joseph's speech together with those of other famous leaders whose words are anthologized whenever Indians are in fashion. He has concluded, "The speeches contain a startling similarity from beginning to end. Speeches by Senecas in the 1790s have the same tenor and outlook as speeches by Nez Perces and Yakimas given a century later. . . . Unless one is intimately familiar with a certain selection, one cannot identify which Indian chief said what." Moreover, "if one were to take the anthologies seriously, one would visualize the Indians of old as a collection of poets who happened to be present while the army was fighting some nebulous group in the hinterlands."[31]

Weirdly, although Tonto himself consistently spoke the broken speech expected of stereotyped Indians, the Lone Ranger and Tonto together once drove Cochise into a similarly poetic speech, and it, too, was a speech of "surrender": "You and Tonto are trusted friends of Cochise," the Apache leader announced during one radio show. "You speak words that are honest and wise. Because of you I shall sit in council with the soldier leaders. Go, my brothers, and tell them the words Cochise has spoken."[32]

We were thus front-row participants in the dreams of every child of our time and place. As much 1940s popular culture suggested, especially in movie country,

My father on his graduation day.

everyone wanted to be what we *were:* Indian kids. We were part of a much sought-after, heavily romanticized image of America's past.

The object of such mass cultural longing was not desired unambiguously, how-ever. In *Love Medicine*, Nector Kashpaw notes that to most Americans, "The only interesting Indian is dead, or dying by falling backwards off a horse."[33] My sister recalls our ironic, "second hand" participation in the creation of less positive In-dian stereotypes. Both with our parents and later with friends old enough to drive, we frequently visited a movie site, Vasquez Rocks, a natural rock outcropping made safe for movie "cowboy and Indian" fights by a covering of soft "false" rocks. Like the television and movie actors who worked there, we played endless games of "cowboys and Indians," falling in terrible mock deaths onto the spongy red "rocks." In these games, as my sister recalls, "we were always exposed to the 'good guys' fighting and winning battles with 'renegades.'" Although we usually willingly played the Indians, we knew that renegades were not "good" Indians, who cheerfully accommodated themselves to "civilization," but rather rare outlaw Indians who continued—pointlessly—fighting the always-white heroes. These were exiles from their own communities, Indians run "amok."[34] The narrative of the myth we repeatedly reenacted was little more than a retrospective denial of collective American guilt.[35]

Despite such contradictory experiences, we learned to be (renegade?) Indians in the epicenter of America's popular culture industry: L.A., where reality *was* "hyperreal," where everything, to employ Umberto Eco's formulation, was already absolutely fake. Every reality—from the curious landscape of desert and sea (then still in transition from the rocky, dusty, live-oak shaded trails and hills of every western movie to the pavement and glass "Lalaland" of today) to our friends and relations in the movies (Uncle Hartley, for example, traded his Navy pilot's uniform for chaps, boots, and lasso to become the first Marlboro man) was "more than," was artifice.[36]

Recently Los Angeles bested itself: "Universal Citywalk," a two-block long shopping mall built at Universal Studios, replicates favorite tourist destinations—Hollywood Boulevard, UCLA, and even that absurd historical gesture toward the city's unsavory history—and racist present—Olvera Street. Yet even here, the Lalaland zeitgeist complicates matters. The architecture critic Herbert Muschamp, explains how Citywalk "summon[s] up sinister visions of a city pushed one step further toward becoming a totalitarian theme-park version of itself":

Actually, the reality that has been edited out . . . is less unsettling than the reality that has been included. The façade [of a U.C.L.A. building] is fake, but real grades are handed out in the extension school inside. The Rossi lighthouse is fake, but the Puck pizza is genuinely worth the trip. There is also an authentically excellent bookstore. And fakery is relative here. Signs for real shops and restaurants along this make-believe boulevard are mixed with signs hung out purely for visual pleasure. Though the signs are fake, the pleasure is real. . . .

Citywalk's artifice doesn't isolate it from the city. It's the cement that joins the two.[37]

Even before its incarnation as that contemporary heaven, the shopping mall, Los Angeles was the North American earthly Paradise. When my sister and I represented Los Angeles at the 1959 Girl Scout Roundup in Colorado Springs, we and our fellow Girl Scouts were literally mobbed by girls from all over the United States and the world. They wanted the signed movie-star pictures we had carted with us (donated by friends of the disk-jockey father of one of our group) as souvenirs representative of our home city. (They stood up well next to the "swaps" brought by others, including bits of anthracite carried by girls from the coal valleys of Pennsylvania, places whose grit we could not even imagine.) But more than that, they wanted *us*. Native "Angelenas" all (European-American, Chicana, Indian), we had not until then realized the extent of the world's love affair with Southern California.

Still, even for its "native daughters," Los Angeles was fantasy, a myth created and recreated by the city's ruling elite, sometimes to attract tourists, sometimes to fool a restive populace. When in 1894 a Pullman strike drew federal troops to occupy the city, Charles Lummis, then an editor at the *Los Angeles Times*, "organized the first Los Angeles Fiesta as a public distraction." "The next year, the class war temporarily abated," continues Mike Davis's account, "he orchestrated the Fiesta around a comprehensive 'mission theme.' . . . Its electric regional impact can only be compared to the national frisson of the contemporary Columbia Exposition in Chicago."[38]

Within a few years, few natives of the city—not even those whose heritage was being stolen, Los Angeles's Chicano community—thought of the annual Fiesta Days as anything but a public expression of deeply rooted "traditions," born in the benevolently recalled "Mission Days."

More recently, on the other hand, Luis J. Rodriguez describes a reappropriation of those days by Chicanos from "the [invisible] other side of town." Recalling his childhood, Rodriguez writes:

The San Gabriel Mission held an annual 'Fiesta Days' celebration to honor the Spanish-Mexican heritage of the area . . . directed for the most part at the Anglos who commemorated a past they were never part of, as if the Mexicans were long dead and mummified, while in the present they'd rather spit on a Mexican than give him the time of day. . . . During the daytime, the *gabachos* put on phony sombreros, rode rhinestone-garnished horses, and applauded one Hat Dance after another. But at first hints of nightfall, they skulked back to their walled estates in San Marino or Pasadena. . . . At night, the fiesta belonged to the Mexicans.[39]

In our childhood time, only a handful of visiting Europeans, exiled to Los Angeles by Europe's wars or lured by movie money, avoided the seduction of the rewritten history. Among the latter was Erich Maria Remarque, who worked in the movies in the 1930s. Fearful of a transformation effected by overexposure to the constant climate of artifice, he warned: "Real and false were fused here so perfectly that they became a new substance, just as copper and zinc become brass that looks like gold. It meant nothing that Hollywood was filled with great musicians, poets, and philosophers. It was also filled with spiritualists, religious nuts, and swindlers. It devoured everyone, and whoever was unable to save himself in time, would lose his identity, whether he thought so himself or not."[40]

Despite the fact that the federal government's postwar Indian policy was again directed at extermination by assimilation, the schools in the city of Los Angeles, assured of the effectiveness of the laundered past, remained solidly "proto-multicultural," promoting a Hollywood version of "America's heritage." In an elementary school where most children were of European background, we two Penn sisters enjoyed two privileges: on Quaker day we were Quakers. On Indian day, we, along with Doug Bison and Jimmy Safechuck, were Indians (all from warrior tribes: Nez Perce, Lakota, Apache). Only our friends Margaret and Irene Rocha enjoyed greater attention because in what was cozily known as "Spanish California" (or "Alta California," the part "we" got, distinct from "Baja California," the part we didn't get—until tourism seized it for "us"), they represented Mexico (usually tamed into "Old Mexico"). Cinco de Mayo (suitably de-historicized, and thus rendered outside politics) was an enormous school fiesta: everyone donned "Mexican" dress and danced "Mexican" folk dances.

The "folk dances" we were taught included shawl dances, performed solely by the girls. But no one told us that these were native dances; rather, we believed they were somehow "Mexican." And because no one told us that Mexicans, and most certainly our friends the Rochas, were likely to be similarly mixed-blood people, we did not make the connection until we began to go to powwows where we realized we already knew how to shawl dance.

For us, those Indian friends were essential. Then as now we met them with a sudden, secret knowledge: "You *too*?"[41] It was a realization that linked us together, close as siblings. And somehow all my teachers knew; Doug Bison shared my double desk semester after semester. Doug—tall, blond, brown-eyed and square-faced—wasn't one of the brainy kids, not one of the dreaded "smart kids" orga-

Best friends. Left to right, top: Irene Rocha, Patricia and Anne-Marie Penn; left to right, bottom: unidentified, Raymond Rocha, Bill Penn, and Margaret Rocha.

nized into the Bluebird Reading Group whose weekly tedium drove me mad. ("Please may I be excused? I'll take a test! I've *memorized* Spot and Puff, Dick and Sally and Jane . . .") But he and I were kin, and so he cared for me, painstakingly clearing my desk, pulling wads of torn and crumpled paper from the back corners, smoothing them flat, puzzling over my discarded poems and comments, saving them. (Where are they now? Home in the Black Hills, with Doug?)

I wondered if Jimmy Safechuck was similarly tending my sister one grade ahead.

That there was anything problematic about an American Indian identity did not dawn on us until we were old enough to begin to grasp two facts about American life: first, that the practice of American racism depended on physical signs, read by a stereotype-dependent mass audience[42]; and, second, that although Americans adored Indians (didn't they name their athletic teams after them?) they preferred them dead, vanished, collected (especially by the camera), and stored away as the "material culture" of ethnographic museums.[43] In the movies, Susan Ball, Jeff Chandler, Victor Mature, Sal Mineo, and dozens of other non-Indians wore the visual signs (identified and "captured" by so many hungry lenses at the close of the nineteenth century) that meant "Indian."[44] In "real life," a site rarely visited by consumers of Native people, the United States government continued its habit of ignoring, controlling, moving Natives onto reservations, off reservations, into boarding schools, out of boarding schools, and on and on, depending upon the whims of changing anthropological fashion or the nation's "need" for more Indian land or labor. In the immediate postwar years most reservations, in a "real life" we encountered only in the form of survivors who made it to the Los Angeles Indian Center of the 1950s, were places of despair, suicide, disease, cultural confusion, and poverty. On their borders (and in their midst on "checkerboard" reservations, splintered into separate plots of land by government policies so that many reservations were soon owned by both Indians and non-Indians[45]) white and red clashed in a manner similar to that the American imagination usually located in the South, a region that played a much less positive role in the collective psyche than did the West.[46]

INDIAN COUNTRY, L.A.

This slightly muddled, urban, Native identity, then, never a problem for us as children, gradually assumed a public, social dimension. And we began to learn—slowly—the elements that rendered this non-reservation Indianness "political." Moreover, the racism that underlies the culture of the United States (born in genocide; born from the active denial of every "value" the invaders claimed to cherish, not least the sanctity of property-ownership, or the crucial importance of "freedom of religion," both of which, our textbooks reiterated, were the [Plymouth] bedrocks of "America") began increasingly to confuse my identity. Although assured by race-identifiers (as well as by joking family references to "our Indian princess") that the shape of my face, the distance from cheekbone to chin, the "shovel" nature of my teeth (such were that era's "scientific" signifiers of Native blood) assured my "Indianness," my light skin, blue eyes, and brown hair together signaled something else to a world that also saw—and pointed out—my sister's "Mongolian eyes" (an anthropology professor's public designation of her eyelids' epicanthic folds), her darker skin, hair, eyes.

That there were confusing ironies in my "whiteness" and her "redness," however, quickly became apparent. Because I was "mainstream" according to the phys-

Dad, me, and Anne-Marie.

ical markers of race in that place and time[47] my Indian blood, however aggressively claimed, was easily contained as "heritage," as a movie of my colorful past. I was, in effect, a vanished Indian, and safe. There was no chance that the civilized, blue-eyed "I" *they* saw, even sitting alone on horseback on a ridge silhouetted against a distant sky, would suddenly be joined by thousands of screaming, murderous sister warriors, riding down the mountain to slaughter terrified "settlers."[48] At the same time, for my grandfather, whose flight from his Indian boarding school had not entirely protected him from the processes of "forced assimilation,"[49] I was a perfect granddaughter, wide of blue eye and utterly devoted to the dark-skinned 6'4" giant who filled our world and that of many of our envious, movie-addicted friends. He chose both of us sisters: I, like my mother "whiter than white," she with a more equivocal racial identity—to hear his stories, to learn the traditions, to know who he was, who his people were. So there we were, the "whitest" child with the "reddest," becoming warriors—defined in the Onondaga language as "those who bear the burden of the bones of the ancestors."

WE LEARN TO BE INDIANS

It must be said at once that my assumption of Native identity was not untroubled by difficulties. My sister reminds me that when Mother, anxious to teach us our cultural identity with every means available to her, bought us beading materials so that we could learn to bead belts and headbands, she immediately set to work, beginning to weave her white, turquoise, and red beads on the tiny weaving frame. I started much less enthusiastically, playing with the beads rather than stitching them neatly onto the warp. Soon Anne Marie had finished her work—meticulously, flawlessly. Her first headband I remember perfectly. As for mine, however, Anne sighs, "You never finished yours."

My sister also remembers that "on one of our regular Sunday visits to Grams and Gramps, once all the other grownups were busy doing other things, Gramps took us into the spare bedroom where he dragged a small chest out of the closet, carefully opened it, and pulled out a feather headdress. I remember it was very old. I think he said it was his father's. But he was very secretive about showing it only to us while none of the other grownups was around. There were other things in the chest, too—a drum and things I didn't recognize—but in my mind's eye, I can only see clearly the beautiful old feathers."[50]

Another time, after we had moved "out to the Valley," Grandfather decided to teach us to make bows and arrows, and to shoot with them. He brought the wood, feathers, and gut, and the knife he carried with him everywhere (even in the pocket of the blue suit he donned for Sunday visits to our ugly San Fernando Valley housing tract). He took us out to the back yard, where for several hours we helped him make us our own bows and feathered arrows. Soon we were learning to shoot them, fitting the grooved arrows into the string, drawing the bow as far as we could, and sending the beautiful arrows toward an old bale of straw he had set up against the back fence. But we never had time to achieve any skill; our

Grandfather, Anne-Marie, Bill, Grandmother, and me.

mother, alert to our extended absence, appeared with horror on her face at the dangers of shooting unprotected wood arrows. She did not forbid us our bows or our arrows. But she did manage to find flat rubber circles to fit over the arrows' tips—circles that were meant to adhere to the "target" she painted on the fence, but which, to our intense disappointment, only flopped unsatisfactorily at contact, dropping the arrows into the dirt.

These were not, of course, the "burdens" of our ancestors and living relations, though we soon began to learn these as well. But before undertaking a more collective look at the "state of Native America,"[51] let me continue the family saga a bit further, disentangling from the mass of memories some few of exemplary importance to this learning of identity.

As the stories of beading lessons and arrows suggest, it was to our "ultra-white" mother that we children owed the constant reinforcement of our pride in our Native background. Although we did not understand it at the time, my father belonged among the assimilationists, those who believed in the efficacy of an Americanizing "melting pot." That Dad wanted to melt into the broader American society is not surprising, of course; even a cursory glance at the attitudes toward Indians reflected by commonly read history texts suggests that few students of In-

Mother in 1937.

dian blood would have learned any pride in their past. Indeed, by the 1930s, few school textbooks even mentioned Indians at all.

My father does not recognize himself in this portrait, though, Indian fashion, he is willing to entertain the possibility that it is accurate. Recently he told me that far from believing in "assimilation," he had simply never wanted to think that he had been given anything in his life because of his race, rather than because of his achievements. He wanted always to be taken on his individual merits. I am glad to record this alternative view here, a view that I have, on and off and with certain variations, shared. Of course his conviction is grounded in that very American ideology that pretends all people have the opportunity, in the school-disseminated myth, to become president. It overlooks the obvious fact that white middle-class and upper-class males routinely reward others of that ilk, usually making exceptions only for those people of color, or those females of all races, who pose no threat to their complete hegemony and who often willingly act as tokens. Moreover, as my generation quickly learned, not claiming one's race does not mean that "they" don't perceive instantly that one is "not one of them." But this desire to be judged "on the content of one's character," rather than "by the color of one's skin," to quote Dad's contemporary, Martin Luther King, does not quite make Dad the "assimilationist" I have long assumed him to have been.

If my father and his brother did learn anything about being Indian, it was primarily that they should be glad they had successfully joined the "civilized" non-Indian world.[52] Los Angeles was, moreover, a very special segment of that world. As Robert Milliken declared from the president's office at Cal Tech, in the 1920s, "[Southern California] is today, as was England two hundred years ago, the westernmost outpost of Nordic civilization [with] a population which is twice as Anglo-Saxon as that existing in New York, Chicago, or any of the great cities of this country."[53]

To ensure such purity, many of the housing subdivisions that began to blanket the desert landscape in the postwar years included "restrictive covenants." Mike Davis notes that "a compliant Superior Court regularly found Blacks as well as Filipinos and Native Americans in contempt for occupying homes within restricted subdivisions or blocks."[54] Although the subdivision to which we moved in 1949 was certainly too proletarian for any such classy appurtenances, it is not surprising that Indians who discovered they could successfully "pass" might keep their real racial identity hidden.

And of course for most Native Americans, "passing" has always been relatively simple, especially as most have some "white" (even "Anglo-Saxon") blood, so that various markers of Europeanness show up in families fairly frequently. Too, the image of Indians promoted in popular culture was sufficiently distant from "real life" to allow considerable leeway for those who desired to move away from the Native world into mainstream "white" culture. True, there was an American language to be learned—or, more accurately (given the fact that only a minority of urban tribal people still spoke their own languages) accent, vocabulary, and patterns of behavior. But these can be learned in public school, especially when encouraged at home.

How easy it is for Indians to pass became evident to me when I showed a film called *The Exiles* to a graduate seminar. The film is about Los Angeles in the 1950s and documents the lives of young Apache people, some "relocated" from reservations, some born in L.A. The immediate reaction of most of the students, who were African-Americans, European-Americans, Africans, and Asians, was surprise that the people in the film did not look "Indian." Except for a night scene showing drumming and dancing—on a hill along Mulholland Drive not far from the one frequented by James Dean's rich friends in *Rebel Without a Cause*—the students insisted they would not have known they were looking at a film about Native Americans. One student thought the protagonists looked vaguely Vietnamese. Only two African students said they recognized them as physically different from most Americans they had encountered.[55]

Thus it was my mother who took seriously—too seriously, we often thought as we were dragged into yet another museum, sent off to yet another reservation, handed yet another Indian book—the task of conveying our identity. Her efforts were unceasing. Conscious, perhaps, of her family's devotion to their important, race-establishing lineage, our mother decided to undertake an equivalent Indian family tree with which she imagined my sister and I could defy the Anglo ruling class and her family. Thus for many months my grandfather found his Sunday repose shattered by Mother's questions: "Who was your mother? your father? your grandfather? your grandmother?" To her frustration, and our amusement, he usually gave as little information as possible—a name here, a name there, and little else. After many such Sundays, Mother's pad of paper boasted sparse information. Undaunted, however, she insisted that we learn one fact about which she felt certain: that Grandfather was descended from "a great chief" of the Nez Perces. For a long time, her confusion about the story he actually told her—albeit in tantalizingly brief fragments—led her to insist that we were the great-grandchildren of the Lakota chief Sitting Bull. Of course, it was to Sitting Bull's camp in Canada that Chief Joseph's band tried to flee. Grandfather was, evidently, reluctant to name Joseph—who was not his relative anyway, but rather the leader of the band to which his family belonged.

When my sister and I were about three and four years old, and still living near downtown, my mother discovered the Southwest Museum.[56] Immediately we were thrust into the 1939 Ford and driven there, where we were, I am sure from dozens of later events if not from memory, introduced to the museum's director as "my Nez Perce children." Left to wander while Mother discussed volunteering (the métier of women of her class, after all), I soon discovered a glass case that contained, just above floor level, the mummified body of a Native girl. I lay down on the floor in front of it, trying to see if we were the same size. My mother discovered me lying there regarding the child's body wonderingly, my sister wandering (terrified) some distance away. Although I was more fascinated than upset, the image stayed with me—and with my mother, who immediately joined a campaign to have the body repatriated and buried by the child's tribe.[57]

The likely "collector" of the child's body was the museum's first director, Charles Lummis, influential editor of the *Times*, "Mugwump," diligent promoter of the myth that became Los Angeles. Even more than he loved his version of the city's "Mission" past, Lummis loved Indians. He had first met them—or their myth—when he traveled west from Ohio in the 1880s. He was at ease in the Southwest because, in the words of one biographer," by 1884, virtually no solid vestige of frontier Indian barbarism remained, and Charles Lummis . . . felt no need to become combative or alarmed or even wary."[58]

No, indeed: Indians were either dead or safely "neutralized," ready to be stereotyped, romanticized, collected, and even—in the case of the Indian child—displayed in museums. So pervasive was the removal of living Native subjects from the collective American psyche that a phenomenon familiar to most contemporary Native people (and satirized by the Native artist James Luna[59]), the "does she mind if I take her picture" syndrome, was born. Lummis decried such "vulgar" behavior (at the same time, he added some details to what was a rapidly growing stereotype of "westerners") when he encountered it in Santa Fe:

Now when a Westerner sees anything novel and surprising, he takes it all in without moving a muscle. . . . But an Eastern tourist will throw up his hands and open his mouth and slop over until the very dogs have to run around to the drugstore for something to settle their stomachs. Right on the streets of Santa Fe intelligent and refined looking ladies have been seen to stop in front of a half-dressed Indian buck [*sic*], gape at him, talk about him, and even pinch him to see if he was honest flesh.[60]

But however appalled he might have been at such behavior before "live" Indians, Lummis had no compunction about "collecting" dead ones. Not only did he assiduously visit burial sites, but he also began to collect both bones and artifacts, most of which ultimately found their way into the museum.

It was, perhaps, ironic that Mother, who came from a "Mugwump" background very like Lummis's own, found herself actively contesting the practices Lummis and his fellows cherished. Perhaps it was the existence of her own Indian children that encouraged her dismay? But whatever the cause, we learned early that museum collecting—of *our* ancestral bones—was morally wrong.

The feeling is widely shared. Wendy Rose has written of another goal of Mother's "culture trips," the Franciscan Mission at Santa Barbara, where archaeologists discovered human bones in the adobe walls:

> I am a hungry scientist
> sustaining myself
> with bones of
> men and women asleep in the wall . . .
>
> They built the mission with dead Indians.
> They built the mission with dead Indians.
> They built the mission with dead Indians.
> They built the mission with dead Indians.[61]

Indian bones, we learned, have as long and dark a relationship with the American public as Indian land.

.2.
ANCESTRAL BURDENS

OF THE BONES

After one hundred and eighteen years of captivity in life and in death, the remains of twenty-six [Cheyenne] men, women and children were buried in Busby, Montana with ceremony and honor.
Harriett Skye[1]

Indiana Jones, leave my people's bones alone.
Roberto Tinoco Durán[2]

Although our mother's campaign to repatriate the body of the Indian girl was successful, similar efforts met considerable resistance. Over many years, until 1989, museums all over the United States—including, most prominently, the Smithsonian—collected and often displayed the bodies, bones, hair, and teeth of Native people. When the law dictated that public museums must inventory all their collections of Indian remains and funerary objects, the Smithsonian Institution alone counted more than twenty thousand Indian remains in its collection, some of which have been "repatriated" in ceremonies like those held by the Northern Cheyenne tribe at Busby.

The origins of this practice lay deep in the American past—a much overlooked period when European settlers paid "bounties" for the heads of enemy Indians (a practice perfected during the English conquest of Ireland in the sixteenth century[3]). Collecting Indian heads (and sometimes scalps alone) was profitable through the entire colonial period. George Russell has recently noted that "bounties varied from $25 to $130 for each male scalp and usually half of that amount for women and children." A notice posted in New England in 1755 recorded Boston's bounties:

For every Male Indian Prisoner above the Age of Twelve Years, that shall be taken and brought to Boston, Fifty Pounds;

For every Male Indian Scalp, brought in as Evidence of their being killed, Forty Pounds;

For every Female Indian Prisoner, taken and brought in as aforesaid, and for every Male Indian Prisoner under the Age of Twelve Years, taken and brought in as aforesaid, Twenty-five Pounds;

For every Scalp of such Female Indian or Male Indian under Twelve Years of Age, brought as Evidence of their being killed, as aforesaid, Twenty Pounds.

It was signed by William Shirley, "Captain-General and Governor in Chief, in and over His Majesty's Province of the Massachusetts-Bay." The bottom of the poster bore the legend "God Save the King."[4]

In the post-Revolutionary period, a newly self-conscious bourgeois ruling class began to develop an elaborate ideological system that allowed no room for such a straightforward, overtly genocidal collection of Indian remains.[5] Thus, in lieu of paying bounties for Indians slaughtered to "remove" them permanently from the land, intellectuals began to employ the reasoning of eighteenth-century "science" to justify their acquisitions. Scientific theories began to explain the dirty work of gathering heads and bodies (and, still, scalps) by referring to the widespread belief that a natural hierarchy of races had, from the first, necessitated European colonization of the Americas. The white race, so these arguments went, stood on the top rung of the race ladder, obliged by its status to dominate all others. Descending inferiority (demonstrated by measuring "collected" skulls), marked those races whose lands and labor the Europeans and European-Americans seized.

As the "civilized" conquerors of North America continued their deadly march across the continent, killing and pillaging Indian country throughout the nineteenth century, intellectuals' explanations for gathering still more Indian skeletons grew increasingly defensive. Motives of those who simply wanted Indian lands and possessions, however, needed no such disguise. In Marysville, California, in 1859, settlers collected money to pay "men . . . hired to hunt [Indians]." They "are recompensed by receiving so much for each scalp, or some other satisfactory evidence that they have been killed." A newspaper reporter described having seen "the scalps of Diggers hanging to tentpoles in the Shasta and Trinity country. . . . The Oregon men," he added, "who first settled that part of the state thought it sport to kill a Digger on sight as they would a coyote."[6]

Considerably less bloodthirsty scientists sat in their Eastern universities constructing much more elaborate arguments to support their continuing collection of Indian bodies and bones. Samuel G. Morton, who held the chair of anatomy at Pennsylvania College's Medical Department in the 1830s, insisted that he could only demonstrate the superiority of the white race by measuring skulls collected from all racial groups, especially those who belonged, in his taxonomy, to the "American" race. (He followed Johann Friedrich Blumenbach's 1775 system which defined five such groups: Mongolian, American, Caucasian, Malayan, Ethiopian.) Caucasians, his science told him, bore the "original skull type"; all others were degenerate versions. His evidence? The Caucasian skull was the most symmetrical when viewed from the top and back, closest to a circle. Because the circle was the most beautiful shape in nature, this skull type had to be God's original design.[7]

Morton's "science" spread rapidly throughout the culture. A few decades later, echoing what was by then a widely popular understanding of the "scientific" method of defining race, General Nelson Miles identified a body found near Fall River, Massachusetts: "it must have been a North American Indian, as it had the conical formation of the skull peculiar to that race."[8]

Although histories of physical anthropology (understandably) tend to keep quiet about the provenance of the bones used in such research,[9] the need for "evidence" encouraged anthropologists and other scientists to employ collectors to rob graves. Many such desperate men, traveling through Indian country in search of Indian bodies, found it a difficult and dangerous occupation. One grave robber, delicately disguised as a "field collector," described his dilemma in a letter from the killing fields to Samuel Morton:

It is rather a perilous business to procure Indians' skulls in this country.—The natives are so jealous of you that they watch you very closely while you are wandering near their mausoleums and instant and sanguinary vengeance would fall upon the luckless—who would presume to interfere with the sacred relics.

But, he added,

There is an epidemic raging among them which carries them off so fast that the cemeteries will soon lack watchers—I don't rejoice in the prospects of death of the poor creatures, certainly, but then you know it will be very convenient for my purposes.[10]

Morton and other scientific defenders of white racial superiority had opponents in these mid-century decades. Alas, however, they opposed only his ideas and not his methods; they, too, bought Native skulls and bones from collectors, measuring them in order to demonstrate that all human bones were the same!

By the final decades of the nineteenth century, more of the fruits of this dubious trade began to find their way into museums and universities as some scientists and collectors lost interest in owning bones and donated their collections to the public. The inheritors of the bones, however, did not treat them with any more sensitivity than had the scientists; indeed, all over America museum curators and the denizens of an emerging academic discipline, physical anthropology, sorted and labeled bones for future study—and sometimes, display.

> *The typical state of affairs at such museums was satirized recently by Tony Hillerman in a novel about the Navajo Tribal Police Officer, Jim Chee.* Talking God *features a part-Navajo Smithsonian curator, who protests the museum's collection of Native bones and sacred artifacts by excavating and "collecting" the remains of his boss's Anglo grandparents which he carefully boxes [in a used microwave oven carton], labels, and ships to their granddaughter's office at the museum.*[11]

The donation of private collections of bones to public institutions in no way signaled an end to "science's" interest in demonstrating race hierarchies. In fact, "craniology" and the study of Indian teeth and other bones is still practiced by physical anthropologists researching America's indigenous populations, though ostensibly not in pursuit of racial judgments.[12] But around the turn of the nineteenth century, those seeking theories of race that would support the "manifest destiny" of European-Americans turned toward blood as their object of inquiry.

This shift toward "blood" as the site of scientific racism did not, however, mean that the trade in Indian bones—or relics—diminished. Indeed, during the Gilded Age, as in subsequent ages of conspicuous material consumption (the "Roaring Twenties," the more recent decade of "Eighties avarice"), the collection of Indian funerary artifacts, including "remains," continued—and, in fact, increased, as museums vied with private collectors to gather the spoils of victory.[13]

Those who collect artifacts—whatever their provenance—are usually not the objects of public obloquy,[14] but private collectors of Indian bones remain a shady and disreputable bunch. "Novelty" collectors, as they are known, work within a black market which has grown steadily in this century. See, for example, the "playful" snapshot of one bone collector, taken recently in the Four Corners area and published in the *Condé Nast Traveler* magazine.[15] Europeans, too, are active participants in the black market for Indian skulls. In *Earthdivers*, Gerald Vizenor's semi-autobiographical novel, a character explains: "It *is* true. . . . Indian heads are most popular with the Germans. . . . They have so many Indian organizations there, perhaps because Karl May wrote so many stories about Winnetou, adventures of the Invented Apache warrior."[16]

> *Winnetou is enormously popular all over western Europe. In 1963, a Winnetou-inspired group was founded in the Netherlands. Ten years later the group, named after*

Karl May, divided into those who wanted to read, write about, and romanticize Winnetou and other Indians, and those more interested in political action. The latter founded the Netherlands Actiongroup North American Indian, which publishes a journal called NANAI-Notes. The Karl May group's journal is called, curiously, De Kiva. This name may be explained by the presence in the club of one Dick de Soeten, described by an acquaintance as "a Dutch Hopi freak."[17]

More "reputable" collectors trade in the lucrative market for artifacts—which, of course, include vast numbers of objects stolen from graves and ceremonial sites, among them many sacred objects such as medicine bundles, pipes, funerary objects, and so on. Their motives, like the motives of museum buyers and curators, are complex. To some extent, those who first assembled museum collections reflected the grandiosity of high capitalist imperialism, a phenomenon which gave birth to the public museum, where individualist connoisseurship was replaced by social collecting during the second half of the nineteenth century. This new phenomenon had developed in turn from earlier social celebrations of imperialist successes, the "world exhibitions," which, in the words of Walter Benjamin, "erected the universe of commodities" where "Fashion prescribed the ritual by which the fetish Commodity wished to be worshipped." This fetish Commodity, moreover, "prostitutes the living body to the inorganic world. In relation to the living it represents the rights of the corpse."[18] But not, of course, the rights of Indian corpses, or indeed even the material objects that lived in both daily and spiritual tribal life. From the moment of "collection" both were transformed from human bodies and living things to "fetish" artifacts.

Unlike most corpses, artifacts take part in the play of the capitalist market. Following the "rituals of fashion," material objects seized from their organic place in the Native American world quickly become "investments." Examples of this transformation fill the glossy pages of glittery, high fashion Indian art magazines. One contemporary advertisement, in *American Indian Art*, characteristically employs the language of Wall Street to sell "antique" Navajo blankets and at the same time to seduce new customers for a Santa Fe gallery:

Many people ask, "Who buys these blankets from you?". . . . My clients do have some things in common. They tend to be entrepreneurial—that is, they make money for themselves rather than for an employer. . . . And because they have succeeded by taking risks, they bring a risk-taking attitude to their collecting. . . . This . . . profile of the Navajo blanket collector makes sense. Navajo weavers were consummate entrepreneurs. Drawing on Pueblo, Plains, Spanish and Anglo influences, the weavers produced singular works of art that appealed to wealthy individuals from all four of those cultures. . . .

Each blanket is a blend of cultural preferences, but each blanket leaves those preferences behind and creates a separate, unique reality in the process.[19]

Here, the conquest of members of the Greed Generation is accomplished by mingling the vocabulary of investment capital with the ludicrously pretentious vocabulary of connoisseurship. As it does so clashingly in a recent argument in favor of including "Native" artists in the capitalist art market, Sally Price's *Primitive Art in Civilized Places,* this advertisement assumes a system of "universal" values that are actually exclusive to the world of finance and capital, of the frenzied American "getting and spending" that reached some sort of awful apotheosis in the era of Ronald Reagan.[20]

Given the long history of the commodification of every aspect of Indian life, it is not surprising that a reversal of the more problematic collecting practices, those involving bones or spiritual objects, was left primarily to the efforts of Native activists themselves. Although there were sporadic protests, most of these efforts awaited the arrival of 1960s politics. As children of the 1950s, my sister and I were precociously politicized by our chance visit to the Southwest Museum; few children, Indian or not, shared a similar awareness of the evils of museum collecting practices.

Our "bone" education, moreover, was not limited to a single visit to the Southwest Museum. Mother "collected" museums as others collected artifacts. We were thus early acquainted with the Indian "dioramas" at the Santa Barbara Museum of Natural History—which frightened us with more-than-life-sized, "authentically" garbed and posed Indian mannequins lurking, "picturesquely," behind doorways, beside pillars, stretched along corridors. We also saw more "mummified" Indian remains in public museums all over California. Most such eerie and troubling displays offered "reassurance" in the form of information leaflets or lengthy captions explaining that these bodies were "prehistoric" or those of California's not-quite-human Indians, barbarian Diggers who had once lived in a pathetic near-tool-less state by "gathering." These, we learned (in school as well?) were distinctly *not* the "noble savages" of the Indian wars (or the movies), but ignoble people who owed to the Spanish missions any semblance of humanity their descendants (however few) possessed.[21]

DIGGER ARCHAEOLOGISTS

By the 1960s, my youthful outrage had begun to spread through Indian Country, particularly once that decade began to witness a new-style Indian militancy.[22] Young Native American activists, an increasing number of them students benefiting from the War on Poverty's educational efforts, prompted legislative efforts to change collecting practices. One of the most important effects of the new laws was a gradual transformation of public views of Indians as commodities into Indians as people with the rights of every other group on American soil.

A first step was to protect Indian burial sites in the same way non-Indian cemeteries are protected from vandals.[23] Strange as it must surely seem, Indian burial grounds have historically been widely regarded as little more than archaeological bonanzas. When archaeologists finished "digging" Indian graves, often publishing their additions to the world's storehouse of knowledge, public officials took over. A typical, though "amateur," excavation of a Mound Builder burial ground in 1927 produced some 234 Indian skeletons, which were quickly put on display at the Dickson Mound Museum in Illinois. Only in 1991 did Governor Jim Edgar close the exhibit of the remains. According to one newspaper story, however, the governor's actions satisfied no one on any side of the issue. James Yellowbank, from the Indian Treaty Rights Committee, said: "We want [the remains] reburied properly and left alone. . . . This is like putting them in an icebox until the next Governor comes along and wants to let people go in there again." Local citizens feared the loss of tourist revenues. Archaeologists, in their turn, found themselves hurrying to "catalogue the site and make any last studies they c[ould]" before access was denied.[24]

After 1989, federal laws forbade future desecrations of Indian burial grounds. The catch was, however, that each state had separately to pass laws to implement the federal regulations; thus, in 1994 there remained states without such laws. A recent controversy in Georgia, which complied with federal regulations in a 1992 state law, suggests that even where protective laws exist, many still believe that

Native American burial grounds should be treated as the proper workshop of scientists. One newspaper story headlined "Controversy unearthed in Georgia hills: research or desecration? A new law and Indian protests may limit what archaeologists can learn from 30–40 burial sites in Brasstown Valley." " 'These are our ancestors, this is sacred ground to us,' said George Martin, a member of the Eastern Band of Cherokee [sic].' " But an archaeologist from Athens, a member of Georgia's "bone court," insisted: "A significant amount of information is obtained by analysis of skeletal remains. . . . Also, the burial objects give you a context for when those objects were used. It's like a time capsule." David Hally, "a University of Georgia archaeologist noted for pre-historic Indian research," suggested patronizingly, "We archaeologists need to do a better job of communicating our findings to Native Americans. . . . It's to their benefit. Just like them, we're trying to get rid of the stereotypes of tomahawks and war bonnets."[25] Atlanta's newspaper disagreed: "The graves should be protected," opined an editor, "from the archaeological dig and from the golf course construction. . . . Showing respect for the dead is almost universal among human cultures. Failure to show such respect can be taken as an insult at the least and, at worse, [sic] as an attempt to deny a people's humanity."[26] The paper's suggestion that the graves be landscaped and left alone did not set well with the Vice President of Southeastern Archeological Services Inc., Chad Braley, however. "It appears that the public cannot distinguish between professional archaeologists and looters," he sniffed. "Archaeologists are not grave robbers. We are anthropologists who study past cultures." Agreeing with Hally, Braley argued, "Archaeology allows modern cultures to know more about their heritage, which serves to demystify stereotypes. One important aspect is objectively studying human remains. . . . Excavate the remains scientifically," he continued, "study them sensitively. . . . Then follow established federal and state guidelines to repatriate the remains to the Cherokee or other nearest living group for a respectful reinterment ceremony."[27]

Chad Braley is being slightly disingenuous in his evocation of the god of modern science. "Archeological Services Inc." is not a disinterested collection of scientists pursuing objective knowledge for the benefit of humankind. Rather, it is a company, a corporation, a group of businesspeople who saw profit in the new Indian burial-site laws. They are, in the words of another article published in *Smithsonian* magazine, "contract archaeologists," working in "an industry that has sprung up in direct response to the new sensitivity to ancient remains."[28]

Capitalism appears here, too, cloaked in the mystification of science. Perhaps because of the link between the market and this kind of "science," protests about

Indian grave-robbing have drawn the ire of vigilant neoconservatives. A recent polemic by Anita Sue Grossman in the right-wing journal *Heterodoxy* gave the game away in her title: "Digging the Grave of Archaeology." In the article, Grossman declares that repatriation will destroy the "scientific" discipline of archaeology. Museums, in her view, are being forced to relinquish their Indian collections solely because of the pernicious spread of "multiculturalism," a phenomenon which has begun to assume the useful role previously played by another "red menace" in the minds of the far right. (Of course multiculturalism, an invention of guilt-ridden liberals, conveniently subsumes *all* the various categories of American race-hysteria under a single rubric. Thus it is no longer necessary to label race problems with a variety of potentially confusing names—"yellow perils," or "Islamic fundamentalisms." Instead, all challenges to European-American cultural hegemony fit neatly into one catchword.)

Demystification of this discourse of politicized, market-oriented science is, however, quite easy. One need only change the race of the remains and all is transformed. After the brutal midwestern floods of 1993 for example, the *New York Times* cried "Cruel Flood Tore at Graves and Hearts" above a story recounting the suffering of those to whom "the unthinkable happened," when flood waters excavated the local cemetery. In Hardin, Missouri, much of the 1810 cemetery was destroyed. Still, Hardin residents are experiencing only a small taste of what is all-too-familiar gruel to Native Americans, including the macabre tourism. "The cemetery itself," one newspaper reported, "has attracted tourists from Illinois and Kansas and as far away as Vermont, who drive past police barricades and ignore the 'keep out' signs to take pictures. 'Is this where the caskets popped out?' a gawker from Vermont asked . . . camera in hand."[29] Compare this event with one recounted by Vine Deloria. In June, 1971, the highway department of the state of Iowa came upon an unmarked cemetery while building a new road near Glenwood, Iowa. They immediately stopped their bulldozing and located a local man who told them it was an old cemetery where many of his relatives were buried. They then dug carefully, eventually unearthing twenty-seven bodies. With one of the bodies were found hundreds of glass beads, some brass finger rings, and metal earrings. This indicated to local officials that this was the body of an Indian girl. So while the other twenty-six bodies received a respectful reburial in the Glenwood cemetery, the Indian girl's body was "seized by the state archaeologist, Marshall McKusick, and sent for display at the Iowa City Museum." "A woman called Running Moccasins tried desperately to claim the body for re-burial," a newspaper report continued. Marshall McKusick, however, announced, "I just can't go giving remains to private individuals." And he forced the local tribe to get a court order in order to claim the body back.[30]

Thus it is with considerable justification that "tribes and advocacy groups have argued since the 1970s" that there exists "a double standard over the protection of cemeteries." As the *Association on American Indian Affairs Newsletter* reports, Indian graves have been "routinely . . . plundered for scientific or medical research or for mere curiosity." "'What would America think if an all-Indian archaeological team went to Arlington National Cemetery and dug up the graves of war heroes to study the type of clothing they wore or the implements of the period?' asked Curtis Zunigha, director of the American Indian Heritage Center in Tulsa." Another Indian commentator predicted a huge outcry (no doubt from subscribers to *Heterodoxy,* as well as from all the rest of the political right) if graves of soldiers from Vietnam were robbed so that "science" could study "the effects of agent orange," or the consequences of the use of other miracles of technology during the Vietnam War.[31]

The new federal regulations guarding Indian remains provide for the "repatriation" or "reburial" of remains held only in *public* collections, such as museums, and by *public* university departments of anthropology. Furthermore, deciding such matters requires first a lengthy and expensive documentation of tribal claims, followed by favorable decisions by "bone courts"[32] before repatriation is accomplished. In the case of "valuable" funerary objects or sacred figures, furthermore, tribes have to demonstrate—usually to the satisfaction of archaeologists appointed by states—a "continuing religious relationship" to the objects. If the loss of the objects to collectors or to museums has effected a change in religious ceremonies, the "continuing relationship" can be shown to have been broken, thus weakening tribal claims.

When laws concerning artifacts are implemented, many objections, just as trivial or substantive as those raised against protecting Native burial grounds, are raised by interested individuals. In recent months, for example, the small town of Barre, Massachusetts, has found itself the center of attention because someone noticed that the hundred or so objects proudly displayed in the tiny town museum were looted from the dead and dying at the massacre of some three hundred unarmed Lakota people by the U.S. cavalry at Wounded Knee, South Dakota, in 1890. It was a bloody and pitiless slaughter of children, old people, women. No warriors were present to defend the Lakota people gathered in camp.[33]

One might think that Lakota claims for these objects would be met without hesitation. And yet the *New York Times* of February 19, 1993, reported that "library officials, stunned by the attention the collection is now receiving, say that they are reluctant to turn over the artifacts. 'Eventually [the collection] will be repatriated,' said James Sullivan, the town librarian. . . . But, he said, 'We've preserved them for 101 years. We're not going to just shove them out the door.'"

The items, it should be noted, include scalps and hair, several dolls taken from the arms of dead children, and cradle boards from which babies' bodies were removed. The donor, a turn-of-the-century town resident called Frank Root, "is said to have bought many of the items from a contractor in charge of clearing the killing field where hundreds of Indians' bodies were tossed into mass graves. . . . Other members of the library association," continued the *Times*, "said they feared the survivors would bury many of the artifacts if they were returned, causing a part of history to be lost. 'It seems a shame to rip a page out of history and bury it,' Mrs. Stevens said."[34]

> *Another page out of United States history: "One survivor of Custer's catastrophe in 1876 was a horse with the highly ironic name of Comanche. He was pampered until his death in 1891, and then his stuffed remains were placed on display at the University of Kansas."[35]*

These, then, are the relics of "novelty" collectors—people like the California dentist who bought Joseph's skull (stolen along with other skulls in 1971 from the burial grounds in Clarkston, Washington, and sold in California's lucrative black market) for use as an ashtray. (Protests eventually convinced the dentist to allow the skull to be "repatriated.") But bone-collecting still hides beneath the white coats of "science."[36] Since the days when Ishi, the last of the Yana people of Northern California,[37] was housed as a "living display" at the anthropology museum of the University of California, "science" has justified the collecting of bodies and body parts from Native people.

Indeed, when Ishi died in the 1920s, the anthropologist Alfred Kroeber was so terrified that his colleagues would treat Ishi's body as they did other Indian remains that he sent a panicky telegram from a Boston hotel to California: "If there is any talk about the interests of science, say for me that science can go to hell . . . We propose to stand by our friends." Less admirable were his further arguments: "Besides, I cannot believe that any scientific value is materially involved. We have hundreds of Indian skeletons that nobody ever comes to study. The prime interest in this case would be of a morbid romantic nature."[38] (Interestingly, the Berkeley museum remains intent upon refusing all Indian claims to its collection of some 10,000 sets of Indian bones, despite strict California laws.[39])

Indian humor—a survival strategy perfected over the course of centuries—includes a story that mocks scientific pretensions. At a recent conference, the story goes, a group of epidemiologists were telling their Indian audience that their work on university-owned Indian bones was helping to overturn the widely held view that epidemic diseases had been introduced into the Native populations by European invaders. Tuberculosis, they claimed, had been found to have killed Plains tribespeople before they had contact with Europeans. So how had this European scourge been introduced? The scientists offered the hypothesis that it came from bovine tuberculosis, carried by escapees from eastern domestic cattle herds, who transmitted the disease to western buffalo when they ranged loose across the continent. These buffalo then gave tuberculosis to Native people when they drank buffalo milk. At this point in the lecture, an elderly Indian in the audience, laughing loudly, was heard to declare in a clear voice, "These white men obviously never tried to milk a buffalo!"[40]

Vine Deloria, with customary wit, summarizes Native America's relations with such social scientists: "The origins of the anthropologist is a mystery hidden in the historical mists. Indians are certain that all societies of the Near East had anthropologists at one time because all those societies are now defunct." Moreover, everyone knows that "the anthropologist is only out on the reservation to verify what he has suspected all along—Indians are very quaint people who bear watching."[41] Gramps, in his turn, used to tell us about how teenage kids at Fort Leavenworth waited for the summer return of the "anthros": all winter long they planned exotic "rituals" and "traditional stories" to tell these outsiders when they arrived. After each telling, painstakingly recorded by the anthropologist, the Indian kids went away and passed the next several hours laughing themselves silly.

The near-mystical claims of "science," however, continue to dilute many people's ability to comprehend objections raised by Native people reluctant to continue to serve as objects. Wendy Rose's seminal essay, "The Great Pretenders,"[42] which attacks the pretensions of anthropologists who "specialize" in Indians, almost always arouses hostility from readers who insist that anthropologists are, in the words of one New York University student, "objective scientists" who "cannot be held responsible for the acts of a few." Given this confusion, it is important to define the problem as clearly as possible.

Annette Jaimes and Ward Churchill have both suggested that the genocide accompanying the founding of the United States lies at the heart of Americans' inability to acknowledge the humanity of Native America. Churchill argues that the

United States needs to undergo a "de-nazification," naming the events that marked European's conquest of the continent, accusing the killers, correcting a historical record that has falsely memorialized some of the cruelest mass murderers in history as "heroes." One aspect of such "de-nazification" would be the acceptance of the idea that moral identity is not discrete, parceled out, act by act, year by year—not in an individual life, not in the life of a nation. As one existentialist wag had it, "Twinkle, twinkle, little star / What you *do* is what you *are*." This is as true of the identity of a nation as it is of that of each individual. All of life thus forms an unfragmented whole (a belief common, of course, to most Native American tradition).[43]

Although acceptance of this concept seems to me to condemn the efforts of most anthropologists out of hand (a judgment widely shared by Native academics, including even those whose degrees were earned in that field) many non-Native students find such an opinion overly unforgiving. Indeed, in a recent class at New York University, my suggestion that anthropology was a deeply suspect discipline elicited extreme reactions: vociferous agreement from the six Native students in the course, and hostility from many others, some of whom were majoring in anthropology. These latter agreed on a common defensive argument: that without anthropologists, tribal traditions, languages, beliefs, and so on would have been (and will continue to be) lost. Tribes themselves, one student insisted, have been very grateful to non-Indian anthropologists who have shared their scholarly knowledge with—to employ admittedly loaded language—the survivors.

Given this not-unexpected disparity, I tried to diagram, using chalk and cartoon figures, an exemplary situation, featuring a prototypical anthropologist, John Shmertz.

John is a graduate student at Harvard, studying linguistic anthropology. Looking around the academic marketplace for a profitable (i.e., "not-yet-done") subject of inquiry, he decides upon a study of the Nez Perce language, Sahaptian. Next, he applies for grants to support his travel, research, and living at the Nez Perce reservation in Idaho. Because he is at Harvard, John has little trouble finding $1,000,000 from, say, the National Science Foundation. With the money he hires assistants and buys sophisticated recording equipment. He then travels to Kamiah, Idaho, where, after renting a place to live and work and adding "Native informants" to his payroll, he sets up shop.

After a year of work, John believes that he has collected sufficient data to establish himself as the authority on the language. He packs up his equipment and household goods and returns to Cambridge, where he transcribes his recordings (again, perhaps with the help of hired assistants) and writes his dissertation. Soon, he finds a job at a prestigious university, teaching Native American anthropology and specialized courses in Native American linguistics. He publishes his thesis ("Sahaptian, the Vanishing Language of the Nez Perce") and many articles outlining new findings.

Decades pass; those old people who acted as his "primary sources," telling him stories, explaining their Native language, putting up with recording after recording, are dead. Fewer and fewer Nez Perce people remember even the barest rudiments of their language, and gradually, its everyday use dies away.

Enter politics, stage left.

With the coming of a new political consciousness in the 1960s and '70s, young Nez Perce leaders begin to realize that knowing a language is also knowing a culture. Many decide to learn Sahaptian—and to begin teaching it to the all-important next generation. In order to begin their work, they send emissaries to Professor Shmertz, Sahaptian expert.

Shmertz, much gratified, agrees to help. Quickly, he teaches Nez Perce to several tribal members, correcting their faults, explaining the intricacies of a language with one usage for sacred matters, a second for the "everyday." Names of vanished animals and traditions are "given back." These markers help the young Nez Perce teachers identify key ceremonies and practices which had disappeared from tribal memory. Not surprisingly, the Nez Perce emissaries are extremely grateful to Dr. Shmertz, and in keeping with the grace for which the nation was always known, they offer abundant thanks.

A few months later, at a conference of Indian anthropologists, Prof. Shmertz is attacked by—let us imagine—Wendy Rose, who questions his life, who questions his "authority," who notes the bitter irony inherent in his colonial relationship to the Nez Perce students, a relationship in which he holds the knowledge of their native language. "But," he cries defensively, "without me they wouldn't know their language! And *they* were really grateful to me for all my work!"

What's wrong with this picture?

First, from the opening moments of this anthropological ritual, the producers of knowledge—the Harvard student, the grant-giving body—were all white (and mostly male).[44] Moreover, they were heirs of other white people: the Europeans who had arrived on America's shores a couple of centuries earlier. And John Shmertz was a more direct heir than most other European-Americans: his career —indeed, his academic discipline—grew directly out of the conquest, which devastated Native populations sufficiently to render their lives, their languages, their artifacts, and even their bones subject to academic "rescue" and "preservation." Thus the historical background, readily occluded throughout the transactions between Shmertz and "science" foundations, Shmertz and his university job, Shmertz and the young Nez Perce students, shapes his work into something rather less grand, something far more equivocal, than his degrees and "fame" as a specialist in the vanishing Nez Perce language might suggest. In a scenario bitter with irony, Nez Perce women and men must request help from a representative of the colonizing power in order to undertake the "decolonization of their collective mind."[45] As Miryam Yataco, a young Andean Indian woman from Peru, exclaimed when one anthropology student in the class reiterated this "gratitude" defense, "Imagine the power of the colonizers whose claim of authority, whose ownership of knowledge, allow them to become the expert possessors of the knowledge necessary for indigenous people to free their *own* minds from colonialism!"[46]

At the same time, despite decades of concerted attempts to rearrange the minds of anthropologists, many, perhaps especially those working with museum collections, still don't get it. At a recent film festival at the Museum of Natural History in New York, Ava Hamilton, a Cheyenne-Arapaho filmmaker, was answering questions following a showing of her film *You Can't Kill the Spirit*, which documents part of the Native American struggle for religious freedom. Most in the audience were anthropologists. One very prominent anthropologist (who, unlike everyone else in the auditorium, rose to his feet to indicate the superior importance of his question) asked Hamilton if she would give her views on a situation that had arisen recently at his museum. New regulations force public institutions holding certain Indian objects to allow them to be "borrowed" by tribal members requiring them for ceremonies. He noted that a young Indian woman had requested a very valuable basket held by the museum. She intended to use it in a ceremonial parade in California. He had, he explained, "very reluctantly" refused the request on the grounds that she might damage the basket. After all, he added, it "doesn't belong to her, but rather to the public." "It is my job," he continued, "to care for the Indian collections for all Americans. The young woman might have *ruined* the basket, letting it get run over by a truck or something!" In self-defensive tones, he concluded, "I'd like you to tell me what you think about this."

Ava Hamilton—to my vast relief—did not hesitate: "The basket," she said firmly, "belongs to the people who made it, not to the museum. If a member of that Indian nation wants it, she should take it." A hiss went round the room as several dozen anthropologists imagined the future desecration of their "collections."[47]

Arnold Krupat wrote his reaction to the above in a letter:

I . . . want to mention my dear friends: Tony Mattina, come here from Sicily as a high school student because somehow he fell in love not with "Indians" but with the Colville people and language. He'll never be at Harvard, never have a grant even approaching six figures. He makes, after 30 years [a modest salary] at U of Montana, but he's on leave for a few years working with the Salish people of Penticton, BC developing language programs for the schools. If Tony lives [long enough] he will complete a Colville dictionary and grammar, which, now that there are only a very very few speakers left, will be important resources for the revival of the language. And there's Don Bahr, after 25 years making [a modest salary] at Arizona State. Never had a grant of any kind. . . . For 30 years he's been working with singers, recording, transcribing, translating. The late Vincent Joseph whom I had a brief chance to meet wouldn't sing a song to Bahr until Bahr had learned the last song Vincent had sung to his satisfaction. Now the last singers of these Yuman, in this case Pima, "dream songs" are gone, but Bahr tells me that a couple of groups of young men—this means guys in their sixties—are meeting once or twice a week, using his tapes of Vincent Joseph and a few others, and are reviving the dream songs. And there's. . . .

And there's . . . my own cousin, from my mother's side of the family, Victoria Lindsay Levine, an ethnomusicologist, working (at modest salary and also without big grants) to transcribe Choctaw music and to show how it has functioned— and continues to function—as a means by which Choctaw people have defied European-American efforts to erase them by destroying their culture.[48]

Arnold Krupat continues his defense of some anthropologists, reminding me— gently—that many founders of my own discipline, history, similarly participated in western efforts to swallow the world:

There is NO western discipline, as I think we both would agree, that is innocent of colonial complicity; social science, history, whatever: as the West has defined those . . . they reek of [Walter Benjamin's] barbarism and blood. . . . And yet, and yet, and yet. . . . I guess I *do* believe that not all anthros living today are as obtuse and miserable as Morgan and the others you . . . cite. I have to think hard about why I want so much to leave at least a corner open to "good" anthropology. . . . But, as someone said about private property, not only do I believe in it, I've *seen* it.[49]

Sigh. All of us who learned history from Jonathan Steinberg, Cambridge historians all, will recognize the master's warning lurking behind all this: it *is* all much more complicated.

COLLECTING INDIANS FOR THE FAMILY OF (MARKETING) MAN

In recent years, a new academic discourse, loosely labeled "cultural studies," has undertaken to "rewrite" the story of relations between indigenous people and colonial "authorities." The origins of this new scholarly undertaking are political, born both from its practitioners' disillusion with what they—and certainly the U.S. media—see as the failures of the practical political work of the 1960s and early '70s and from a comforting sense that "politics" in the '80s and '90s requires only an enthusiastic (and profitable) participation in abstruse and arcane exchanges of "discourse." So long as the ostensible subjects of such exchanges are clearly "the oppressed"—women, members of racial minorities, gays and lesbians, and so on— comments about them (and, increasingly, comments about the comments about them), particularly if couched in the jargon invented by the big guns of the genre and replete with "self-deconstructive," criticism-deflecting personal remarks pass as militant political action among the academically successful.[50]

One of the most representative of the new genre in its anthropological (or ethnographical) guise is Sally Price's much-celebrated *Primitive Art in Civilized Places*. Given Price's opening assertion, that she intends to investigate "some of our [*sic*] most basic and unquestioned cultural assumptions—our 'received wisdom'—about the boundaries between 'us' and 'them,' "[51] it is clear that the work's motives are political. Moreover, the book's enthusiastic acceptance by the "cultural studies" community suggests that many "academic leftists" welcome it as a stride forward. But is it? Or is the book merely an exercise in "digging up and replanting" the same old garden?[52]

I think that Price gives herself away at the very beginning of the book: "Dedicated to those artists whose works are in our museums but whose names are not." In a wash of logocentrism, the author insists from the outset that *names* matter more than anything. It is thus the duty of new art historians, alert to an injustice committed by earlier collectors of the work of "nameless" primitive artists, to erase the namelessness that afflicts "Native" artists. Not even death or the passage of time need pose insurmountable obstacles to those engaged in this worthy work: "Even for objects crafted in the early or mid-nineteenth century, [Robin K. Wright] has demonstrated the potential of careful stylistic analysis for delineating the work of particular individuals, creating epithets such as 'Master of the Long Fingers' where retrieval of the carver's proper name is no longer feasible." Before Wright (and Price) and other more sensitive art historians, Native art had occupied a unique and marginal place in art historical scholarship. Price notes:

One exception [was] made . . . to this general focus on individual creativity and historical chronology. In the Western understanding of things, a work originating outside of the Great Traditions must have been produced by an unnamed figure who represents his community and whose craftsmanship respects the dictates of its age-old traditions. The present chapter will suggest a closer look at this composite fellow and the restrictions on his creative spirit. And it will attempt to establish the authorship of his famous anonymity and traditionalism.[53]

How? Price continues:

Over the past few decades . . . growing numbers of scholars who are applying an art historical background to the study of Primitive Art (most notably in Africa) are significantly nuancing this image, as they contribute to our knowledge of individual artists' lives, document art historical developments through time, and refine the stylistic distinctions that identify the proveniences of particular pieces . . . attempting to differentiate the work of individual Primitive Artists *much as they would that of their European or American counterparts.* (emphasis added)[54]

Alas, however, there remain those unwilling to enter her world of improved cross-cultural relations:

An editorial in *African Art* confused "tribality" with "anonymity" and went on to discuss the implications of this characteristic for the recognition of individual artists. With the artist himself thus reduced to anonymity there cannot develop that cult of the individual that can surround the works of a single European or *even* Japanese master carver or painter. (emphasis added)[55]

Clearly, Price intends to "recuperate" the individuality of these overlooked individuals. But why? Aside from the very western privileging of the individual—especially "geniuses"—in bourgeois society, there is (always!) the question of money. In a capitalist society, the value of individuals is measured—almost exclusively in U.S. society—by money. Thus it is money that matters to Price. Writing of the "collection" of "primitive artifacts," for example, she notes critically: "nowhere is there any mention of such matters as [note the order] appropriate compensation, native opposition to scientific collecting, or other issues touching on the personal relations or ethics of the enterprise."[56]

Compensation, then, is the primary goal. The market is the essential factor in shaping relations between the "supplier" cultures and the "collecting" ones:

The creation of a "market" (*however undervalued it may be in comparison with that in the West*), inevitably affects the nature of a community's encounters with outsiders, its economic workings, the role and meaning of the classes of objects that are collected, and ultimately the physical forms that are produced.[57] (emphasis added)

Will cash debase primitive artists? Price admits that the problems are multifold:

Although some commentators have proposed that a monetary incentive disqualifies an object of native manufacture for inclusion in the category of "authentic primitive art," producing art for money is not really the problem. As Edmund Carpenter has pointed out, "A recent book on Inuit souvenirs reminds us that Michelangelo worked for money without loss of integrity. *Yet he never mass-produced debased Christian altar pieces, suitably modified to meet Arab taste, to peddle on the wharfs of Venice.*"

Still, there are problems inherent in relations between "Haves" and "Have-Nots": "I would suggest that paying artists for their labor and their talent is one thing when it occurs within a well-defined cultural setting in which both the curator and the owner-to-be share basic assumptions about the nature of the transaction. . . . It is quite another thing, however, when a Western traveler in Africa spots an interesting looking wooden figure and offers to purchase it for a price that represents a negligible amount to the traveler and a large sum to the owner; in this situation, the buyer lacks understanding of the meaning of the object in its native context, the seller lacks understanding of its meaning in its new home, and there is no common ground in the evaluation of the price for which it has been exchanged."

Worse still are the demands of "tourists":

[Carpenter] decries the development of soapstone carvings because it was imposed from outside and because it *has deprived the Inuit of something that gave value to their life.* Collectors decry tourist art with equal vehemence but tend to view it as a ruse perpetrated by wily natives and to resent its existence because it deprives them of value for their money.[58]

Collecting, the quintessence of commodity fetishism, provides a special First World experience: "Above all, make your collection a part of your life," Price quotes one collector. "Live with it, look at it, fondle it."[59] In this capitalist art market, value for money depends upon names—or at least individuation—because the question is one of *authenticity.* Authenticity is determined not by qualities intrinsic to a work of art, but rather by the relationship of a named artist to the work.

Price intends to rescue primitive art from its secondary place in the modern art market by "authenticating" it. But the goal of her recuperation is to make "them" . . . *just like us!* With diligence, "they" can become individualistic, competitive, capitalistic, and responsive to *universal* standards. They *even* possess [western] humor: "the complex humanity of these artists who (as far as I can tell from having known at least a few such people first hand) are absolutely as disposed as Calder to the full range of thoughts and emotions that bring out the lighter side of the human comedy."[60] Moreover, Price continues in a flood of self-congratulatory condescension, "many Primitives (including both artists and critics) are also endowed with a discriminating 'eye'—similarly fitted with an optical device that reflects their own cultural education."[61]

Primitive Art in Civilized Places, then, simply turns the western world upside down, or, speaking politically, right side up. Sally Price proposes no revolution— in thinking, or anything else. Nor, indeed, does she suggest stepping outside European-centered presumptions in order to imagine a world rather different from the one into which she generously proposes to welcome "natives." Indeed, the underlying argument of her book, that "universals" *do*, in fact, exist, *even among the primitives*, should reassure even the neoconservatives, so fearful of the lengths to which the "political correction" of "cultural studies" threatens to take "us" from our proper origins in the Enlightenment ideal. For what she means by "universals" is just what the Enlightenment meant: under their problematically varicolored skins, "they" are *just like us*! It merely requires a bit more effort from progressives to demonstrate "our" similarities. (Price writes, "In the case of early twentieth-century art from the rain forest of Suriname, for example, I have found specific attributions to be a challenging task, dependent on language learning, methodological skills, and theoretical background, but no more of an impossible undertaking than research described in traditional art historical scholarship."[62]) But "whew!" it can be done.

I had gotten it backwards all along. Not "seeing is believing," you ninny, but "believing is seeing."
    Gerald Vizenor

In addition to the hoots of derision such patronizing efforts deserve, there are calmer tribal responses to Price and her colleagues—

The Hopi Arts and Crafts Guild:

Each artist is paid the same for work, whether well or poorly made, whether it sells to tourists or not. The Hopi artist gets money for his or her work even though it has no market value. A spokesperson said, "We can't sell it? We display it anyway. We charge the tourist more for good work, a certain percentage, so that we can pay for the bad work. We mark the things in code so the poor craftspeople won't be hurt, and the good ones won't be jealous. We have to be fair to every Hopi."[63]

Simon Ortiz:

My mother was a potter of the well-known Acoma clayware, a traditional art form that had been passed to her from her mother and the generations of mothers before. My father carved figures from wood and did beadwork. This was not unusual, as Indian people know; there was always some kind of artistic endeavor that people set themselves to, although they did not necessarily articulate it as "art" in the sense of western civilization. One lived and expressed an artful life, whether it was in ceremonial singing and dancing, architecture, painting, speaking, or in the way one's social-cultural life was structured.

Jimmie Durham:

One's Indian community cannot authenticate or designate a position in the world of art because that world is of the colonizer. One must approach the colonizer for the space and license to make art. The colonizer, of course, will not grant such license, but will pretend to under certain circumstances.

Mel Thom:

The tribal Indian doesn't think of making money—and certainly would not see that as a purpose in life! Just wants to make a living and live—not live to make a living.

Robert Thomas:

Americans confuse consumption with experience.[64]

Not oblivious of the ethical dilemmas vexing their discipline, anthropologists have increasingly attempted to reform, sometimes by adding (dis)ingenuous "prefaces"

or other marginal notations in which they "confess" their First World or colonialist complicity in the "research" they are describing. Barbara Tedlock, in her book about "her" Zunis, *The Beautiful and the Dangerous: Dialogues* [sic] *with the Zuni Indians,*[65] employs a first-person present narrative as such a disarming device: "I fall in love with the beauty of the high desert and native peoples [note the equation]. . . . In my person as an ethnographer, I record ancient myths, rituals and ceremonies. Zuni was . . . our [she collaborates with her husband, Dennis Tedlock] first serious encounter with Otherness. . . . Time spent not so much in the living of a particular life, but rather in the [she means "our"] searching for an alternative life." Furthermore, she admits to "moral" qualms: "During participant observation, ethnographers move back and forth between being emotionally engaged participants and coolly dispassionate observers of the lives of others. This strange procedure is not only emotionally upsetting but morally suspect in that ethnographers carefully establish intimate human relationships and then depersonalize them—all, ironically in the name of the social or human sciences."[66] The problem can be rectified if ethnographers now undertake, as Tedlock herself has, to include the Self [sic] *along with the Other:* "both Self and Other are presented together within a single multivocal text focused on the character and process of the human encounter. This emergent form of writing is known as 'narrative ethnography.'" According to Tedlock, "The world . . . is re-presented as perceived by a situated narrator, who is also present as a character in the story that reveals his or her own personality. This enables a reader to identify the consciousness that has selected and shaped the experiences within the text." Wait a minute! You mean, Ms. Tedlock, that we never knew before that you, the author, the "anthro," were "selecting and shaping the text"? You really think Indians haven't noticed the anthropological forked tongue emerging from one side of the mouth as the "absolutely fake" Zunis, and from the other as the scholarly "situated narrator"?[67]

Once again, the anthros circle their rusting wagons against marauding "Native" critics. Their discipline, their livelihoods, their raisons d'être at stake, they send out clouds of disguising smoke while calling for heavy artillery reinforcements. The cavalry's big guns are, of course, those connoisseurs whose "hobby" is Native America. Fully aware of the hobbyists' continuing lust for their blood and bones, Native intellectuals repeatedly prick the collective memories of tribal people telling and retelling the story of missing bones and bodies.

One of the more prominent participants in the 1973 siege of Wounded Knee, Anna Mae Pictou Acquash, was mutilated by the FBI after she was found, mysteriously murdered, three years later. The FBI, already suspect in Indian Country because of its merciless—and corrupt—war against the American Indian Movement, explained that its agents had cut both hands from the body and sent them to Washington "for identification." The event horrified Native America. Joy Harjo wrote a poem, "For Anna Mae Pictou Aquash, Whose Spirit Is Present Here and in the Dappled Stars (for we remember the story and must tell it again so we may all live)." The work includes the lines, "You are the shimmering young woman / who found her voice, / when you were warned to be silent, or have your body cut away / from you like an elegant weed."[68]

The historical desecration of other Indian bodies is similarly the subject of poetry. Adrian C. Louis has written a "Christmas Carol for the Severed Head of Mangas Coloradas," which commemorates the beheading of the body of the murdered Mimbres chief: "Later, an Army surgeon removed / his savage brain and measured it somehow. / Scholars at the time were amused / and amazed that it measured / the same weight as Daniel Webster's." The poem concludes, "if one could imagine / an Apache warrior ever crying / One tear of Mangas Coloradas would outweigh / all the Indian history books ever / written by white men." Wendy Rose, in her turn, not only condemns Indian bone collecting in many poems, but extends her condemnation to such treatment of all indigenous people. One poem, "Truganinny," records the history of the last survivor of the original inhabitants of Tasmania. As she approached death, Truganinny begged not to be stuffed and displayed as her husband had been before her. The Australians, no more decent than their U.S. counterparts, ignored her wish; her corpse remained on public show for eighty years.[69]

Thus, perhaps, the origin of the title of a recent travel article, "Corners of Tasmania Are Forever England." The piece, written by a Russian, Vitali Vitaliev, describes the wonderful variety of "different cultures" accommodated by Tasmania. Unlike America, however, Tasmania shows no trace of the island's original indigenous culture. The sole lament for what was before comes in a paragraph describing indigenous animals: "Despite the fact that the last known specimen of the Tasmanian tiger died in captivity in 1939, there have been thousands of sightings of the beast since then." Vitaliev was entranced by the place built on the bones of murdered Tasmanians by the English: "It was a landscape straight out of my childhood dreams: neat houses under red-tiled roofs, quiet streets running down to the River Dervent, the hunched back of the Tasman bridge, tiny antiques shops in Salamanca Market." And not only the "improved" landscape seduced him: "it was not only the natural [sic] beauty of Tasmania, it was also the profound spirituality of the island, the nostalgia for good old Europe." "The first English settlers," he continues, "fell over themselves to recreate in Tasmania their native country, which they knew they would never see again." This process, perhaps, overdetermined their slaughter and subsequent exhibition of those to whose land their English compatriots had condemned them.[70]

One group of mid-nineteenth-century Anglo-Californians discovered a similar impulse to collect and display Indians when the so-called "Lone Woman of San Nicolas Island" was discovered living on the rocky offshore island from which her people had been captured to work ashore as "Mission Indians" several years earlier. Because, like Ishi after her, she was an artifact of a vanished—and no longer threatening—tribe, she was quickly assimilated, transformed from a wild "Lone Woman," whose lost language prevented her from telling a name, into a Victorian heroine. According to the quickly disseminated story, her infant had accidentally been left behind during the "removal" of her tribe to the ship that would carry them into Mission slavery. Realizing this, the Lone Woman had leapt overboard to swim back to her baby. With this maternal gesture, she forever removed herself from the category "Indian" and made her place on the female pedestal. By thus attaining an unusual bourgeois perfection she was spared the fate encountered more than sixty years later by another "last of his (Yahi) tribe" (and last of the Yana people), Ishi. But it was a near miss. In 1880, *Scribner's Monthly* published an account by Emma Hardacre that described what happened soon after the Lone Woman's capture: "Captain Nidiver conducted the woman to his home and put her in charge of his Spanish wife. The news spreading, Father Gonzales, of Santa Barbara Mission, came to see her; many persons gathered from the ranches round about, and the house was crowded constantly. The brig *Frémont* came into port soon after, and the captain offered Nidiver the half of what he would make if he would allow her to be exhibited in San Francisco. This offer was refused, and also another from a Captain Trussil. *Mrs. Nidiver would not hear of the friendless creature being made a show for the curious*"[71] (emphasis added).

This apparently did not halt public speculation about this unusual woman, however. Hardacre explains, "The gentleness, modesty, and tact [she could not speak any language her captors understood] of the untutored wild woman of the Pacific were so foreign to ideas of the savage nature that some parties believed that she was not an Indian, but a person of distinction cast away by shipwreck, and adopted by the islanders before their removal from their home. . . . The old sailors who rescued her affirm that she was an Indian. . . . The representative of a lost tribe, she stands out from the Indians of the coast, the possessor of noble and distinctive traits; provident, cleanly, tasteful, amiable, imitative, considerate, and with a maternal devotion which civilization never surpassed."[72]

Thus exempted from more common attitudes, protected by a woman who admired her "maternal" nature and pitied her "friendless" plight, the Lone Woman escaped the rapacious collecting instincts of the American public. (Not entirely, however. Her "rescuer" recognized the value of all her possessions, including her clothing. "When the schooner was reached, she went aboard without any trouble, sat down near the stove in the cabin, and quietly watched the men in their work on board. To replace her feather dress, which he wished to preserve, Brown made her a petticoat of ticking; and with a man's cotton shirt and gay neckerchief, her semicivilized dress was complete."[73]) She did not live long in "civilization," however; only a few weeks after her removal from San Nicolas, she ceased eating. Soon thereafter, she died. And even in death her character protected her: "In a walled cemetery . . . close to the Santa Barbara Mission, under the shelter of the tower, is the neglected grave of a devoted mother, the heroine of San Nicolas."[74]

The tale ends with the advice that "her grave will be pointed out to any one by the Franciscan brothers on the hill." During our repeated summer trips to the Mission, however, it was never pointed out to us, despite my mother's tales to the Mission's priests about her Indian children.

That first encounter with my Indian analogue, lying in her case at the Southwest Museum, elicited an internal rage that has never died. Ironically, it was death that brought horribly to life the fulfillment of one Oka chief's prophecy, recorded in 1869: "This land is ours—ours by right of possession; ours as a heritage. . . . We will die on the soil of our fathers, and our bleaching skeletons shall be a witness to nations yet unborn."[75]

Fuel to feed our burning witness was everywhere in our childhood: more bodies, more bones, stories of smallpox blankets, Grandfather's murderous boarding school, suicide and despair in the home nations of our friends at the Indian Center. Although I have no memory of didactic lectures about my responsibilities to my grandfather's people, I cannot recall a day—after age four or so—when I did not know that I had been born to try to bear the burdens of brave, decent, and (above all) honest ancestors, repeatedly murdered, deceived, cheated, captured, and imprisoned by the other ancestors, who, in our family taxonomy (simplified by our white grandparents' avoidance of us) were mean, bigoted, rich, people.

Looking out for "them," then, *inside* myself as well as everywhere outside, became my mixed-blood imperative.

It wasn't easy; like Indian kids everywhere I ran away—from myself, from school—constantly.

> It is difficult to recount this story without acute embarrassment, but when I was in the third grade, and escaping school almost daily, the principal summoned my parents to explain that my "behavior problem" was due to the undo pressure they put on me. When asked to explain, she told them (in deathless "eduspeak") that I was creating constant trouble because I was trying to achieve beyond my potential. My parents demanded that I be given an intelligence test. If I did turn out to be less intelligent than they thought, they promised to see that I did not run home from school. The principal agreed and I was removed from my regular classroom for three full days of testing. I remember being relieved that I did not have to be bored in my classroom for those days, at least. I also remember that the test seemed very stupid; at one point I was given a string of wooden beads, together with a bunch of unstrung beads and a string and told to duplicate the first string, matching shapes and colors. "Pretty dumb," I thought. I do not remember—though I've been told often enough since then—that the principal called my parents to apologize for her mistake. From then on, I was a cheerful participant in all the variety of supplementary programs (including much longed-for visits to hear the Los Angeles Symphony, with Leonard Bernstein conducting several children's concerts) given to "gifted" ("culturally deprived" avant la lettre) children in the Los Angeles City School System of that era. But I still kept on running.

Unlike most boarding-school children, I could make it home; I could run to the dry, sandy, scrub-dotted wash behind our housing tract to catch horned toads, to wait for coyote.

.3.

BUFFALO BILL'S DEFUNCT[1]

In . . . celebration [of Los Angeles] . . . some reminders of the intercultural heritage were to be seen, but the Indian element in the parade was in the nationwide stereotype. . . . [There were] half a dozen representatives of the noble red man of the forest, who, with their lay figure of Captain Jack of the Modocs, contributed not a little to the hilarity of the occasion.

J. J. Warner, Benjamin Hayes, and J. P. Widney, 1876[2]

In the United States we are known and visible, but not as ourselves in our real situations. In fact, we are romanticized almost to death. I believe that every U.S. President so far has been presented with a plains Indian headdress as part of his campaign strategy; not to win Indian friends, but to prove to the public that he is a straight-shooting frontiersman. . . . Every year we lose more land. Every year we get poorer and more desperate. Every year more Indian young people commit suicide or are committed to prisons. Yet we are exploited by every "movement" and cause, from the political parties to the hippies to the ecologists, and this has always been true.

Jimmie Durham, 1993[3]

The extent to which popular culture has rendered American Indians—as a group or as a handful of "desirable" tribes—the objects of mass nostalgia or spiritual longing is captured in a letter from Hawaii, published recently in *Indian Country Today*, the nation's largest Native newspaper. I quote it in its entirety:

I was born and raised in Hawaii. I have always loved the Sioux because of a special man. *Tashunke Witco*—Crazy Horse.

I love *Indian Country Today*, and will always subscribe until the day I die.

This year is the first time I have gotten some Native American items. I feel since I am not over there, these items make me feel like being there.

The letter from Tim Standing Soldier was right on. We had a bar named Crazy Horse,

but it was soon changed in a matter of weeks. Also Claudia Iron Hawk Sully's letter
made me feel warm and proud.

I am a white man, but my heart has always been Lakota.

Thanks for the crossword puzzles for I am trying to learn the Lakota language.

Can you imagine trying to take away all Indian languages and customs?

Then during World War I, the Navajo code speakers came through.

They were honored for their deeds by the same people who were against native
peoples' ways.

     John J. Mastusovic Jr.

     Honolulu, Hawaii

Initially, the writers' syntax and tone seemed pitiable: here, surely, was a barely educated person, reaching out to those the movies had taught him to admire—indeed, sufficiently to drive him to fall in love with Lakotas, to study the Lakota language, and to declare that his "heart has always been Lakota" (whatever that might
mean). Moreover, his confusion about the era of the Navajo Code Talkers, who,
along with their less well-known Hopi counterparts, foiled Japanese attempts to
decode secret military transmissions in the Pacific Theatre in World War II, underscored the possibility that the writer is only semi-educated.

    And yet, on second reading, another thought struck me. Perhaps Mr. Mastuso-
vic usually writes and speaks "standard" English. Perhaps this strange semi-co-
herent syntax was invented—a "whiteman's" response to the "Tonto-talk" which
almost always signals "Indian" to consumers of American mass culture?[4] Perhaps,
as he wrote, his mind accompanied his efforts with the sounds of indistinct, but
formal, measured (even "poetic") gruntings, such as those almost always heard by
white people listening to Indians?

> One Glenn Baxter cartoon mocks such stereotypes. It shows two fur traders faced by an
> Indian who holds a sign reading "White man's head on fire." The trader, "Thune-
> grench," whose hair is indeed blazing, is saying, patronizingly, "Quite good, Running
> Elk—your work on the apostrophe is coming along—but there is still much to learn."[5]

    The contradictory stereotype of Indians speaking both in "poetry" (a sign that
the speakers were great leaders) and in brief, guttural phrases (reduced to their
simplest elements, as is the language of children) was born long before Mr. Mas-
tusovic put pen to paper. Debates about most Indians' evident inability to use a
variety of pronouns, conjunctions, or complex verb forms (in any of the European languages of conquest) raged from the moment of contact. At the same
time, many late sixteenth-century European intellectuals (particularly those who
traveled to the Americas) were struck by the rhetorical beauty of Native people's

public recitations (even when they were hearing or reading them in translation). Of course this did not suggest to most of them that Indians were in any way the equal of "old world" orators. In a world in which systems of writing were taken as markers of "civilization," the exclusively oral cultures of Native America identified indigenous people as hopeless "barbarians." Once that hierarchy was established, however, the invaders often felt free to compliment the formal and aesthetic skills of Native orators doing the necessary work in "preliterate" societies of passing culture from generation to generation.

One Franciscan, Bernardino de Sahagún, writing in the final quarter of the sixteenth century, remarked the cultural significance of Native orators in the mixed terms that came to dominate this discourse:

All nations, however savage and decadent they have been, have set their eyes on the wise and strong in persuading. . . . There are so many examples of this among the Greeks, the Latin, the Spaniards, the French. . . . The same was practiced in this Indian nation, and especially among the Mexicans, among whom the wise, superior, and effective rhetoricians were held in high regard. And they elected these to be high priests, lords, leaders, and captains, no matter how humble their estate.[6]

Thirty years later, Juan de Torquemada, another Franciscan, described didactic speeches given by Native parents to their children (including a rare women's speech—from mother to daughter). According to Walter D. Mignolo, Torquemada found these speeches hard to translate:

We have not been able to translate them into Spanish with the gentleness and mildness which these people used in their own language, and we have dwelt more on translating the meaning of the doctrine plainly and clearly than the eloquence of the language they used themselves; for I confess that when these people express themselves, be it either to tell of their good or their bad fortune, they are outstanding rhetoricians.

Lest this imply that they might therefore contend with European orators, however, Torquemada quickly explained that theirs was a skill imbibed from "nature":

They have [not] heard the rhetorical precepts of the type taught by Quintilian or Cicero in his divisions, but rather . . . they have a natural capacity, and they are so eloquent that they can talk about anything they desire with great ease. Any high-minded person . . . would conclude, given the said conversations and notices, that these poor wretches, and native Indians of Mexico, Tetzcuco, Tlaxcalla, and its environs, were able to understand and sense things by dint of natural reason, some more so than others, as with any culture.[7]

At the same time, the link between written languages with "pure" and firm grammatical structures and intellectual superiority was clear to every European. (As we shall see, the Lone Ranger's writers also insisted on this connection.) Their languages, replete with complicated grammatical cartographies, thus constituted the appropriate languages of imperial conquest. Antonio de Nebrija, writing in August 1492, began his Spanish grammar by arguing, "language was always the companion of empire; they began, grew and flourished together."[8]

Although many among the educated invaders initially combined Nebrija's principle with praise for the (startling) rhetorical abilities of indigènes, their successors, increasingly caught up in the genocide of conquest, soon dispensed with admiration in favor of assigning Native people to a linguistically debased category.

The exigencies of occupation, together with the necessity to "Christianize" the Native populace, led to another debate over language, a debate in which the indigenous population once again found itself tossed from side to side without any "say" (despite their admittedly superior orality) in the matter. On the one hand were those who argued that Native people should learn religion in their own languages—thus necessitating considerable language learning on the part of would-be missionaries, who would then, at least by implication, acknowledge the worth (by whatever measure) of indigenous languages. On the other were gathered the language nationalists. "On the one side of this conflict," writes Anthony Pagden,

there were those, for the most part members of the religious orders, who claimed, as did for instance the Jesuit historian, José de Acosta, that not only were the autochthonous American languages fit vehicles for acculturation, but that as they were the only possible road into the unsettling minds of the Amerindian peoples, they were also the only possible means to true evangelization. No people, he argued, will willingly adopt the religion and the culture of another, unless it can be persuaded of the desirability of what it is being asked to accept in terms which are immediately and powerfully intelligible to it. . . . On the other side were the regular clergy, and increasingly, the crown and its agents, who shared the view that the belief systems of a culture were too closely tied to the language spoken by that culture for any form of instruction to be possible in any other tongue. "Speaking Christian" came to mean speaking Spanish, or possibly Latin.[9]

As the debate raged through the centuries of conquest, the belief that "Christianization" (which of course also meant "civilization") was achieved only through dominant European languages meant that Indian languages were more and more linked to barbarity and paganism. Moreover, connecting the inferiority of native peoples with their "inferior" languages helped to justify the mass slaughter of the "uncivilized" people who spoke in debased tongues. "All the participants in the battle over the worth of Amerindian languages agreed, *mutatis mutandis,* on one premise: that language was the prime indicator of rationality, that what a man spoke was, to a very large degree, what a man was."[10] Needless to say if "he" (and doubtless even more if "she") spoke only what was by definition an "irrational" (non-literate) language. . . .

By the end of the eighteenth century, the debate had become obsolete: the question of language had been settled firmly in favor of Europe's tongues, and obviously, in most of North American, in favor of English. Most subsequent scholars (increasingly through the nineteenth century, anthropologists) who took up the question of Native American languages agreed that their colonial subjects, Indians, could never appreciate the complexities and wonders of European civilization because their Native languages simply had no words with which to comprehend the various manifestations of European superiority. An entire epistemology soon emerged from this self-serving conviction. "[Hurons] are ignorant of the ceremonial and complimentary terms and of a number of verbs which Europeans employ to give force to their discourses," wrote one Frenchman. "They only know how to speak in order to know how to live. They have not a single word which is either useless or superfluous."[11] In his *History of America* (1777) William Robertson wrote in a similar vein: "'the mind of man, while still in the savage state' recognizes only such objects 'as may be subservient to his use, or can gratify any of his appetites, attract his notice; he views the rest without curiosity or attention. Satisfied with considering them under that simple mode in which they appear to him, as separate and detached, he neither combines them so as to form general classes, nor contemplates their qualities apart from the subject in which they adhere. . . . Thus he is unacquainted with all the ideas which have been denominated *universal,* or *abstract,* or of *reflection.*'"[12]

Thus were planted the scholarly and ideological roots of a simple, childlike, and above all practical, Indian, who expressed himself or herself in "Tonto-speak." Although the middle of the twentieth century continued to idealize key Native orators—especially those long dead in the Indian wars—it was generally believed that most Indians, good or bad, "renegade" or "hang-around-the-fort," talked in an instantly recognizable combination of the first person singular subject (in the objective case: "me"), simple, present-tense verbs ("want"), single syllable nouns ("meat"), and a variety of hand signals.

As usual, however, tribal tricksters quickly turned all these language assumptions on their heads. Vine Deloria tells one typical story. In 1963, a conference was held for trainee missionaries to the Navajo nation:

A Navaho interpreter was asked to demonstrate how the missionary's sermon was translated into Navaho. So the white missionary gave a few homilies and the interpreter spoke a few words of Navaho. The trainees cooed with satisfaction that meaning could actually be transferred into a barbaric tongue like Navaho.

One missionary was skeptical, however, and asked if there were specific words in Navaho that were comparable to English words. He was afraid, he said, that the wrong message might be transmitted. So he asked what the Navaho word for "faith" was. Quickly, the Navaho replied with the desired word. "Yes," the missionary commented, "that's all very nice. Now what does that word *mean?*" "Faith," replied the Navaho, smiling.[13]

A mere sharing of a lingua franca, however, does not necessarily ensure understanding between would-be theologians. That it is all much more complicated than that was demonstrated in another meeting between European Christian and Navajo, this at Emory University in Atlanta in 1993 during a visit by Stephen Plummer, the Episcopal Bishop of the Navajo Nation. I arranged for him to talk informally with a group of students and faculty, one of whom was British and fervently high Anglican. After watching the expressions on the mostly white faces as he spoke briefly about life as a Navajo Episcopal Bishop, Stephen Plummer began to realize the depth of ignorance in the room. So he reached for a story that might allow these strangers access to his world. He began talking about the way in which he "translated" English spirituality into "Navajo," drawing parallels, for example, between Navajo creation stories and Christian ones. When he finished, the British professor asked in earnest tones, "If you draw these comparisons in your theological teaching, how do you then distinguish between which version is true and which is myth?" The Bishop stared at him for a very long time, visibly perplexed. Finally, he said, "But they are both true." The professor was thunderstruck. Eyes wide, he insisted, "But what about the story of Christ's crucifixion and resurrection? What about the redemption? How do you, as a Christian, make it clear that this is the revealed word of God?" The Bishop simply gazed silently back across a cultural abyss, willing, but equally stymied.

In the case of the cultural history of the United States, it is not entirely clear when observers (including both popular and canonical writers) began to shift from allowing some Native speech the poetic qualities noted by the first invaders to putting the laconic, terse, "Tonto-talk" of western movies into the mouths of virtually all Natives. It should be possible to track the literary move; nineteenth-century American literature was—not surprisingly, given the near-constant self-congratulation of those manifestly destined conquerors—replete with "Indians." And for a child who read steadily—from the age of three and a half, when, early one

Sunday morning, looking through the thick comics section of the *Los Angeles Times,* I realized quite suddenly that I was actually reading for myself—every mention of Indians, in the thousands of books (from culture high and low) avidly consumed over the years, taught me a complicated, often bizarre, tale of America's tribal people. (Of course, such learning could not become conscious until I grew up, and then only after I recovered a sense that literature had a history, an idea nearly erased by the satraps of New Criticism who ran the English faculty at Berkeley in the early 1960s.)

James Fenimore Cooper (whose work I loathed) offered early nineteenth-century Indians who did not grunt, but spoke instead a rather formal, deliberately exoticized, English, accompanied by the familiar "sign" language. At one point in *The Last of the Mohicans,* for example, Uncas speaks in Delaware, demanding:

"Do any of my young men know whither this run will lead us?" A Delaware stretched forth a hand, with the two fingers separated, and indicating the manner in which they were joined at the root, he answered: "Before the sun could go his own length, the little water will be in the big." Then he added, pointing in the direction of the place he mentioned, "the two make enough for the beavers."[14]

Despite Cooper's evidently strenuous efforts, James Russell Lowell was not fooled: "[Cooper's] Indians, with proper respect be it said / Are just Natty Bumppo, daubed over with red." These same implausible characters drove Mark Twain to satire in an essay which helps date the establishment of common Indian stereotypes in America's collective psyche:

Cooper's gift in the way of invention was not a rich endowment; but such as it was he liked to work it. . . . In his little box of stage-properties he kept six or eight cunning devices, tricks, artifices for his savages . . . and was never so happy as when he was working these innocent things and seeing them go. A favorite one was to make a moccasined person tread in the tracks of the moccasined enemy, and thus hide his own trail. Cooper wore out barrels and barrels of moccasins in working that trick. Another stage-property that he pulled out of his box pretty frequently was his broken twig. He prized his broken twig above all the rest of his effects, and worked it the hardest. It is a restful chapter in any book of his when somebody doesn't step on a dry twig and alarm all the reds and whites for two hundred yards. . . .

If Cooper had any real knowledge of Nature's ways of doing things, he had a most delicate art in concealing the fact.[15]

And Hiawatha (as Mother recited it to us frequently) featured no monosyllabic "Tonto-talk":

Only Minnehaha softly
Whispered, saying, "they are famished;
Let them do what best delights them;
Let them eat, for they are famished."[16]

In Herman Melville's *Moby-Dick*, in stark contrast to the African-American ship's cook, "old Fleece" who spoke a music hall dialect ("Stop dat dam smackin' ob de lips!") the Indian harpooneer, Tashtego ("an unmixed Indian from Gay Head") passed most of the novel speaking the same English as the Pequod's other sailors, though he was—in keeping with the mid-century stereotype—considerably less verbose. Until near the end of the novel, the only hint of Tashtego's linguistic savagery was his recurring use of a sound that would become "Ugh" a few years later. When the sailors are gathered one midnight, singing, dancing, and telling tales, Tashtego, "quietly smoking" amid the noise, reacts to the physical antics of the "French Sailor" with: "That's a white man; he calls that fun: humph! I save my sweat." Later in the same scene, "A row a'low, and a row aloft—Gods and men—both brawlers! Humph!" Sometimes, he utters a "war whoop": "Woo-hoo! Wa-Hee!" (echoed by the two other "savage" harpooneers, the African Daggoo—"Kee-hee! Kee-hee!," and Queequeg: "Ka-la! Koo-loo!").

Near the end of the novel, however, perhaps signaling the imminence of death, Melville abruptly alters Tashtego's language: "Um, um, um. Stop that thunder! Plenty too much thunder up here. What's the use of thunder? Um, um, um. We don't want thunder; we want rum; give us a glass of rum. Um, um, um!" (Except for the Pequod's lone survivor, Ishmael, Tashtego is the last of the crew to be seen, "a red arm and a hammer hover[ing] backwardly uplifted in the open air.")[17]

However scornful of Cooper's fake Indians, Mark Twain provided his own version a few decades later in the problematic *mixed-blood* "Injun Joe." This character, featured as a primary villain in *The Adventures of Tom Sawyer,* did not grunt, or speak in gutturals. Introduced as one of what Huck Finn and Tom Sawyer at first perceive to be three devils come at midnight to the graveyard where the boys are attempting to cure warts with a dead cat, Injun Joe murders one of his companions, telling him first, "Five years ago you drove me away from your father's kitchen one night, when I come to ask for something to eat, and you said I warn't there for any good; and when I swore I'd get even with you if it took a hundred years, your father had me jailed for a vagrant. Did you think I'd forget? The Injun blood ain't in me for nothing."[18]

From the moment they witness the murder—and Injun Joe's successful deception of his partner, the drunken Muff Potter, who believes he did the deed—Tom

and Huck live in terror of the "half-breed" who "never forgets." Mark Twain's Injun, then, thus reveals another character trait that will remain in the American folk
lexicon: he never forgets a wrong.

(How curious these white people! Once most tribal people have been slaughtered, once all desirable land stolen, once the tiny remaining Native population
has been successfully imprisoned on "reservations," the conquerors tell themselves
that their victims will forever carry the memory of the terrible injustice—*because
they carry that memory in their blood.*)

> *Anne and I saw this story on television at our aunt's and uncle's tin-roofed house when
> we were five and six years old. Without children of their own—yet—our relatives prob-
> ably thought that watching the movie of "Tom Sawyer" on their new black and white
> TV would be a treat for us. Instead, their two little nieces, protected from most televi-
> sion or film and thus not at all defended against the sound and light effects of television
> (exacerbated by the scary crackling of their roof, cooling in the evening air), were ut-
> terly terrified—especially by Injun Joe's malevolent presence in the graveyard. I don't
> know if the fact that our 6'7" uncle was also an Indian—and looked like the actor
> playing the character—made us more frightened than we were already. Certainly we
> never forgot.*

This elephantine quality was not always deployed to create fear of Indians in
popular culture. Many of the children's books we read and reread featured Indians whose memories of earlier white kindness "saved" settlers from the wrath of
their fellows. One widely read series of children's books were (and are) those by
Laura Ingalls Wilder, which purportedly told the tale of her mother's "pioneer"
adventures as her family moved "west" from Wisconsin to Kansas and onward.
Like most other American girls of my generation, I knew every detail of the lives
lived in *Little House on the Prairie, On the Banks of Plum Creek, By the Shores of Silver
Lake*. What those of us who were tribal children learned from Wilder's books was,
however, a bit different from what non-Native children learned.

Little House on the Prairie takes place in "Indian country": "In the West the land
was level, and there were no trees. The grass grew thick and high. There the wild
animals wandered and fed as though they were in a pasture that stretched much
farther than a man could see, and there were no settlers. Only Indians lived there."
But not for long: when Laura queries her mother's unexplained dislike for those
whose land the family was invading—"This is Indian country, isn't it? . . . What did
we come to their country for, if you don't like them?"—Ma replies, "Pa had word
from a man in Washington that the Indian Territory would be open to settlement
soon" so "the Indians would not be here long."[19] But before the Indians leave, at

Uncle Bob, Aunt Phyllis, Bobby, and Robin Penn.

least one Encounter is inevitable. The scene is set: for several nights running, a pack of howling wolves surrounds the family's tiny shelter. Only the Wilders' faithful dog, "Jack," stands between them and those wolves as they all lie awake, listening to the eerie, fearful sounds outside.

One day soon after the ominous arrival of the wolves, Pa goes hunting, leaving Jack tied up guarding the house. As Laura and Mary play nearby, the dog suddenly growls a warning: "The hair on his neck stood straight up and his eyes glared red." Laura looks around: "she saw two naked, wild men coming, one behind the other, on the Indian trail." (Indians, we all know from the movies, *never* walk along side by side. It is probably something about those moccasin trails.) "They were tall, fierce looking men [of course, "squaws" never left home]. Their skin was brownish-red. Their heads seemed to go up to a peak, and the peak was a tuft of hair that stood straight up and ended in feathers. Their eyes were black and still and glittering, like snake's eyes."[20]

What happens next is familiar from dozens of westerns. Without noticing the two little girls nearby, the "terrible men" enter the house, where "Ma" is alone with the baby. The two sisters hiding outside, terrified, decide to obey Father's earlier order not to release the growling, salivating dog (who would, of course, kill Indians just as readily as he would kill wolves: they are all dangerous animals). Bravely, they join their mother in the house, which has begun to stink from the "horrible smell" of the Indians. Laura examines them carefully:

First she saw their leather moccasins. Then their stringy, bare, red-brown legs, all the way up. Around their waists each of the Indians wore a leather thong, and the furry skin of a small animal hung down in front. The fur was striped black and white, and now Laura knew what made that smell. The skins were fresh skunk skins. A knife like Pa's hunting-knife, and a hatchet like Pa's hatchet, were stuck into each skunk skin. The Indians' ribs made little ridges up their bare sides. Their arms were folded on their chests. . . . Their faces were bold and fierce and terrible. Their black eyes glittered. . . . Both Indians were looking straight at her. . . . Two black eyes [still] glittered down into her eyes. The Indian did not move, not one muscle of his face moved."[21]

Of course, these preposterously garbed fakes speak only in "short, harsh sounds." Of course Ma feeds them and they eat greedily, crouched on the floor like animals, making animal noises, while the four females watch in silent terror. Of course, too, they "grunt" before they get up from the floor, then, making "harsh sounds in [their] throat[s]," they "walked across the floor and out through the door. *Their feet made no sound at all*" (emphasis added).[22] The rest of the plot—though replete with other "natural" hazards, each of which is overcome by the stalwart pioneers—is obvious. Ma, despite her vicious prejudices, has made some crucial Indian friends, who—because they never forget—will rescue them, and indeed all the would-be settlers in Indian Territory—when other Indians decide to chase them out.

There are only a few variations on this time-worn theme. One evening, as the family rests beside the fire, Ma begins to sing the words to a song Pa is playing on his fiddle:

> Wild roved an Indian maid
> Bright Alfarata
> Where flow the waters
> Of the blue Juniata.

Strong and true my arrows are
In my painted quiver,
Swift goes my light canoe
Adown the rapid river

This story, intriguing for its female "lead," ends ominously:

Fleeting years have borne away
The voice of Alfarata,
Still flow the waters
Of the blue Juniata.

Laura, again with an annoying curiosity, asks, "Where did the voice of Alfarata go, Ma?" "Oh," Ma finally answers, "I suppose they went West. That's what the Indians do." When Laura presses the issue (such an explanation must surely have seemed absurd even to a fairly stupid child), asking "Why do they go west?" Pa steps in: "When the white settlers come into a country, the Indians have to move on. The government is going to move these Indians farther west, any time now. That's why we're here, Laura. White people are going to settle all this country, and we get the best land because we get here first and take our pick. Now do you understand?" She doesn't, continuing her obtuse inquiry into manifest destiny: "But Pa, I thought this was Indian Territory. Won't it make the Indians mad to have to—" But Pa interrupts: "No more questions, Laura."[23]

Of course, Pa soon realizes the Indians *are* "mad," and not only in the sense of "angry." When they gather in a war camp nearby, the family spends several more "nightmare" nights—this time hearing the ominous "throb" of Indian drums and the "wild yipping" of the Indians. "The Indian war-cry," is, Pa tells his family, "the Indian way of talking about war." But for a while, at least, "the Indians were only talking about it, and dancing around their fires."[24]

After many sleepless, terror- and drum-filled nights, the family is finally rescued by one "good" Indian. Guess who? Of course, he is one of Ma's earlier guests. On other occasions, he had even been treated "with kindness" by Pa. (The author adds that this Indian had tried to talk French with an ignorant Pa. Thus their Osage rescuer was not an ordinary Indian, lost in grunting, yipping savagery. Instead, he was "educated": he possessed a European—real—language.) This friend to the Wilders not only convinces the others not to attack the Wilders but he also rescues their neighbor. In the end, they accept the "inevitable" and move on.

Needless to say, this Osage was a chief. Moreover, despite his natural barbarity, he possessed what every other good, if defeated, Indian man possessed by the late nineteenth century, a "nobility" in defeat which Laura Wilder acknowledges. The closing scene sees the Indians riding—in a great long line (again, single file!)—past the Wilder house on their way west. Laura looks up at the Osage's "fierce, still, brown face. . . . It was a proud, still face. No matter what happened, it would always be like that. Nothing would change it. Only the eyes were alive in the face, and they gazed steadily far away to the west. They did not move. Nothing moved or changed, except the eagle feathers standing straight up from the scalplock on the shaved head. . . ." " 'Du Chêne himself,' Pa said, . . . and he lifted his hand in salute."[25]

How ubiquitous the clichés! By the 1930s, when the Laura Ingalls Wilder books were first published, these tired images, these overly familiar sights and sounds of "Indians" were repeated again and again in children's books (producing in their readers all the reactions—of disgust, fear, self-justification—needed to ensure the wild popularity of the coming decades' western movies). Tales of Indians good and bad, of massacres carried out and massacres foiled (each involving a white female alone with male Indians, thus suggesting, even to child readers, the dangers that an interracial society posed for white womanhood) filled the libraries and bookstores.

But the favorite book of my early childhood, *Caddie Woodlawn* (also first published in 1935), featured a twist on the familiar tale and perhaps my annual rereading of it was partly a result of my preference for this unusual version of "settlers and Indians." In this novel, the heroine, a "tomboy" who never played with girls and who despaired of her mother's general feminine wimpishness (the other reason I loved the work), befriends some Indians. (Grown men, again, of course; the author was not that advanced.) When she overhears the adults discussing an attack on her friends, she is stunned: "Massacre! Were the whites to massacre the Indians then?" Immediately she flees to the barn leaping onto the bare back of the "trustworthy" Betsy to ride to her Indian friends to warn them, despite the fact that she has heard from the grownups that the Indians are "on the war path."

Arriving in the Indian camp, Caddie again encounters a series of counter-stereotypes. "Dogs ran at her, barking, and there was a warm smell of smoke in the air. A fire was blazing in the center of the clearing. Dark figures moved about it. Were they in war paint and feathers? . . . But no, surely they were only old women bending over cooking pots. . . . There was no war paint! No feathers! Surely she and father had been right! . . . More and more Indians kept coming toward her. But they were not angry, only full of wonder." She calls for her special friend "John," and when he arrives, with "unhurried step" and "unsurprised eyes," he asks (speaking

Tonto-talk *avant la lettre*), "You lost, Missee Red Hair?" As Caddie explains, John sees that the child is trembling with cold. Helping her off her horse, John gets "the squaws" (another stereotype) to see that she is carefully fed and warmed. The differences between this scene of Indians feeding Caddie and the Wilder females feeding Indians are striking:

> One spread a buffalo skin for her to sit on. Another ladled something hot and tasty into a cup without a handle. . . . Caddie grasped the hot cup between her cold hands and drank. A little trickle of warmth seemed to go all over her body. She stretched her hands to the fire.

Once she is warm and fed, John—with "Indian patience"—asks gently, "You tell John 'gain." When he hears again the plot to massacre his people, he agrees that the band must move on. First, though, he insists upon returning Caddie safely home. Once there, he meets up with Caddie's Indian-respecting father: "For a moment they stood silent, their hands clasped in the clasp of friendship, their heads held high like two proud chieftains."

Of course, John is not really Caddie's father's equal. He continues to speak "Indian." Thus when he gives Caddie his dog (to replace—temporarily—her Nero, lost by her uncle in Cincinnati) and "scalp belt" to keep for him he says, "You keep . . . John come back in moon of yellow leaves. John go now far, far. Him might lose. You keep?"

Caddie and her brothers, American capitalists all, immediately determine to make money showing the scalp belt to the other children at school, who will pay for a chance to view the horrid object. But while planning their exhibit, Caddie is faced with another dilemma—this, too, treated in an unusual manner by the author. At their one room school the next morning, an Indian woman comes to drop off her "half-breed" children, bidding them a final goodbye because her white husband, ashamed of her race, has sent her away. The children, naturally, are deeply distressed: the youngest cries through the school day. Upon returning home, Caddie asks her mother for an explanation. Caddie's mother, unlike the parents in the *Little House on the Prairie*, is shocked. She struggles to find an explanation. "Folks seem to hate the red men more than ever they did before. Though why they should, I can't say. . . . Sam Hankinson hasn't a very strong character. Now if your father had married an Indian . . . you may be sure that he would never have sent her off because he was ashamed of her. No, not a good man like your father."

> *She is dead, so we cannot know, but it is possible that it was this sort of behavior that turned the tongue of my "three quarter breed" great-grandmother "sharp," a charac-*

teristic that made most of her grandchildren, including LaRue Bettis, who told me this, give her very wide berth. It might also explain why her father, a half-breed himself, chose to marry a woman described on their marriage certificate as "full-blodded [sic] Indian."

Caddie broods and broods until she remembers that she has been keeping a silver dollar wrapped up in her chest. After school the next day, she takes the three little Hankinson boys to the nearby general store where she indulges a fit of *noblesse oblige* buying them candy, tops, combs ("your mama would like you to keep your hair combed nice and tidy"), handkerchiefs ("nice, cheerful, red handkerchiefs, if you please"). Of course this child's actions are pure condescension: "The red was like music to their half-savage eyes. . . . 'Now you can go home,' said Caddie, [in patronizing tones—but how like those our mother used in similar situations!] giving each of them a friendly pat, 'and have a good time, and mind you remember to have clean noses and tidy hair on Monday when you come to school.' "[26]

The book—uncannily—had one more minor similarity with my history: at one point the family receives a letter telling them that their father, who had been born in England, had inherited a title and estate from an uncle. "Oh, the big house with the peacocks, Father will it be yours?" one of the children cries. Only Caddie hesitates, asking, "Would we have to leave Betsy and the animals?" Told that there would be "many fine horses" to replace them in England, Caddie thinks of another problem: "how soon would we have to go? Would it be before John came back for his dog and scalp belt?" Ultimately, the family—who had heard of these rich English relatives who had rejected their father in much the same way our rich white relations had rejected us—votes to remain "Americans." Of course, when I was reading the book, and approving her choice to remain what she was, I never guessed I should one day spend several uneasy years among England's upper classes.

The book ends with two returns. First

the Indians came back. . . . John came in and sat at the kitchen table and ate. He had no [English?] words to tell them of the strange, far wilderness where he had been, what game he had caught, what leafy trails mottled with sunshine he had traveled, what portages and shining lakes he had seen. [No problem, obviously, for the book's non-Indian author.] All he said was "John him back," and ate his pie in silence. But something of the beauty and mystery of far-off places hung about him.[27]

John has brought a pair of "moccasins, decorated with the brightly dyed quills of porcupine" for Caddie, who thanks him effusively. "But John had nothing more to say. He spoke in deeds. He took his scalp belt, grunted to his dog, and mounted his pony."

WHEN NICKELS WERE INDIANS

But of course the book is a western fairy tale and could not end on that note. So,

Still another traveler had been on his way for months now. He had no steamboat tickets; he could not ask nor understand directions. He only knew that his nose and his heart were keeping him headed in the right direction. He was footsore and muddy and full of burrs. Sometimes he was hungry and heartsick and filled with despair, but he knew that he must get home. . . . [He] trotted through a tangled wilderness, lying at night beneath the stars to lick his weary feet and sleep. One day he trotted into the farmyard—so thin, so dirty, so footsore, and covered with burrs! . . . But Caddie Woodlawn knew him. "Nero!" she cried. "Nero! *Our own dog!*"

The late afternoon sun flooded her face with golden light. . . . Her face was turned to the west. It was always to be turned westward now, for Caddie Woodlawn was a pioneer and an American.[28]

Although by no means free of familiar clichés, *Caddie Woodlawn* was a major exception to many of the rules that rendered most children's books of the era—and after—deeply offensive, sometimes in the relatively mild manner of Laura Ingalls Wilder,[29] sometimes in much more overtly racist terms. And American children were not the only consumers of disgusting stereotypes. Children's fiction from Europe, including the works of Karl May,[30] promoted (and continues to promote) a vicious stereotype of Indians (always male, warriorlike, nearly inarticulate).

One contemporary example, a brief excerpt from a popular novel by the British author Lynne Reid Banks, demonstrates my point. *The Indian in the Cupboard* (one of a successful series of "Indian tales") features a small boy, "Omri," who discovers that when he puts his plastic Indian doll into a magic cupboard it comes alive. A single scene suggests the level of the entire work:

The Indian stood there, his feet, in moccasins, planted apart on the white-painted metal floor, his chest heaving, his knife held ready, and his black eyes quite wild. Omri thought he was magnificent. "I won't hurt you," he said. "I only want to pick you up."
The Indian opened his mouth and a stream of words, spoken in that loud-tiny voice, came out, not one of which Omri could understand.
"Don't you speak English?" asked Omri. All the Indians in films spoke a sort of English; it would be terrible if his Indian couldn't. . . .
"I speak," he grunted. . . . "You touch—I kill!."[31]

Nineteenth- and twentieth-century novelists were not the only purveyors of the Tonto-talking stereotypical Indian, of course. All kinds of government officials and soldiers added their "eyewitness" evidence. As had always been the case, observations about language were often accompanied by self-serving assumptions about "mentalities." General Miles, no doubt accustomed to translator-Indians' dependence on the present tense, once noted, (cozily) "Our Indian, strange in many respects, is especially peculiar in his lack of history. He is a man who lives in the present, interested in only so much of the past as affects the present condition of himself or his tribe."[32]

To others, the way Indians spoke English was not a result of their ahistorical natures but rather a straightforward reflection of the simplicity of their own, inferior, languages. Lewis Cass, who was governor of the Michigan Territory in 1826, described the Wyandot language: "Of all the languages spoken by man, since the confusion of tongues at the tower of Babel, it least deserves this character [of being harmonious and musical]. It is harsh, guttural, and undistinguishable; filled with intonations, that seem to start from the speaker with great pain and effort." By these signs, Cass concluded, "The range of thought of our Indian neighbors is extremely limited. Of abstract ideas they are almost wholly destitute."[33]

One more recent writer has remarked that the rhythm heard by whites in many Native languages reminded the listeners of Indian drumming. Thus many translators—perhaps without realizing it—replicated the beat of drums as they repeated Indian speeches. Of course, even the most entrancing rhythms did not mean that Indian languages were in any way the equal of English. Their orality was forever the problem. As one turn-of-the-century commentator noted, "The Indians themselves are full of poetry. . . . Their eloquence is proverbial, soaring and figurative. . . . They, indeed, live poetry; it should be ours" she added generously, "to write it out for them."[34]

And indeed, "they" did write it out—for "them." In doing this writing, however, translators immediately began to create what became the stereotypical "Indian" English. It was not all "Ughs!" or "Me follow white mans," however. Often, as with Joseph's famous speech, the translation became poetry. Sometimes the translator's hand was obvious, sometimes not. (In Joseph's curious formulation, "From where the sun now stands I will fight no more forever" there is surely a mistranslation, however mysteriously "poetic" the result.) One case where the work of the translator should be abundantly obvious, though perhaps not to those who believed all Indians spoke in the accusative case, was the 1832 speech of Black Hawk, chief of the Sauk tribe. He is recorded as having said,

Black Hawk is a true Indian and he disdains to cry like a woman. He feels for his wife, his children, and friends. But he does not care for himself. He cares for his nation and the Indians. They will suffer. He laments their fate. The white men do not scalp the head; but they do worse—they poison the heart, it is not pure with them. His countrymen will not be scalped but they will, in a few years, become like the white men, so that you can't trust them.[35]

In Los Angeles in the late 1940s and through the '50s, we heard what was by then the "movie Indian" language everywhere. In the first place, we had Tonto himself, faithfully riding along beside the (white) Lone Ranger ("lone" because his only company was an Indian?[36]) whom he called "Kemo Sabe," a bastardization of the Spanish "¿Quién Sabe?"—Who Knows? Tonto ("fool," in Spanish[37]) reproduced his strange guttural language in countless radio shows, prefacing his every move with "Gettum Up, Scout!" My sister and I listened faithfully to this race-nuanced Hollywood version of Don Quixote's travels with Sancho Panza (his "fool," though one created in keeping with the European tradition of jesters and their aristocratic masters rather than one determined by race). After all, Jay Silverheels, who played Tonto, lived nearby—the target (happily a willing one) of another of our mother's "culture journeys." I recall that he reacted well to the two little Nez Perce girls on that first visit, and thereafter thrilled us by letting us ride his horses. (I also recall being shocked that he was wearing "ordinary" clothes. Such is the power of mass media to re-represent Native people, even to themselves.)

Tonto never broke into standard English, regardless of how many years he rode by the side of the impeccably grammatical Lone Ranger.[38] Even in interviews, Tonto was expected to perform his role, though occasionally he attempted irony. When one newspaper reporter jokingly asked Jay Silverheels about Tonto's tendency to "get conked on the head" in almost every show, "Tonto" replied "Oh sure. Indian play dummy part to build up situation of story. . . . Tonto get hit on head heap many times but always make drama." The interviewer then switched into a more serious tone, discussing the show not with Tonto, but rather with an articulate and "pure English-speaking" Jay Silverheels. But for all his admitted awareness that the actor was not the character, the reporter could not contain his excitement at meeting a childhood hero: "As I arose to leave," he confessed, "I squared my shoulders and cried, 'Tai-ee Kemo Sabe!' 'It's been a pleasure,' said Tonto."[39]

Indian humor counters Tonto's dilemma a bit differently. A "last episode" is told and retold in Indian country, in many different versions. One features a battle between the Lone Ranger and Tonto and a large band of ferocious Indians. Though they fight with their usual bravery and skill, the "masked man" and his Indian companion are hopelessly outnumbered. Completely surrounded, they have, in western parlance, reached the end of the trail. The Lone Ranger, true to the movie code of honor, draws his gun ready to die fighting. One last time, he turns toward Tonto: "Well, my friend, it looks like we're done for." Tonto looks straight into his eyes. The silence grows. Then Tonto speaks: "What do you mean 'we,' Kemo Sabe? What do you mean by this 'we,' Paleface?"[40]

Although it was completely clear that the Lone Ranger—whiter than white, as were his horse, his hat, his bullets—conveyed appropriate lessons in perfect English to little white fans, it was less apparent what the show's creators meant to indicate to the non-white audience.[41] At one point the show's agent, Raymond Meurer, "confided that Tonto . . . provided Negro children in the audience with an opportunity to 'identify' themselves with a hero." If Indians were "safe" role models, however, African-Americans were not. Fran Striker complained, "I'll never bring another Negro into a story again. We had one just once and he spoke in a dialect. We got hundreds of letters from Negroes all over the country." As though even more baffled, Striker added, "We've had some letters from Indians who don't like the way we show *them* either."[42]

> *This link between minorities was played out in a shameful episode of our childhood. When we were about three and four years old, Mother's women's church group— a "mission society" of some sort—chose us to "play" African children in a mission tableau. We both recall having our recalcitrant "Indian hair"—"arrow" straight and nearly uncurlable—tied into dozens of "rag curls" by grown ups, who then used burnt cork to "blacken" our faces, arms, and hands. We had little to do but stand still in a "jungle," moving out to center stage when the narrator began telling the story of the African missions. Because neither of us has forgotten this relatively trivial event— though we have both forgotten much else—it must have left a strong impression.*

Learning to be mixed bloods from Tonto and the Lone Ranger was simple: three times every week we tuned our tiny brown plastic portable radio (set on a bookshelf above my sister's bed) to the *William Tell Overture*, which signaled another episode of our favorite program.[43] On many Sundays, we got the visual version, watching a televised Lone Ranger and Tonto ride through the West righting wrongs while our own Indian, Grandfather, snoozed (apparently untroubled by this program, as he was not by some of the westerns we tuned in) in his armchair just behind us.

Although the audience for the heroes' various incarnations (in comic books—which we were forbidden—as well as in film and on TV and radio) suggests that nearly every child in America in the late 1940s and early '50s longed to become one or the other of the heroes, there were two special reasons for our devotion. First, Tonto. He reinforced all kinds of lessons we were learning about being Indian: he could track anything, anywhere; he was much more observant of people, of the natural world, than non-Natives; he was utterly honest; he was absolutely loyal; he carried a special medicine, bandaging wounds, caring for the injured, gently and with an eerie skill. And he could ride; although (in keeping with western movie custom) Scout was deliberately much smaller than Silver, a compact, speedy Pinto pony, he was fast.

Scout's modesty and smaller size held far more appeal to me than the size and demeanor of the much more phallic Silver, who evidently could not begin any action without rearing up on his hind legs. We, at least, believed that all Indian horses were special. Perhaps we secretly shared General Nelson Miles's belief, that Indian "ponies [were] as suspicious of the white man as the American horse [was] of the wild Indian."[44] And we knew which ponies *we* wanted to ride.

On the other hand, one lesson, reiterated in countless stereotypes as well as at home, proved personally very difficult (though not for *my* constant "sidekick," my much more taciturn sister). Like other Indians, Tonto was extremely reticent. Indeed, that was one reason for the choice of an Indian as the Lone Ranger's companion. As George Trendle put it, the character had to "be someone who wouldn't detract from the glory of the Ranger . . . someone who would talk little, contribute much." As perhaps the present evidence of my lifelong graphomania attests, Indian silence was one piece of Indian "lore" I was unable to replicate.[45]

At the same time, Tonto was more than a mere silent "dummy," foil for the hero Ranger. Ariel Dorfman has suggested that such "companion-servant" characters, "are problematic and rebellious beings who come from submerged but seething zones of reality. They have agreed to subordinate their energies to the superhero in order to better serve their own pure, essential natures." Thus "all who are mutilated or vexed, all who are excluded from power, either too young or too old, all who are resentful and sensitive, all the exploited and all the potentially disobedient have their place alongside the Lone Ranger." And Tonto was "our" rebel: not only because he was an Indian (and even, like us urban mixed-blood children, an Indian "without a past"), but "he speaks like an Indian, loyally follows the trails of people that must be found, has a sniffer that anyone could envy, says 'ugh' whenever it's convenient, sends smoke signals, and knows all about medicinal herbs." In a curious twist of "double consciousness," Tonto embodied, "A Post card. A caricature. He even cooks. *Practically a woman*" (emphasis added).[46] Dorfman's suggestion that Tonto was a "closet" rebel, and a feminine one at that, argues that he in fact subverted the "Americanizing" intentions of the program's creators as thoroughly and as subtly as Indians had continuously subverted efforts to draw them into the mainstream of capitalist America.

Needless to say, perhaps, such subversion was far from the consciousness of either George Trendle or Fran Striker. Both believed that their discourse—at least as embodied in the Lone Ranger—echoed that habitually used by a wide variety of government officials and other scholars interested in the "Indian problem" as I have noted. Even before educational prescriptions were promulgated to transform "shiftless" Indian children into capitalists in the 1901 *Course of Study for the Indian Schools of the United States,* the anthropologist Lewis Henry Morgan—who, let me remind readers, belonged to a white male "secret society" called "the Grand Order of the Iroquois"—believed that the objects of his romantic worship, the men of the Iroquois nation, would never "progress" until they exchanged their "ruling passion" for the hunt, for white people's overwhelming lust "for gain." The latter, according to Morgan, was the sole underpinning of "civilization."[47]

The Lone Ranger's *overt* ideological underpinnings, articulated repeatedly by the show's authors and owners [!] embodied these same virtues, those of bourgeois capitalist society. As they repeated endlessly in press releases, "free enterprise" was the primary message carried by their masked hero. However, as Tonto demonstrated, these were lessons that Indians had a great deal of trouble learning. Decades after Lewis Henry Morgan, the writers of Tonto and the Lone Ranger unconsciously created a portrait of one representative Indian that was ironically accurate in one important particular: he was *still* unable to learn the anthropologists' lessons.

Another television cowboy of the era encountered a similar dilemma, though this with "real" Indians. Gene Autry was fond of repeating a story about when he took six American Indians with his troupe on tour through England and Ireland just after the war. He described "the unique way" his quaint primitives "worked out [to] pay . . . their bills in an unfamiliar foreign currency":

"We all had a lot of trouble keeping track of the exchange rates," Autry said. "But those boys didn't even bother. They just filled their pockets with shillings. . . . Well, whenever they'd take a taxi ride or go into a shop to buy something, they'd just pay the bill with a shilling. And when the cabby or merchant would protest, they'd add another shilling or so on until the protest stopped."[48]

The Lone Ranger's creators also insisted (curiously, given North America's recent war against the authoritarian Nazis), that because the program taught children unquestioning respect for the Lone Ranger, it also taught them "to respect anyone in authority."[49] In imitating the Lone Ranger's personal cleanliness, chastity (there were no love scenes), and keen sense of order (expressed in the perfectly parsed sentences dear to the hearts of 1950s English teachers across the United States), children would quickly become patriots, presumably as devoted to the authorities who ran their country as Tonto was to the masked hero.

But, as Dorfman's analysis suggests, there were more troubling messages hidden within this quintessentially American myth (just as there were in the equally anodyne Davy Crockett shows of Walt Disney's America, as we shall see below). One such message, that of racial tolerance, was meant to overturn some common American practices. "Nowhere in the stories is any minority group referred to in a derogatory manner," boasted one agency press release.[50] Moreover, Raymond Meurer repeatedly cited one occasion in 1951 when the Lone Ranger (and Tonto, though he was not mentioned in this tale) attacked segregation directly during a benefit appearance in Miami, where the Ranger and his "handlers" were shocked to discover two separate audiences of black and white children. As Meurer reported it, because "The Lone Ranger stands for tolerance," he—and again, presumably Tonto—crossed the barrier dividing white children from black to shake "everybody's hand." Supposedly the gesture elicited great cheers from the entire crowd.[51]

> American childhoods of the 1950s were filled with (smug) admonitions against bigotry. Our Girl Scout and Brownie Handbooks included long lists of words "good Scouts" would never use. We had never heard of most of the words and had to ask Mother to explain "Spic," "Wop," "Kike," and so on. On the other hand, we knew "Nigger," as well as its companion, "Red Nigger," both terms overlooked by the Girl Scouts, as were "Injun," "Redskin," and the like. We had learned these early. Mother's method of dealing with the ubiquity of these terms was efficacious but extreme. When I was three, I came home from playing in the grounds of our apartment to ask the meaning of a word I had heard some local ladies using to describe the Chicano gardener. The word was "nigger." My mother reacted to my question by washing my mouth out with laundry soap. I had to wait until my father got home from work to find out what the women had meant.

Tonto and the Lone Ranger are riding along through the dusty countryside. Suddenly, they hear the sounds of a vicious battle raging nearby.

Lone Ranger: *"Tonto, Indians must be attacking a wagon train."*

Tonto: *"Ugh."* [52]

However well-intentioned the show's creators, the message of genuine racial tolerance—rather than self-congratulatory noblesse oblige—was continually contradicted. Not only did Tonto consistently *act* against other Indians, repeatedly joining the Ranger to rescue whites from his counterparts' savagery, but the show itself featured almost no other "good" Indians. In fact, David Wilson Parker's analysis of some 120 stories discovered only five Indian characters who were portrayed as other than the traditional barbarians of countless western movies. Most Indian characters, good or bad, appeared only to utter stock "Indian": "Me get revenge."[53] Worse, the show defined those among these "Ugh-talkers" who were "good" Indians as those with a demonstrated willingness to help outsiders settle the West.[54]

Fortunately for us, the show included some unconscious subtextual subversions. Tonto was, above all, silent. In the silent gaze of this Native, we learned, rested two qualities: one, an honesty too unswerving to be entirely "American" (whatever the protestations of the Lone Ranger); and two, a scathing judgment. When Tonto looked long and hard out of black, all-seeing Indian eyes at white strangers, the effect (unintended by the show's creators) was unsettling. "Looking someone down," as most tribal people know, has deep historical roots. One of D'Arcy McNickle's tribal characters is typical: "She had a way, all unconscious, of making other people seem small and squirmy, like something you might pluck out of your hair."[55] (It is an effect that does not endear: much of the savage brutality employed by vigilantes, "volunteers," or soldiers, doubtless resulted from seeing themselves reflected in Indian eyes—at "half their natural size"?—as the members of an unholy band of thieves and murderers they actually were.)

We had reinforcement for the lessons we were learning from Tonto. We found them included with another of America's "miracles" of modernity, cereal. Our weekly box of Nabisco Shredded Wheat held three cardboard cards dividing rows of wheat biscuits. These "Injun-uity" (get it?) cards featured lessons taught by a radio and comic book character called "Straight Arrow."[56] Straight Arrow reversed one key essential of the Lone Ranger; his "sidekick" was not an Indian, but rather a grizzled ex-prospector called "Packy" (presumably, though I don't remember, after the "pack-mules" ubiquitous in mining regions of the West). Straight Arrow was also considerably more complicated than the Lone Ranger. For one thing, he lived two identities, in the manner of Superman: one as Steve Adams, respectable white rancher, the other as "Straight Arrow," war-painted "Comanche chief," beloved of a beautiful Indian maiden, whose band was always camped a convenient horse ride away, called by the suitably infantilized name "The Fawn." During ordinary times, Steve Adams lived the life of a celibate, handsome, rich cattle rancher—a nice guy, popular with his unsuspecting neighbors, but no hero. When trouble loomed, especially when injustice threatened, Steve, accompanied by the loyal, "in the know" Packy, rode swiftly into a "hidden gold canyon" where his "real" horse, a Palomino stallion called "Fury," awaited his master's voice. (Like the Lone Ranger's silver horse, bullets, and hat, the color scheme of Straight Arrow's horse, weapons, and canyon—as well as Packy's former occupation—were all part of the capitalist twist to this creation of Hollywood and Madison Avenue.) According to the origins tale told on the introductory "Injun-uity" card, Straight Arrow was the fulfillment of an unusually a propos "old Indian legend": "Some day," the prophecy promised, "a mysterious Indian would come . . . taller and stronger and braver than any other who rode the plains. . . . When this great warrior was born, a gold arrowhead was hung around his neck. And he was called Straight Arrow. He will ride a golden horse, and shoot golden arrows." All that gold, needless to say, placed him squarely at the heart of the American dream. Yet there was one more curious aspect of this legend, this one weirder still. Despite the "manifest" origins of Straight Arrow's creators and sponsors, their creation story seemed to prophesy white doom: "He alone," the legend concluded, "will save the Indian tribes."[57] Or did this actually mean that Straight Arrow would save Indians by teaching them to be white? or by keeping them pacified? The cards, alas, did not tell.

Once safely hidden in the golden canyon, Steve transformed himself, stripping off his rancher's clothes in favor of breechclout, moccasins, feathers, and face paint. Dropping his rifle, he seized his trusty bow, arrows, and "Indian knife." And then, sometimes with Packy, sometimes alone, Straight Arrow rode off to right wrongs, signaling *his* coming with his trademark cry to his horse, "Kaneewah, Fury!"

What were Fury's origins? The name implies that the horse carried a battler against injustice. The single phenomenon that aroused Straight Arrow was that which also awakened the anger, the fury, of his white analogue, the Lone Ranger. But here again there is a second possibility. The Indian horse and his Indian rider— savior of the tribes—might also be seen to have embodied the overwhelming American injustice, the history that all 1950s Americans, including the creators and fans of Straight Arrow, lived to deny. Doubtless this possibility, like the ambiguity present in the Straight Arrow creation myth, never occurred to the show's writers or indeed, to most listeners. A "rational" reason for Indian "fury" was impossible for them to credit.

Similarly, a prominent University of Pennsylvania historian writing a half century earlier could not imagine his compatriots' complicity in the dark phenomenon of genocide. When he described the sorrow in a "characteristic Indian countenance" in his 1904 *History of the United States,* a countenance noted for "a certain serious, almost sad expression, which is readily noticed by strangers," Henry William Elson offered no hint that this might have been due to real historical events. Safe inside the conqueror's heroic myth, he explained instead, "This may result from the fact that he is never free from superstitious fear. He lives in constant dread, not of the armed foe [!] or the wild beast, but of the myriads of invisible spirits that inhabit everything in nature about him. . . . His unceasing fear of them for ages has probably set his stamp indelibly upon his face."[58]

Straight Arrow's life featured several stereotypical elements familiar to Lone Ranger fans. He bore what the American public recognized as an "Indian name." The history of these names was typically problematic. Unlike other unwilling participants in the American historical narrative, for example, enslaved Africans, Native people did not regularly suffer the erasure of their given names, although some boarding schools followed the custom practiced by colonizers elsewhere in assigning European or "Christian" names to incoming children. Instead, Indian names, particularly those carried by tribal people whose resistance earned them a grudging white respect, were often "translated" into English. When Charles Lummis visited our grandfather's school, Haskell Indian Institute, shortly after its founding in the mid-1880s (when Grandfather may well have been one of the students he "observed"), he included among the school's "wonders" the names given the boys. "You would be amused," he wrote in languid, superior tones, "if you could hear the names of these young savages. The Native titles are entirely un-pronounceable by English-speaking jaws, but the English translations—by which the pupils are now known exclusively—are ridiculous enough. They are given a gratuitous Christian name, to which is appended a translation of their father's name. For instance we have Fred Eagle, Frank Buffalo, Joseph Fireshaker, and many others. The funniest," he assured his readers, "was Moses Bear-ears."[59]

As a result of this name translation, most mid-twentieth–century white Amer-icans believed that Indians have always been called—in English!—"Standing Elk," or "Thunder Rolling in the Mountains," or, when gender called for infantilization or softening, "Fawn," "Doe," "Little Feather," "Prairie Flower," and so on.[60] (By contrast, few children of immigrants from Japan have been taught to call them-selves "Plum Mountain," though it is an English translation of a common Japan-ese name. Similarly, few German-Americans think of themselves as "Rose Tree"; few Italian-Americans answer to "Wolf Kisser.")

Despite his name, however, Straight Arrow did not ordinarily speak "Tonto-talk" (though "bad" Indians, such as "Two Paw," did: "Grass on prairie plenty tall"; and "White man, look"[61]). Nor did he shift languages once his "war paint" was in place, though when talking as an Indian he did lapse into the curiously "formal" vocabulary and nature-imagery of better-known movie Natives. In one 1948 episode, "Stage From Calvaydos," Straight Arrow first assumes his Comanche clothing then warns Packy, "My friend, we must go as quietly as the prairie wolf." On another occasion he was made to say, portentously, "Among the teepees of my people the paleface child will know safety." He was also prone to cry "Great Man-itou!" when shocked. (According to an unself-consciously ignorant Charles Lum-mis, "Manitou" was "a name for God, current in nearly all the varying Indian di-alects [sic]."[62]) Straight Arrow also enjoyed a phallic moment similar to that the Lone Ranger invariably indulged. Before riding off, Straight Arrow made his horse rear: "Up, Fury!"

Although they avoided some of the more blatant clichés, Straight Arrow's story writers were not entirely immune from pervasive stereotypes. In the course of one story, a "paleface" baby, rescued by Straight Arrow from the nefarious plans of an uncle greedy for the child's inheritance, soon learned the language of movie In-dians—despite the fact that those he was hiding among, Straight Arrow's Co-manche band, themselves spoke ordinary English. Thus when the baby's fear-crazed mother is brought to the Indian camp to be reunited with her child, she finds him waving one tiny hand in the air and calling, "Me Ind'an chiefs!"[63]

Injun-uity cards were collected by all the kids in our grade school. From them we, and our friends, learned several things about "generic" Indians which we took quite seriously. In our case, many of the lessons found support from family cultural practices—values and behaviors we Penn children were taught as our unique legacy, both Quaker and Indian. These lessons varied from the trivial to the serious, and included:

Indians walk silently.

Their silent movement was often described as "melting," as though Indians were not corporeal. One superintendent of Indian Affairs described the Indians on the Tule River reservation in California in the mid-nineteenth century: "Such of them as longed homesickly for their own lands melted from Tejon like quail in nesting time, by unguessed trails, to the places from which they had been drawn."[64] A variation on "melting" was "gliding." General Oliver O. Howard described the Little Crow's Sioux band: "They would murder a settler's family and glide on, serpent-like, to strike another."[65]

Although the requisite elements for melting or gliding silently in space were (at the very least!) moccasins and unpaved land, we practiced such actions barefoot on the pavements of L.A. Because all our friends believed this stereotype as fervently as we did, we were much in demand for such "hiding" games as "capture the flag," or "hide and go seek."

Indians could ride any horse, preferably bareback.

That most Native inhabitants of the United States were never horse owners escaped the notice of the writers of the Injun-uity cards, as it escaped the knowledge of the general U.S. population as well. Moreover, both groups seemed ignorant of the fact that mounted Indians often made, and used, elaborate saddles. Perhaps this indigenous technology would have complicated the belief that Indians were above all "close to nature," a belief that supported the justificatory view that they must inevitably disappear before the forces of nature-taming, railroad-building "civilization" and "progress"?

When I was nine, the depth of my belief in Indians' natural ability to ride any horse was tested. A horse I was riding in the San Bernardino Mountains, spooked by something on the trail I didn't see, bolted. Though I quickly dropped the reins and my feet lost hold of the stirrups, I was never afraid. I fastened my hands in the horse's long mane and enjoyed the ride, jumping ditches and gullies, climbing up

and racing down hillsides, until we were caught and stopped by a grownup, riding hard after. (My "Native" stoicism was further reinforced when I was told how
brave I had been.)

Indians always tell the truth, and, moreover, can always tell a liar.

We learned early the lesson Barney Bush teaches in these words: "Our people
were not listening closely enough to what the white folks were saying, since in our
cultures, a person's voice was the sound of the heart." This conviction that Indian
people always spoke the truth was a basic principle in our family myth. That non-
Quaker white people, by contrast, spoke with "forked tongues" was a constantly
repeated lesson, though it was a lesson I found impossible to learn and at the same
time to continue to live in what constantly stood revealed as a lying world. Only
recently have I learned Jimmie Durham's salutary motto, which life in two of
America's private universities has me repeating as a personal mantra: "Don't ask
a white man to walk a mile in your moccasins because he'll steal them and the
mile too."[66] Most non-tribal people can never understand that liars, to most Indians, are people with a disgusting personal habit. Hearing a lie, we react exactly as
though a guest has spat on the carpet. A deep embarrassment for the liar evokes
a behavior Wendy Rose has described as that of "potted plants." Of course, this is
not an efficacious reaction in a world utterly dependent upon self-deception, upon
hypocrisy and upon the willing acceptance of what Richard Nixon's minions described as "inoperative statements." Nevertheless, it is a common Indian one.[67]
Thus we all learn to accept that most Americans speak double-speak, a language
that—like all dystopian languages, including those we read about during adolescence in Aldous Huxley and George Orwell—obscures, veils, rewrites, self-justi-
fies. The evident inability to tell the truth renders the "struggle of memory against
forgetting" contemporary Native America's primary battle. It isn't easy.[68]

One of the most surprising aspects of this constant lying is people's ability to
begin believing their own lies. Perhaps "literacy" means a loss of memory; what
isn't written down, signed, dated, notarized (preferably by a member of America's
high priesthood, the bar) disappears into an *oubliette*.

Indians are stoic in the face of pain, whether emotional or physical.

At Haskell Indian Institute, my grandfather learned that Indians stood the heat of
fires better than white people. He used to demonstrate this by roasting marsh-
mallows in the fireplace using an ordinary table fork. Similarly, Mohawk men are
widely believed to be immune to the fear of heights which afflicts other people.

Thus the famous Mohawk "ironwalkers" predominate among the men who built, and continue to build, Manhattan's great skyscrapers.

A belief in Indians' emotional stoicism was born early in the conquest of North America. Our 1950s Disney hero, the "King of the Wild Frontier," Davy Crockett, described one bloody encounter with Native people in his diary:

I recollected seeing a boy who was shot down near the house. His arm and thigh were broken, and he was so near the burning house that the grease was stewing out of him. In this situation he was still trying to crawl along; but not a murmur escaped him, though he was only about twelve years old.

But lest this killer (Ride on, Santa Ana!) misunderstand, and find himself admiring his Indian child victim, Crockett went on to "reread" the scene:

So sullen is the Indian, when his dander is up, that he had sooner die than make a noise or ask a quarter. The number that we took prisoner, being added to the number we killed amounted to a hundred and eighty six.[69]

A few decades later, General Nelson Miles recounted one "singular tragedy" involving a captive band of Sioux, imprisoned after a battle in the mid-1870s. "One morning, soon after sunrise, a sharp pistol shot was heard in one of their tents, and the officer of the day and one of the guard went to ascertain the cause. He found that a young and handsome Indian woman of about 22 years of age had committed suicide." When the others learned that she was dead, "the male Indians maintained their accustomed stoical silence and dignity. One was noticed to pick up a little child and hold it in his arms during the scene of mourning, but upon his face you could discern no more emotion than upon that of a bronze statue, although the [white] officers and soldiers were greatly moved."[70]

A century later, the stereotype was little changed, though its vocabulary had shifted. One 1950s group of educational researchers, working in a social scientific frenzy, compared white children from the midwest with Indian children from Pine Ridge, Hopi, Zuni, and two sites in the Navajo nation. Their research results show a persistent inability to comprehend that Indian children might not all share a genetically determined stoicism. Any differences they discovered between Indian groups were explained by the aberrant group's "degree" of "acculturation" (by which they clearly meant both "civilization" and mixed blood). Thus they decided that the Sioux children, all mixed bloods, were much like their white counterparts in terms of their emotional "development" (another favorite word). By contrast, "the Southwest Indian children" were distressingly recalcitrant. Indeed, the

Navajo, Zuni, Hopi, and Papago children remained incomprehensibly silent and still in the face of external provocations that immediately elicited aggressive anger from Sioux or white children. The "pure-blooded" Southwestern children, concluded the researchers, shared "a more passive attitude and become angry only when other people are directly aggressive or punitive toward them."[71]

Indians never discuss with outsiders "what is in their hearts."

Herein lies one of the greatest gaps between mainstream U.S. culture (in so far as there is a single one) and Native practice. As any European caricature will attest, Americans share a fervent belief in the efficacy of self-revelation. Everyone is expected to show friendship by telling everything about themselves to everyone. Not only will each individual thereby "feel better" ("problems shared are problems halved"), but he or she is signalling emotional access, declaring "openness," that much-(over)valued American characteristic. Too, Americans believe—unquestioningly—in the value of information. Secrets are disliked, feared, shunned. "We have a *right* to know," most Americans will declare, confidently.[72] And yet few traditional Native cultures would agree. Most, indeed, believe that the most cherished secrets of the group—or of individuals—should be known, if at all, by only a few. Knowledge, in other words, carries with it a variety of dangers and responsibilities from which the young and the foolish should be protected. "Freedom of Information Acts" do not exist at Hopi.[73]

 Grandfather embodied this stereotype. There were only a few, rare occasions when he allowed access to what was in his heart. One day I was practicing the piano, playing the only Stephen Foster song I had learned, "'Way down upon the Swanee River. . . .'" (True to form, I loved it for its melancholy, understanding nothing of its contents.) Grandfather came in the house and stood just behind the piano bench, listening. When I finished, he asked if I could play any other Foster songs. I said I didn't think so, but which one would he like to hear? "'Old Black Joe,'" he replied, "It's my favorite song."

Where had he learned it? Why was it his "favorite" song? Of course an eight-year-old child doesn't think to ask. Instead I said, "But you're not black, Gramps, you're red!" He only smiled a big smile and hugged me.

Only many years later does it begin to make sense:

> Gone are the days when my heart was young and gay,
> Gone are my friends from the cotton fields away,

Gone from the earth to a better land I know
I hear their gentle voices calling
"Old Black Joe."
I'm coming, I'm coming, for my head is bending low;
I hear those gentle voices calling "Old Black Joe."[74]

How many friends had he left behind in Kansas? How foreign was Los Angeles? I am certain of only one thing: like my sister and me, like my father, he wasn't happy in a city. And of course as far as we knew, he had left behind in Kansas almost everything he had known and loved. (We were to discover, though only many years later, that this was not exactly the case, that in fact all his living brothers and sisters had lived in Los Angeles for a period during our childhood. Why we, and, as far as we know, he, had no contact with them, however, remains a mystery. Only his thoroughgoing proscription of alcohol in any form, plus his oft-repeated "Beer is for bums," hints at one possibility for his distance from his siblings.)

His reticence extended even further. Although Nez Perce tradition does not proscribe the public telling, we never knew Grandfather's *wyekin* song, or the identity of his animal guiding spirit. Perhaps it, too, found L.A. a difficult scene in which to function—unlike mine, which roams the Los Angeles foothills, troubling suburbanites even today with her constant howling and canny thefts.

Reading Linda Hogan recently, I was reminded of Grandfather's constant preference for the outsides of buildings, his reluctance to sit indoors, no matter how hot—or, much more rarely—cold it was outside. Living in this terrible dead city of New York, I know now how he must have grieved for Indian Territory, for those things Hogan so vividly recalls: "the songs of the first frogs in springtime, the red light of morning, the red earth, the heartbeat of trees and waters."[75] As here, watching filth from the rooftop incinerator fall in great scary clouds onto my balcony where it collects in ominous, dark mounds, I long for the frogs and toads, the slithery desert lizards, the "horny toad" I kept in one sandy corner of the back yard, catching him every afternoon when school was finished (or I was finished with it), whispering to him—was it a "he"? I thought it was—stroking him until the throat pulsing stopped and he breathed quietly in my hand. Or the smell of grass at 5 o'clock on an L.A. summer morning, when it is wet with the dampness that blows in from the ocean, or the sounds of that ocean, whose comforting pounding was our summer lullaby—first at camp on Catalina Island, then at the tiny house on a beach near Santa Barbara. Perched precariously on top of a dune, surrounded by layers of green, lizard-sheltering ice plant that crunched when we stepped into it off the wooden steps that linked the beach to the house, that house, small, tacky, shared with one or two other families, was our childhood paradise. . . . Far, far from home, "I hear the voices crying. . . ."

All of these lessons, and many more, were repeated, weekly, on our Straight Arrow cards. Some examples of more trivial stereotypes included one showing how both whites and Indians could learn to gallop stallions down the sides of whatever mountains we might have encountered on our travels through L.A.'s (mean) streets. Another showed us how to track animals—cats, dogs, and rats, as well as horses, cattle, moose, or even buffalo! (The general air of unreality of these cards is highlighted by this lesson, which described a particular configuration of rat paw prints as made by an animal "traveling at a trot." Surely not even a New York subway rat "trots"?)

In addition to cards, comics, radio shows, and the like, our generation's children had many other sources of what was known as "Indian lore." One was advertising. (Shredded Wheat had Straight Arrow, but Land O' Lakes butter and Mazola margarine had their "Indian maids." "Indians" sold cigars and cigarettes, romance and detective novels, summer camps, and recently an aerosol can labeled "Money House Blessing Gold Spray with Indian Spirit," sold in great quantities in New York City's *bodegas*.[76]) The other was school, where "higher culture"—poetry—had its Indians, the maiden, Minnehaha ("Laughing Water"), the elder, Nokomis, the "brave," Hiawatha. Longfellow narrated their story in the rhythm of the Indian tom tom, deploying every stereotype in the process.

In one sequence, for example, the poet describes the trio's typical reticence in the face of provocation from unwanted guests:

> Never once had Hiawatha
> By a word or look reproved them;
> Never once had old Nokomis
> Made a gesture of impatience;
> Never once had Laughing Water
> Shown resentment at the outrage
> All had they endured in silence . . .[77]

History, too, had Indian maidens. The two most prominent, Pocahontas and Sacagawea, were portrayed as brave heroines in most textbooks, though both betrayed their people by saving precursors of the conquest. Everyone also learned to sing "My Little Mohee," and "Shenandoah's Daughter," both of whom were desired by white men. (Of older women we learned little. Except for *my* heroine, the Osage ballerina Maria Tallchief, married women disappeared instantly into a

STRAIGHT ARROW

HORSEMANSHIP- HANDLING YOUR MOUNT

To start from a standing position Straight Arrow leans forward.... at the same time running the reins up along Fury's neck and tapping him with his heels. This is a motion to urge him forward which any riding horse will understand. After Fury starts, Straight Arrow takes up the slack in the reins but does not pull on Fury's mouth.

Most riding horses are "bridle-wise" which means they respond to the pressure of the reins across the back of their necks. To turn Fury, Straight Arrow moves his left hand to the left for a left turn and to the right for a right turn.

To put Fury into a gallop, Straight Arrow briskly brushes Fury's sides with his legs and at the same time flaps the reins in a forward motion on Fury's neck.

When going down grade, Straight Arrow gives Fury his head (that is slack in the reins)...and leans forward (not back) ..... this helps Fury obtain better footing. To stop Fury, Straight Arrow pulls on the reins and leans back.

Card No. 33　In a series of 36 STRAIGHT ARROW INJUN-UITIES

An "Injun-uity card" from our Nabisco Shredded Wheat.

nearly invisible domesticity; no longer sexually desirable maidens, they became mere "squaws.")

Male Indians, in their turn, found other reflections in popular culture. Even in our "multicultured" elementary school, there were children's songs: "We are the red men / Tall and quaint / In our feathers and war paint / Pow Wow. Pow Wow. / We're the men of the olden cow. / For we are the red men / Feathers in our head men / Down among the dead men / Ugh! Pow Wow." And counting games: "One little, two little, three little Indians." There was a negative Indian in Al Capp's "hillbilly" comic strip. Lonesome Polecat, much smaller than all the other male characters, sold "moonshine" called "Kickapoo Joy Juice." There were "positive" images evoked by the words "brave," "warrior," and—to some extent at least— "chief." (This latter term, however, became pejorative when used to address every adult Indian male, including, on more than one occasion, Grandfather.) There were cars called after Indian leaders like Pontiac, or, more recently, after entire tribes: Cherokee, Navaho. And there were thousands of athletic team "mascots."[78]

But most important for my learning of race *and* gender in these years was another children's novel, given me by my fourth grade teacher, Mrs. Hunt. I loved her because she was the only teacher not to fail me in the ridiculous report card categories that signaled the philistine presence of John Dewey's "progressive educationists": "citizenship," "cooperation," "tidiness." Despite the constant efforts of Doug Bison, my desk remained a mess. And as for "cooperation," I never saw the point of being forced to correct other children's desultory efforts to construct accurate maps of Brazil, or their equally problematic attempts to read "Dick and Jane" aloud. They—naturally—resented me. I was bored witless. Mrs. Hunt's was the only class I never ran away from, not once in the whole year.

Ramona, published in 1884 by Helen Hunt Jackson (and regularly republished up to the present decade) quickly replaced *Caddie Woodlawn* in my affections. The novel tells the story of an Indian girl who—according to the book jacket of my 1949 edition—"though brought up on a great Spanish estate in Southern California, chooses the life of her own people." Alas, however, Ramona discovers that her people are dying. In the end, she is rescued by a Spaniard, who takes her and her Indian child to Mexico, where they escape the racism that dogged Ramona's life in California. The critical judgment of the 1940s, recorded in *The San Francisco Chronicle*, was that *Ramona* was "the greatest story of California ever written." "It will," the paper predicted with two-edged optimism, "always remain as an eloquent plea for justice for a rapidly disappearing native race."[79]

This novel carried three (mixed) messages. The first was that it was proper to "choose one's own people"—especially in the face of racism. The second and third lessons, however, embodied the "Indian plight" paradox: as a people, Indians were done a terrible and continuing injustice; but there could be no rectification, alas, because this noble people was "rapidly vanishing." *Ramona* thus both stimulated readers' anger and simultaneously quelled it with the information that contemporary Indians were doomed. (Here, then, was another difference between Native people and African-Americans: the descendants of slaves could get angry, organize, and do something about it—albeit at considerable cost—in the here and now. But if the only Indians left were the "dregs" of a dying race, then only passivity or acceptance remained.[80])

MY BABY LOVES A WESTERN MOVIE

Despite the careful censorship our parents applied to movies and television, Anne and I had the occasional treat of other westerns in addition to Tonto and the Lone Ranger. For several weeks running the whole family was invited to a neighbor's to watch Walt Disney Presents Davy Crockett, "King of the Wild Frontier." It was, as everyone knows, a major craze of the fifties: documentary film footage suggests that children all over New York, all over the suburbs of Chicago, throughout the rural South, were glued to their TV sets on successive Friday nights as Davy and his "boon" companion, invented for the sake of mythical symmetry (questing heroes must have their companions), fought Injuns (Creeks), fought bad (white) guys, fought Congress, and finally fought the Mexican army. "Coonskin caps" proliferated. Children ran through neighborhoods warbling "Born on a mountaintop in Tennessee" and waving B.B. guns named "old Betsey."

These things were not for us: not only were we gun-shunning pacifist Penns, but I was the sentiment-ridden Emmeline Grangerford of our neighborhood. I learned only the opening lines of the show's cheery theme song, but I can still sing almost all of the sorrowful lament written by Davy Crockett and sung, in Walt Disney's version, at the Alamo: "Farewell, to the mountains / Whose mazes to me / More beautiful far / Than Eden could be." I didn't realize that I was also sentimentalizing, "The home I redeemed from the savage and wild / The home I have loved as a father his child."

The ideological message of Davy Crockett was considerably more mixed than that purveyed so innocently by Tonto and the Lone Ranger, or by Straight Arrow. Despite the notorious conservative Americanism of Walt Disney—despite his personal preferences for the anticommunist witch hunters of our youth—the hero's behavior is not that of an authority-respecting patriot. Instead, Crockett spends most of the series defying authority: first the army, during his months as a volunteer in the Creek War (when the army lieutenant who commands the Tennessee volunteers repeatedly proves to be an overdressed, over-"civilized" fool next to the homespun wisdom of Davy Crockett), then his fellows in Congress, then President Andrew Jackson himself, whose Indian Bill he speaks and votes against because of its injustice to the Indians.[81] (Although no mention is made of it in the series, this is the bill that launched the Trail of Tears.) Our hero's final foray into rebellion, defending Anglo Texas against the Mexican army's efforts to defend Mexican territory, was accomplished both in real and TV life, in company that was highly dubious: a British riverboat gambler (played by a family friend, Hans Conried, whose Davy Crockett fame made his visits to our house cause for great envy), an Indian (who was "good" because he had chosen white over red, and whose looks—more suitable for a city gangster—made us laugh that anyone could be fooled into thinking he was Indian), and the "boon companion." In the terms prevalent in McCarthyist America, Davy Crockett, anti-government rebel, defender of (some) justice for the Indians, should have been anathema to would-be commie-hunters. Had he been teaching elementary school in Los Angeles in those years, he'd have been fired (as was one of the teachers in our school, to the horror of our mother, president of the PTA).

How interesting—and pleasant!—to think that by teaching us that the standard to which we should hold government was a very high one, that lying was pure evil, that telling the truth, defending minorities, scorning material wealth, and judging others on the basis of their character (did Martin Luther King watch Davy Crockett?), Walt Disney may have been an unwitting part of the youth explosion of the 1960s!

MIXED BLOOD AND THE MOVIES

Parental vigilance prevented us from seeing most of the western movies that apparently shaped childhoods all over the United States in the 1950s.[82] But there were two films we did see, one after we had moved to Palo Alto, where we were allowed considerably more social latitude than we had enjoyed before, and one on a never-to-be-repeated family expedition to a drive-in movie theater in Los Angeles.

Although I had forgotten the content of the two films, their titles remained locked in memory, and I found both at the video rental store. Watching them again, more than thirty years later, I was struck by two things: first, the extent to which race—and especially white and red racial identities—troubled that era; and second, the enormity of the reasons why "passing" families like ours kept quiet about their real racial identity.

John Ford's *Two Rode Together* (1961) stars Jimmy Stewart and Richard Widmark. Like most westerns of the era, it is based on a novel, this one Will Cook's *The Comanche Captives* (serialized, together with dozens of other "movie" westerns, in the consistently anti-Indian *Saturday Evening Post*). It tells a story replete with racial confusions. Jimmy Stewart plays the mildly amoral marshal in a small Texas town who is dragooned into a brief service with the U.S. Army, rescuing those taken captive by Quanah Parker's band of Comanches over a period of many years. On his expedition to Parker's camp, he is accompanied by Richard Widmark, a young lieutenant.

At the Comanche camp, they discover that several of the captives have "gone native" and prefer to remain where they are. (*Pace* Conrad, there is no suggestion here that the captives' decisions were made because life among the Comanches was in any way better than white life. Those who have chosen to stay are portrayed either as mad or as terrified "concubines" of cruel Indian men.) Although two captive females, whose sexual relationships make them at the same time the inviolable private property of male Indians and "goods" irreparably soiled for future white consumption, are left behind, Stewart and Widmark take two captives back with them. One is a young Mexican woman; the other is a teenage boy, taken against his will (when not spitting like an animal, he repeats one line in Comanche which translates "Me Comanche! Not White!") because one of the settlers has promised a $1000 reward for any teenage white boy brought back.

When he sees the "savagery" of the boy, however, the wealthy settler refuses to claim him. And the other whites react negatively as well. One by one they pass by the small cage where the Army displays the rebellious and dangerous boy, a circus animal in a fairgrounds freakshow. Each decides that the boy is far too "Indian," too "wild," too far from civilization. In the end, only a woman driven mad by the loss of her baby son wants him. Her husband, fearful of her reaction if he refuses her, takes him in.

The result is overdetermined by the demands of melodrama as well as by those of his "Native nature." The boy turns on his adoptive "mother" the moment she releases him from the post where he has been chained like a wild dog. She is killed.

The settlers hold a court and convict the boy of murder, sentencing him to be hanged. The group—only one step removed from the lynch mobs ravaging the American South—then carries out their sentence, hanging him as an Indian. The hellish death scene is made even more appalling when the boy suddenly recognizes a music box, treasured by a young woman (Shirley Jones) whose brother had long ago been taken captive. As he is dragged toward the hanging tree, he is heard screaming the only English he speaks: "Mine, mine, mine." (The Mexican woman, whose "foreignness" evidently renders her less problematic, ultimately falls in love with Jimmy Stewart. Because he is different from the others, he reciprocates her feelings. Together, they catch the next stage west.)

The troubling subtext of this film is thus an exploration of the nature of racial identity and of the problems of cultural inheritance. As the music box makes clear, the boy (who remains nameless) was captured when eight years old. Only ten years have passed since his recapture. Yet he has forgotten English, and learned to scorn those who speak it. "Me Comanche, not white," he cries over and over and over in that language. He accompanies the Comanche word for "white" with spits and grimaces of disgust. Moreover, he *looks* Indian. Though his sister is pale, blonde, and blue-eyed, this boy's hair is blue-black, his skin "red," his eyes black. Although very short (much shorter than the characters playing the other Comanches), he looks at least as "Indian" as those actors playing Quanah Parker and his Comanche band. And he certainly looks much more "Indian" than most western movie Indians, including Davy Crockett's doomed companion. There is a suggestion, therefore, that race, and even its physical markers, can be lost or assumed rather easily. In this nation of immigrants, especially in the 1950s, a decade when each individual's "Americanism" was so constantly suspect, the movie seems to embody a thoroughgoing confusion about the nature of identity, of race, of culture, and even of nationality. But then of course, as America's Everyman, Ronald Reagan, assured us, Hollywood was a hotbed of "un-Americans."

The other film we saw was much more disturbing. John Huston's *The Unforgiven* (1960) (also based on a western novel, this one by an appalling bigot, Alan LeMay, whose work was frequently serialized in the *Saturday Evening Post*) is a striking and terrible representation of the virulence of America's (and John Huston's) racism. Seeing it again I wept. Seeing it again I thought "No *wonder* my grandfather kept quiet! No *wonder* they were afraid."

The story features Audrey Hepburn (!) playing a young "orphan" woman adopted into a pioneer family, the Zacharys. The father is dead. The head of the family is the oldest son, played by Burt Lancaster. Although a stalwart, hard-working, "American" family, they have a secret, known only to the mother and to a mad Civil War veteran who follows them from homestead to homestead, taunting them with it, driving them further and further west in search of peace.

The film reaches its climax when the veteran convinces the Zacharys' neighbors to suspect that Audrey Hepburn is not a white orphan, but rather AN INDIAN. "Red nigger" is the epithet in the mouths of many neighbors as one family "friend" tries to get Hepburn to strip before the women so that everyone can see if her "tan" continues where the sun can't reach. Meanwhile, her real brother, a Kiowa chief, has come round to the homestead several times trying to reclaim his sister. Driven away time and again by Lancaster and his two brothers, the Kiowa and his warrior friends continue their quest. The two stories come together when the Zachary brothers discover that Hepburn (with whom Lancaster has fallen in love) *is* an Indian, a "red nigger." One brother, an Indian-killer of some renown, leaves home immediately. The other two, however, remain: unsure of how they feel about "Indians," they clearly love their "sister."

The climax comes during another attack by Kiowas. This one, unlike those before, seems likely to succeed because Hepburn's revealed identity has lost the Zacharys the friends who might have ridden to their defense. Hopeless but brave, the Zacharys fight: the mother is soon killed. The youngest brother is gravely wounded. Lancaster, alone, fights on. Just as death is imminent, however, the missing brother (Audie Murphy) suddenly returns, single-handedly turning the battle in the Zacharys' favor.

Soon all the Kiowas except Hepburn's real brother lie dead or engaged in hand-to-hand combat with Lancaster and Murphy outside the house. Inside, Hepburn stands guarding the wounded youngest "brother," a pistol in her shaking hand. Suddenly, her Kiowa brother breaks in: "I am your brother," he tells her, "Come with me." There is a long still shot of Hepburn's face as she stands between her "real" brother and the adopted white one. Then, her face set, she resolves her dilemma (and the film's), pulling the trigger and shooting her brother in the stomach. The blood problem is solved: Lancaster embraces her, declaring his love. Together they walk outside to a victorious silence. Standing together, the bodies of Kiowas lying all around, these two "whites," one old, one new, watch a flock of geese flying a perfect V across the clear blue western sky.

This, then, was the world of the western movie *and* the world in which such movies were possible—indeed, in which such movies were both popularly and critically acclaimed.

One recent writer, who interestingly and unwittingly transformed Audrey

Hepburn's character into a "mixed blood," only "part Kiowa," applauded the "realism" of another LeMay authored western film. "The character of the Indians is respectful," she wrote, "but their savagery is not disguised. Illustrations of Indian cruelty are not hard to find. They are there in newspapers and contemporary accounts; eye witnesses have got it all down on paper. . . . Men are tortured with burning sticks and babies swung against trees." Although, she admits grudgingly, "The U.S. cavalry was not renowned for restraint when confronted with captive Indian women," they, at least, had good reasons: "Retribution spurred many white men on to savaging the bodies of their red enemies."[83]

One movie critic described *The Unforgiven* as "entertaining . . . though . . . with little lasting power." This writer noted the film's "anti-Indian bias," but insisted that LeMay "attempted to deal dramatically with the cultural differences between the races, placing most of the blame on tradition." Moreover, the director, John Huston "improved upon the novel and made the story far richer. . . . *The Unforgiven* is . . . filled with a strange mysticism." He concludes, "Although *The Unforgiven* is good-looking and enjoyable, its underlying racist attitude ultimately makes the film less satisfying than it should have been."[84] (Thus does white America skewer its racist entertainment on the double-edged tongues of its movie critics!)

Given the enormity of the American racism reflected by the popularity of westerns, it is easy to see why caring mixed-blood parents avoided telling children that their heritage was less than 100 percent blue-blooded European. As I watched *The Unforgiven*, I kept thinking over and over, "*That's* why Dad rarely said . . ." Indeed, especially given our Hollywood childhood and the fact that we could all "pass," it is surprising that we learned who we were at all. Even more surprising was the fact that this was the side of us we valued most—at least most of the time.

Soon, however, there was a dramatic change. In 1959 we left our mixed-race, working-class neighborhood to move again, this time into "white country." Our sudden feelings of dislocation, however, found some relief in the politics of the era just being born. In the year we moved worlds, what seemed like our whole generation began to live what one movie critic described as "a smoldering problem that would burst forth into both ideological and real conflagration in the civil rights turmoil of the [next] decade."[85]

◆4◆
DISLOCATIONS

It's not a comfortable territory to live in, this place of
contradictions.
Gloria Anzaldúa[1]

In 1959, Palo Alto exuded taste, charm, money. And the
material wonders of our new house—though small and
utterly inconsequential by local standards—soon taught
us scruffy L.A. proles how some other Americans lived. So backward were we that
we had never heard of those familiar wonders of 1950s domestic prosperity, dish-
washers and garbage disposals, clothes dryers and two-car garages.

Not even the strident voice of television advertising dented our blissful ignorance: we
had never owned a set in L.A. and we did not get one, even after ascending to a techno-
logically more sophisticated Palo Alto. Our main childhood source of television, our
grandparents, followed us north, but not to affluent Palo Alto. Instead, they moved to
what was then a small, sleepy rural town, Napa. Grams found work as a secretary at
the high school. Gramps, now "retired" rather than "unemployed," planted a loved
garden, made gifts for us in his tiny welding workshop under the carport, washed and
rewashed his black 1939 Plymouth, and broke his happy, leisurely country routines
playing checkers with the other old (Chicano) men at the general store down the road,
or napping on the front porch, waiting for the mail.

The world outside our new house was different too: a stunning English cottage
garden, complete with "herbaceous borders," replaced our vast sandy wash of an
L.A. backyard. No horned toads here, though I quickly discovered a suitably tasteful substitute in the elegant little purple-grey (the Palo Alto word, which I didn't
yet know, was "mauve") tree frogs that filled the tulip trees, magnolias, cedars, and
gingkos that shaded the wide "patio" (our first private patio!) bordering the garden. The big two-toned, rear-finned 1957 Plymouth, not yet the "classic" it would
become twenty years later, did not sit easily in all its bright yellow and white splen-

dor on the pebbled drive alongside the little redwood picket fence that marked our front garden. It soon vanished, replaced by two cars more representative of our new status. This city of wealthy bohemianism demanded exotic foreign cars and our parents quickly conformed, buying two German-made Opels: a dark blue sedan for Father, a pale green station wagon for Mother.

Despite such efforts to fit in, the house turned on us shortly after we moved in. It began with an event that became a metaphor for all our relations with the people that town sheltered in smug leafy comfort. But though we didn't realize it then, it was actually our second warning that there would be more to our Palo Alto lives than affluence and material comforts.

We missed the first hint that life in Northern California might prove startling. It had come in a letter written by our father during the six months he lived in a rooming house in San Francisco, working as a researcher for Standard Oil and waiting for our move north at the close of the school year. Wifeless, he ate canned soup heated on a hot plate in his room and took his laundry to a commercial establishment down the street. Like the laundries of "Old San Francisco" stereotype, this one was owned by a Chinese family, all of whom, white-haired grandparents and children alike, could be seen working long hours just behind the front counter, folding, pressing, scrubbing.

Not least because my parents had always had many Asian and Asian-American friends, many of them neighbors in our racially hodge-podge L.A. neighborhood, my father sought to alleviate his loneliness by spending considerable time in the laundry, chatting with the owners. One day, he wrote us in his weekly letter, the father of the family remarked shyly and cautiously that my father looked a little "Chinese." To his new friend's surprise, Dad smiled, explaining why a racial similarity might exist: the "land bridge" theory of Indian origins put American Natives' roots in Asia.[2] At that, the Chinese man, hitherto extremely reticent, broke into smiles, called his whole family to the front of the shop, and introduced them all to "this white man who is not a white man at all." My father was very curious about this strange designation, and asked why it made a difference to his new friends that he was "not a white man." After all, he thought, these were not Japanese-Americans with reason to suspect every non–Asian-American they encountered.[3] The man then invited him back to the family's small sitting room where he poured some tea before explaining that he, all his relatives, and indeed every Chinese-American in San Francisco bore the brunt of the most terrible bigotry. Not only were they the constant objects of public hate, but they were virtually restricted to a ghetto—San Francisco's famous Chinatown, its tourist façades celebrated in *Flower Drum Song*—and limited in their choices of occupation. Because Chinese men had first been lured to California to build the railroads and serve the thousands of greed-driven immigrants from the east, the gold-seeking Forty-Niners, they had found themselves limited after the Gold Rush to making a living in personal service occupations, doing laundry (both as domestic servants and as commercial launderers) as well as serving food, cleaning houses, and so on. Soon everyone in non-Asian Northern California believed that Chinese people possessed a genetic proclivity for the domestic arts. To avoid attracting the dangerous attentions of vigilant guardians of America's "whiteness," Chinese-Americans opened "racially suitable" businesses, including those that washed and cleaned clothing. Hidden behind these stereotypical roles, they remained safe, invisible through several generations.[4] Dad was astounded. Perhaps it was naïveté or ignorance, he wrote, but he had never before encountered the story of Northern California's virulent anti-Chinese racism.[5] His letter about these new friends mingled his anger and surprise at this blatant evidence of America's untiring efforts to protect its "Europeanness."

We might, therefore, have known what we could encounter in our new little city a few miles south of racist San Francisco. But we, like our parents, believed Palo Alto's self-serving myth: it was a liberal city, populated by eccentrics, especially Quakers, and open to all sorts of folks.

The fates, however, soon threw us a second, even more blatant, sign that our comfortable assumptions were awry. Soon after we moved in, our two dogs sickened and died. As usual, I was the child and Mother was the parent who carried my Rusty (a red cocker spaniel given me years before by a baby sitter as a reward for my "stoicism" during an asthma attack), and my brother's much-loved mutt Butchie to the vet for the last time. Given the mystery of their sudden deaths, the vet asked to perform autopsies. Soon we learned—as we were to learn in different contexts over and over during those Palo Alto years—that all the glory of our garden's beauty had hidden a dark secret: the lethal germs of canine ileitis, which had killed the previous owner's dog, got Rusty and Butch the moment they stepped out of their traveling cages.[6]

So perhaps we might have known sooner what we rapidly discovered: we, mixed-blood, not really white, not really middle class, had moved in to one of the whitest, most upper-middle-class societies America had to offer. ("White?" my sister exclaimed when I made this remark. "It wasn't just white, it was white*washed!*" And rewashed, if anything threatened its placid cold surface.)

And here, at a tiny, exclusive high school, replete with intellectual pretensions (the principal, they all boasted, had a Ph.D., though we never learned in what field) and the requisite overlay of "bohemianism" (the school forbade exclusive social clubs and experimented with an honor code, abolishing all the usual rules of public high school, rules of dress, of behavior, even of attendance), we quickly went underground.

Perhaps because I looked the part, perhaps because I was younger and had more time, I learned to inhabit this nether world of our dual identity much more easily than did my sister. Soon, in fact, I blended in almost completely, competing assiduously and sometimes successfully for the myriad academic prizes held before our privileged noses, and this despite the overwhelming realization that our schooling (especially in the hallowed canon of European writers, philosophers, artists) had been woefully, indeed unbelievably, inadequate.[7] Not everything about our Indian selves proved unhelpful: both of us employed the "potted plant" reaction frequently, turning away intrusive questions, blocking impertinences, rejecting rejections. But here our other skills, trivial or essential—our moccasined silence, our stoicism, our bareback riding, our peculiar dancing, our lack of acquisitiveness, our emotional inaccessibility—went unvalued or even misunderstood. And, looking around at an ocean of white faces, topped by a stunning blondness only California seems to breed in its young, we knew our mixed-racial selves were best hidden away for the duration. This did not mean we did not grieve: we were adolescent girls in the unforgiving *Seventeen/Glamour* magazine beauty culture of 1950s suburban America. I recall many hours spent twisting a mirror sideways and backwards, wondering at the peculiar shape of my face, the abrupt slant from cheekbone to prominent chin. Why, I wondered, does no one else have this funny face, these wide lips ("liver lips," the L.A. neighborhood kids had called me), these oddly shaped teeth? And in our high-school years, "Indian hair," stick straight and worn long, parted down the middle, had not yet become fashionable, so we both suffered the pains of curlers and hair spray, desperate in our attempts to duplicate the frilly blonde hair of most of our friends.

On the other hand, it was there in Palo Alto that I learned what that intelligence that had embarrassed me through my Los Angeles years meant. I discovered delight. From random reading of every sort of fiction or poetry, the good tossed mindlessly in with the bad, the sentimental with the serious, the verse with the poetry, pulp fiction (*Saturday Evening Post, Reader's Digest*) with middlebrow "culture" (*National Geographic*), I began, slowly, to discover the joys of form and of thought. It was Palo Alto's first—and only, in our years—African-American teacher, my eleventh-grade English teacher, John Turner, who began what became a long process of reeducation, giving me an American literature (albeit a lily-white, male literature) with which I was only lightly, and very eccentrically, acquainted. Another cultural "displaced person" (almost totally assimilated to the Eurocentrist convictions foisted on him by his English professors at Berkeley), Mr. Turner took my case very personally. "What junk are you reading *now*?" he would cry when he saw me crouched over some novel he thought unworthy. He tried everything. On one unforgettable occasion, after we had all produced a description of a scene recalled from childhood, he was so horrified by my sentimental, mawkish prose that he read out loud to the class what he described as "the worst piece of writing I have ever been forced to read."[8] He did not name the perpetrator, of course. But throughout that most painful of salutary experiences I groveled in my chair, terrified that my hot face would give the game away to my deskmate, a handsome blond aesthete and poet called Bill Pease who was, in my callow eyes at least, the embodiment of anarchistic sophistication. (I was most fascinated—both by the hint of religious blasphemy and by the fact of alcohol—when he casually described "getting high" on communion wine at his Catholic Church.)

John Turner was equally appalled by my social life. Soon, I had joined the "in-group," dating the school's athletic hero, going to all the "right" parties. "What *are* you doing?" he would shout. "How can *you*, of all people, join that elitist bunch, that bunch of rich snobs?" I didn't know; the social "in-group" he decried included the academic elite of the school, all those who read poetry, who wrote, who discussed Dostoevsky's novels over lunch on the school's lawns. I did not realize all that he meant until near the very end of those two years in high school.

We were signing yearbooks—that most hallowed of traditions, where the in-group marks off whole pages for themselves and the out-group hopes desperately that one of the chosen will write something fond or memorable or even friendly which will mark them as "almosts" rather than "nevers." Not very practiced in the arts of exclusion, I offered my book indiscriminately to everyone in all my classes, willingly signing those offered me in return.

After the first day of signing, I sat in my room at home, reading and rereading the inscriptions. Suddenly I encountered a strange message in a hand I didn't recognize: "To my best, and only friend at Cubberley High School. I'll never forget you. From C— H—." C— H—, who sat next to me in senior English, was, I had always assumed, one of the handful of African-American students in my year, albeit a girl with very light skin. But now for the first time I realized: "You *too*?" she was saying. "Yes," I replied silently that evening curled up on my bed, "Me, too." She had known; it was I who had been walking blind (but *blue-eyed*) through the pale world all around us.

Did John Turner realize? I don't know. I do know that he instantly recognized my father when he walked into my English classroom for Parents' Back-to-School Night. "I knew at once that was your father," he told me the next day. I never asked him how he knew that the black-haired, dark, slant-eyed, very tall man was related to me.

I was not entirely blind, of course. I knew who and what I was. But this was a new world we had entered, and it was not an easy one. It held its own contradictions: along with the football games, proms, and Friday nights at the beach, this little society included an adolescent life of the mind. In place of rock and roll (essential to our childhood, where Ritchie Valens was the first to escape our ghetto, where pachuco dancing meant Friday nights, where Ritchie Valens's death marked our final months in the north Valley[9]) we had the emerging world of folk music. We all took up the guitar and memorized the words to countless Joan Baez and Pete Seeger folk songs. (The more sophisticated among us bought the recordings of black artists: from Bessie Smith, Mahalia Jackson, and Billie Holiday to the newly discovered "folk" heroes—Leadbelly, Brownie McGhee and Sonny Terry, Odetta.)

Joan Baez was a "local," preceding us through Palo Alto's schools by a few years. But her experience was much worse; rather than the self-consciously avant-garde high school we attended, she went through Palo Alto High, where old money reigned supreme and where color and class definitions utterly excluded half-Mexican children, despite Baez's father's position as a physicist at Stanford University, alma mater of most "Paly High" parents. This was the high school whose rich and privileged students reacted to defeat in a football game by yelling "niggers" at my high school's team, which, like the school itself, included a handful of African-American students.

We also had politics: memorable evenings organizing ourselves to travel to San Francisco to protest the House Un-American Activities Committee hearings at City Hall, arguing with the Christian Anti-Communists, who came to a student-sponsored talk by a member of the Fair Play for Cuba Committee, or debating America's lack of civil rights for Negro citizens. (We self-consciously elected a black student body president in my senior year and laughed down a woman from the DAR, come to "award" a scholarship to the senior girl with "the best citizenship.") We debated the justice of a standardized college entrance exam even as we collectively bicycled over to Stanford's exquisite Mission-style campus where we dutifully performed our intellectual magic on the test's pages.

And on weekends we drove to San Francisco, where we stood around the streets of North Beach, posing ethereally in white lipstick and black dress, pallid imitations of our chosen elders, the city's beatniks. They were then on the wane, even in their native habitat. But they still held boundless attraction for suburban adolescent admirers (and imitators) of Lawrence Ferlinghetti's "Christ came down from his tree today / and ran away to where. . . ."[10]

John Turner, uncharacteristically tolerant of our collective tastes, allowed us to read our favorites from this volume one day in English class. His face, however, wrinkled into a horrified grimace, betrayed his utter scorn for what he described as "overly trite" poems.

Thus Palo Alto gave me a certain intellectual delight muddled with personal alienation, the latter reflected in a constant restlessness, an unarticulated sense of "foreignness" that did not go away. We were, suddenly, in our mother's world, whose patterns and ways we had never learned. And the ways we *had* imbibed—proscriptions against acquisitiveness, competitive aggression, and confrontation, a reliance upon dry ironic jokes to indicate displeasure or embarrassment, the utter inability to value wealth, or titles, or status, our intense dependence upon grandparents, in our case especially Grandfather—all were alien to the Protestant, middle-class world we had joined willy-nilly.

Although these things could not be explained so that my friends understood my differences, most earned me a valued reputation as a special kind of eccentric, a status devoutly pursued in my curious high-school milieu. Only one of my Indian traits proved an intractable problem, then and through the years to come. I did not understand the extent to which my emotional difference from my non-Indian friends posed an insurmountable difficulty for me and for them until many, many years of incomprehension (and some months in the Berkeley student health center's psychiatric wing, recovering from what I now recall was an overdetermined nervous breakdown in the final semester of university) had passed. Instead, I just kept trying and trying to act in the ways my friends seemed to require.

And what was it they needed from me? Although hesitant to reinforce romanticized stereotypes about Indian behavior, I think I must quote one white teacher of Indian students, writing in 1971, inasmuch as his view of his students seems to capture some of what non-Indian friends have complained about in my actions. Utterly baffled when he encountered his students for the first time, he tried to counter his mystification by analyzing their behaviors in the accepted European-American manner. (These included many that were accepted by my close high-school friends as eccentricities.) He concluded with what he described as the most intractable of these "Indian" traits:

Finally and most difficult to describe, the Indian people I have known are *non-intrusive*. They speak and act as if always aware that every human being is surrounded by an invisible sheath of emotional privacy. It is inexcusable to intrude into this privacy—inexcusable to coerce people to show strong emotions when they do not wish to do so. Deep emotions are precious. They are to be expressed without coercion at the proper time, with the proper people. They are cheapened by indiscriminate or forced display . . .
  Thus, many Indian people I know are embarrassed by exuberant public displays of affection or anger, and refrain from such displays themselves.[11]

In the relatively restrained world of Palo Alto, my inability to ooze emotion or to "share" what was most deeply personal (the offensiveness of which only got worse once I joined that era's feminist movement, which invented "consciousness-raising"), meant only that many of my closest friends believed that I deliberately distanced them from my most intimate thoughts and feelings. "You are so *closed*," my friends would complain, "You never tell us what you *really feel* about anything." I tried to compensate by learning to talk a lot about experiences. I thought sufficient factual information—a kind of reportorial account of who, what, where, when—was what they demanded. Of course it was not. Friends insisted, often bitterly, that my withholding of the confidences that marked "intimacy" (especially those that signalled the need of support or help) suggested that I thought I was "better" than everyone else, that I didn't need anyone, that I didn't care enough for them to share my secrets, or even, much later when it was fashionable, that I needed a psychiatrist to "unblock" my repressed self![12]

I didn't know then that most people simply cannot walk outside the compelling ideological world they inhabit, so I kept trying to explain that what they saw as an offensive reticence was simply my *self*, that I was different in some essential ways from them, and that they should try to accept those differences. But I met only frustration; even those who said they could accept cultural differences could not, in fact, accept them in me.[13]

Still, here too the issues can quickly wind inside out, not least when well-meaning people describe "Indian traits" to tribal people themselves. Michael Winerup, writing in the *New York Times*, described a school exchange arranged between Choate and Window Rock High School in the Navajo nation. Before the Navajo students arrived at the posh prep school, teachers, anthropologists' studies in hand, carefully prepared their European-American charges for The Encounter. One earnest Choate student explained to Winerup, "One of our teachers told us there's a rule in the Navajo culture not to look in people's eyes. . . . I said, 'O.K., I'll be careful about that.' " What she didn't tell her teachers, however, was that she intended to discuss these "rules" with the Arizona students themselves. And when she subsequently asked a Navajo student about this eye contact restriction, the young woman replied "No . . . I don't think so. I never heard of it."

Of course this does not mean that the piercing eye-to-eye gaze considered essential to "honest" interactions in European-American society prevails in Navajoland. The reporter did not consider the possibility that fish, asked about water, would deny the existence of "fish rules" about living in it.[14] As is always the case with newspaper articles of this kind, the point of view is entirely European-American; the article is written for readers who are assumed to share—or at least to be aware of—the Choate perspective. An anthropological attitude, in which hosting a strange and exotic people demands memorizing detailed information about "their" cultural ways, prevailed here, as it often does in encounters between non-tribal people and Indians. Like the young Navajo woman, we could all tell stories of occasions when people asked us about "the correct Indian way" to do this or that. And when one is visibly mixed European and Native (and perhaps even more if one is also female), one is even more readily assumed to be a natural informant, an accessible negotiator between cultures. Such situations are, not surprisingly, the object of much joking among tribal people themselves.[15]

MOVE ON OVER OR WE'LL MOVE ON OVER YOU . . .

In at the birth of the 1960s, we, America's rebellious young, loathed "conformity,"[16] the lies of American history, American imperialism (both smugly promulgated by our high-school texts: Samuel Eliot Morrison's *Oxford History of the United States* and Ray Allen Billington's *Manifest Destiny*), the idiocies and injustices of the Cold War (we saw the HUAC hearings at San Francisco's City Hall, watched the older demonstrators "washed down the stairs" by police wielding firehoses[17]), and most authority. We were as yet unsure of what to do about all these matters;

we were, after all, but sixteen or seventeen years old in 1961 when we graduated from high school. But almost all of us expected to do *something*.

Thus those years in Palo Alto, however odd, however dislocating, were, for me at least, preparation for life as a student radical at Berkeley in the coming years. What is sometimes forgotten when the 1960s are discussed is that most of the student movement's "foot soldiers" (all I, in my intense shyness and wariness about white students' real motives, ever was) came from America's white upper-middle class, the group we half belonged to by birth if not by familiarity, and the group we joined with the family's move in 1959. These were our "white" cousins and their friends, the kids who carried the confidence of privilege: beneath the deliberately scruffy hair and self-consciously "folkloric" clothing walked children who knew which fork, which glass, which gesture, which words marked them as inhabitants of America's ruling classes. These were the children who would once have moved smoothly and automatically into Berkeley's sororities and fraternities, children whose families bore the pedigree required for such entry—and whose refusal to join such elitist groups thus constituted serious rebellion against parents and kin.[18]

Although I readily imbibed most of these social lessons (so that years later I could pass easily into the elite world of Cambridge High Table) one lesson I never quite learned was a longing for money or for other material objects. Avarice was, of course, then only in its infancy. (It did not reach maturity until the Reagan-Bush years.) But in Palo Alto, the lust for possessions (for the right clothes, cars, jewelry, for expensive vacations in exotic locales, for big, ornate houses), drove our friends as it drove their parents. We were, however, still "poor," and even had we lacked a cultural proscription against such behavior, we still could not have hoped to participate.[19] Moreover, what I loved, and longed for, was not for sale. It struck me then as it strikes me now: if one has this ocean, this desert, these redwood forests floored by tiny glowing manzanita, these great granite mountains and soft alpine valleys, these paths shaded by elegant, white and red-skinned madrones, by those eternal emblems of California native survivance, the squat, fragrant live oaks, or the fragile summer sighing inside stands of tall, silver-leaved aspen, who could want *things*? *These* are alive; things are not. Or worse, I began to understand, things breathe a dangerous "anti-life": "stuff" sucks vitality from those humans who fill their days in its pursuit until they discover—if they do before they die—that they haven't been part of the living world at all, that they are surrounded, they are captives, almost as surely as those whose bodily captivity allowed their possessiveness free play.

Choate's Navajo exchange students suggest that most tribal people carry this need for their natural home place wherever they go. "Having been away," reported *The Times,* "Shelton was struck by how much he has missed seeing the prairie and the entire sky. Navajos say life thrives where the sky meets the earth, and Shelton Laughing has grown accustomed to always being able to find that spot. Le Andrea felt she'd lost her sense of direction at Choate. She is used to waking up in her home as the sun rises through her front door. At Choate, trees and rolling hills blocked the early morning sun." Not only Navajos feel this: all the people from western tribes in our talking circle at NYU would recognize the young people's feelings of dislocation.[20]

My friends' intense concern to drive a particular car (the 1957 Chevy was *the* car of my high-school years), to wear particular labels (both "I." and "J." Magnin were preferred), to walk in one brand of shoes (de rigueur were Bass penny loafers), to date star members of the school's athletic teams, never moved into the center of my life. Perhaps we were simply too old by the time we encountered these curious raisons d'être?[21] Perhaps we carried other, more important, beliefs which blocked the importation of this most American of values, greed. Whatever the explanation, it was this materialism, more than anything, that ensured, from my side at least, that the split between their world and ours was irreparable.

But the school tried its best. American history trumpeted the victories of those heroes who had populated the continent's growing cities and towns, who had torn away mountains for splendid concrete and asphalt paths for the newest pioneers, "freeways" leading to more and more housing developments, more and more (white) people, more and more money for the denizens of America's vaunted progress.

Alfonso Ortiz, with tongue in cheek, suggests a psychological problem might explain Americans' collective urge to "develop" the land: "The general American view seems to be that empty space is intolerable. It must be filled with objects. It never ceases to amaze me how white Americans can never gaze upon a landscape without wanting to fill it with sheep, barns, plowed fields, or something else. They just can't seem to let it be."[22]

Even without the soon-to-come revisionist historians, however, contradictions in our progressive high-school curriculum were rife. Though we read novels like Ole E. Rølvaag's *Giants in the Earth,* which stimulated our retrospective sympathy for the heroic Scandinavians who bravely "peopled" an "empty" midwestern wilderness in order to bring us bread and fruit and cheese and steak, we also read Sinclair Lewis's *Babbitt,* a satirical attack on the peopling and people of America's prototypical booster-driven town, Zenith. We read Ruth Benedict's *Patterns of Culture* in order to learn that there were people in other, quaint, exotic parts of the world who did not live as "we" lived. Some of the anthropologists we read even suggested that *National Geographic* was wrong, that the social organizations of some [select] "primitives" were not only different, but just as good as ours. Indeed, some of the most daring scholars we read argued, with a heady radicalism, that some exotic cultures were *better* than ours! Though we listened to Aaron Copland's celebration of America's captivity of tribal peoples' sacred Grand Canyon, we *sang* Malvina Reynolds's condemnation of the suburban paradise; "Little Boxes": "made of ticky tacky / Little boxes, little boxes / And they all look just the same." Instructed in the perfidy of everything Russian, we read that Stalin was the sole world leader to support the Republicans in the Spanish Civil War. Then we read further, about Leningrad and the Battle of the Elbe, where the same horrible, deceitful Russians—or their brothers, sisters, mothers, and fathers—had finally made possible the defeat of our other Satan, Hitler. Told that communism was always bad because it restricted people's "natural rights," we learned of America's favorite fascist allies—Batista, Franco, Chiang Kai-shek—and the methods they used to ensure their citizens' "rights." No longer made to recite "one nation, under God," an inappropriate patriotic school ritual in progressive Palo Alto, we began to wonder *what* god?

When I left Palo Alto for Berkeley, then, I carried heavy, unwieldy baggage, baggage in which squirmed tens of mixed messages, contradictory beliefs, competing values. For my two years of high school, there had been little Grandfather, no Indian Center, no powwows—indeed, no fiestas, no Cinco de Mayo. The only words of Spanish we heard were strange and lisping—Castilian Spanish, the Spanish of Europe, not that of the Americas and certainly not that of the neighborhoods of Los Angeles. The only hint of indigenousness was flamenco dancing, taught us by the school's Spanish teacher, Señor Gomez. Weekends we went to watch him dance in a tiny cantina in San Francisco's North Beach. But this dancing—presented as quintessentially Spanish, with no word of the Gypsies and Moors whose joint creation it was—was little more than another symbol of our madcap, anxious efforts to avoid identification with our fathers' grey-flannel-suited suburbia.

 Were there any other Indians in Palo Alto? I asked my sister. We think there was one, one of our, and later, at Berkeley, my, closest friends, Jim Mott.

Even if he did not share our ethnicity, he certainly shared my literary pretensions,
though like most of the kids who had gone through Palo Alto's schools, he was much
more advanced. When I was fifteen, for example, I recall telling him proudly that I was
reading Ayn Rand's Atlas Shrugged *with much admiration. He laughed at me: "I*
suppose you think you're one of the Nietzschean chosen few? Or do you just naturally
love fascism?" As I had with John Turner's writing lesson, I kept quiet until I hung up
the telephone. Then I ran for the family's Encyclopedia Britannica *to look up*
"Nietzsche" and "fascism."

But if he was Indian, as we now think, we never spoke about it. We were entirely cut off (as cleanly as though we had moved countries) from our mixed-
blood, working-class birthright. I substituted the politics fashionable among my
friends. But they were not Indian politics. Through these years, the sounds of an
insistent Indian drumming remained underground, an "ophiolatrous liturgy," living deep below our conscious daily world. (We were so completely detached, in
fact, that it was not until several years later that I learned about the excitement
bursting out all over Indian Country, prompting rebellions, many of which took
shape in the neighboring cities of Oakland and San Francisco.)

Despite being cut off from what mattered most before our move, a Palo Alto
adolescence left its marks. I now knew how to "pass"—out of my class and out of
my muddled race—when necessary. More important, I knew how to live under
water.[23]

"WESTWARD THE COURSE OF EMPIRE
WENDS ITS WAY . . ."[24]

In 1961 Berkeley was a paradise, preaching a comforting liberal message aimed at
people like me. In those first years of the decade, the Berkeley faculty, like the rest
of the intellectual world, claimed a benevolent cultural universalism. Symbolized
by half a dozen coffee-table photography books—most striking, and most popular Edward Steichen's *Family of Man*—the commitment of our professors' generation to a "utopian" (or better, dystopian) world of non-violent sameness (*"Everyone is just alike under the skin,"* they assured us) sprawled through our daily lives.

We soon caught on. When I arrived at Berkeley, virtually every women's dor-
mitory room (and most women's apartments) held three objects: a Modigliani
print, usually of a long-necked female figure, a Che Guevara poster, and a paper-

back copy of *The Family of Man*.[25] For us, Steichen's book was more than just a token of that era's belief in universality. It was a religious text, daringly celebrating sex, daringly countering (we thought) Cold War insistence on immutable difference, radical in its implied equation of the world's cultures, its quoting of spiritual texts other than "ours."

Alas, however, *Family of Man* was actually only a "Family of White Men." Its claims to "universality" veiled its reassuring subtexts: an insistent privileging of "us," a celebration of "woman" as Mrs. Cleaver, visual representations that assured viewers that everything white and American was so fine that, despite superficial semiotic differences, it was shared by all sorts of folks. Beneath their exotic dress and nakedness (familiar to readers of *National Geographic*, dark-skinned breasts were here, too, emblems of American liberalism) they represented not themselves, but merely exotic versions of characters familiar from the *Saturday Evening Post*.

As though the Norman Rockwellian message might prove too subtle to viewers of the photographs or readers of the epigrammatic captions, the book offered an explanatory "Prologue" from America's Norman Rockwell of poetry, the relentlessly middlebrow Carl Sandburg. Here are Sandburg's opening lines, a Midwestern Babbitt's shout of praise for American individualism: "The first cry of a newborn baby in Chicago, or Zamboango, in Amsterdam or Rangoon, has the same pitch and key, each saying, 'I am! I have come through! I belong! I am a member of the Family.'" Whatever side of Sandburg's binary globe one might land up on—whether the "white" side or the "colored"—every baby, the poet argued, is *really* born into America's midwest. Thus, Sandburg reassured readers as they entered this visually "exotic" world, "You might catch yourself saying, 'I'm not a stranger here.'"

Well, whew! If everything "they" do is exactly like what "we" do, the book implies no threats, no challenges, no odd exotic ideas to disconcert the certainty. "They mate [!], toil, fish, quarrel, sing, fight, pray, on all parallels and meridians having likeness." In fact, a daringly progressive Sandburg continued, we are all even very like those true strangers, our ancestors, "early man": "The earliest man, ages ago, had tools, weapons, cattle, as seen in his cave drawings. And like him the latest man of our day has his tools, weapons, cattle." Of course progress has been made: "The earliest man struggled through inexpressibly dark chaos of hunger, fear, violence, sex. A long journey it has been from that early Family of Man to the one of today which has become a still more prodigious spectacle." (This confident encomium to human "progress," it should be remembered, was written against a background featuring thousands of husbands and fathers, starched shirtsleeves rolled up, digging holes in their suburban gardens, preparing underground shelters against the possibility that the same bomb that incinerated Hiroshima and Nagasaki might doom "us" to "dark chaos"!) Sandburg's concluding mantra left readers with no doubts:

> There is only one man in the world
> and his name is All Men.
> There is only one woman in the world
> and her name is All Women.
> There is only one child in the world
> and the child's name is All Children.[26]

Steichen himself was slightly more sophisticated in his introduction, but no less smug. "I believe the Family of Man exhibition . . . now being circulated *throughout the world* (emphasis added), is the most ambitious . . . project photography has ever attempted. . . . The exhibition, now permanently presented on the pages of this book, demonstrates that the art of photography is a dynamic process of giving form to ideas and of explaining man to man. It was conceived as a mirror of the universal elements and emotions in the everydayness of life—as a mirror of the essential oneness of mankind throughout the world."

Ah, but is that what "photography" is about? And even if it were a "mirror" of the quotidian, would that mirror—and does this collection of photographs—really provide evidence to white male Americans that everyone all over the world is, in fact, just like them?

Steichen's unsophisticated claims for photography's transparency aside (they were even then being explored in the United States by Susan Sontag, and had already been analyzed in Europe by a variety of critics, not the least of them Walter Benjamin) his claims reek of self-congratulation. But he spoke too soon: both the visual and the written texts that follow, despite their seemingly radical provenances, provide something rather different from evidence of a warm universality. In fact, their overriding impact offers a startling insight into the totality of the hegemony of mainstream American values and beliefs about race, about gender, about class, among America's intelligentsia.

> *In the present decade, full of challenges to European-American, male hegemony, many liberals have resumed citing "what bonds us all together as humans," compulsively reprising Steichen's Family. The New York Times Magazine is full of letters and articles citing some encounter between a European American and some "exotic" that demonstrated—to the letter writer, at least—just how similar "we" all are. Two examples: Marvin Weinbaum, who lives on Long Island, reacted to an article about*

the African-American youth practice of "snapping"—using good-natured insults to "one-up" others—by pointing out that his boyhood chums, in "white, Jewish Pelham Parkway . . . forty years ago" played an identical game, known as "sounding." He concluded his letter to the magazine, "if anything is to be celebrated, it is an acknowledgement of all that binds rather than separates us." In the same issue of the magazine, Roger Rosenblatt (a committed universalist) found himself faced with the daunting task of trying to explain how the massacres in Rwanda are a horrible exemplar of "universal" human behavior. His solution was slightly dubious and layered with intellectual dead-ends and unfortunate double meanings, but he finally reached it after explaining (in good universalist fashion) that the slaughters are due not to recent history (in which Belgium, and before that Germany, are hideously culpable) but rather to "buried ethnic hatred": "Yet there is something deeper even than historic horrors and tribal hatreds in all this. It owes more to evolutionary biology than to history; it reaches into hearts of darkness located far beyond Africa. Under certain circumstances, not always predictable, people will do anything to one another. Going by the descriptions of events in Rwanda, it is doubtful that the Hutu killers felt any twinge of conscience as they went about their torturing and murdering. The same is true of Americans, Europeans, and Asians when they have been caught up in their own spasms of depravity." (One doesn't like to exude chauvinism, but in the midst of jettisoning history and "blaming" evolutionary biology instead, Rosenblatt might have noted that the killers here—and in those contexts he adduces to ensure his political correctness—were almost entirely males of the species.)[27]

Moreover, the choice of written texts underscores the extent to which America's Native people—in this case in their collective stereotype as wise, spiritual observers—provided 1950s America with a philosophical heritage that could be deployed to echo, but never to challenge, the overwhelming Judeo-Christianity of those whose celebratory text this is.

The Family of Man contains forty-seven epigrams that act as unifying thematic captions for groups of photographs. Of these, eleven are quotations from British men, mostly poets, but also including Bertrand Russell and Thomas Paine. Next in frequency (with six each) are quotes from three sources (thus rendered equivalent): the Old Testament of the King James Bible, English translations of Greek and Roman writers (Ovid, Euripides, Plato, etc.), and "Indians" (Sioux, Navajo, Kwakiutl, Pueblo). There are five from male Asian thinkers and poets, four from continental European men, two from European women, two from non-Western religious texts, one each from indigenous people in New Zealand and Africa, one from a European-American man (Thomas Jefferson), and two from institutions (the Atomic Energy Commission, the United Nations).[28] The Family of Man thus had one main progenitor, and he was British. Only slightly less important, however, was a classical European paternity—Hebrew, Greco-Roman, and . . . *American Indian!*

Here's some of what these Indian wise men (although gender is not indicated, the overwhelming absence of female tribal people from the sort of coffee-table "texts" quoted suggests that they were all males) say, and what their "sayings" are used to illustrate:

We shall be one person
Pueblo Indian

This captions three photographs: two of marriages (Japan, Czechoslovakia) and one of an Andean man playing a flute with an Andean woman smiling behind him. (This latter becomes emblematic: it is repeated several times in the course of the work, and used as part of the logo for the book itself. The relative positions of man and woman are entirely representative of the book's assumptions, as is the "universal" happiness depicted in the picture.) Photographs of weddings in Mexico, Sweden, France, India, and the United States follow on subsequent pages. Next, without a new epigraph, follow eleven pictures of pregnant women (three giving birth): eight from the United States, one from "Kordofan," one from Japan, one from the "Arctic," one from Mexico.

Having captioned—and "universalized"—marriage and maternity, another anonymous "Indian" now provides a translated, de-contextualized (and thus hopelessly trite) chant for "manhood":

When I am a man, then I shall be a hunter
When I am a man, then I shall be a harpooner
When I am a man, then I shall be a canoe-builder
When I am a man, then I shall be a carpenter
When I am a man, then I shall be an artisan
Oh father! ya ha ha ha
Kwakiutl Indian

This kind of de-contextualized language is familiar. "Non-Indian readers with little knowledge of American Indian cultures reading the foregoing," Geary Hobson argues in a similar context, "are left with the impression that Indians, as they have always heard, are a people with a 'simplistic' way of life. Such readers look at the 'simple' phraseology and are further confirmed in that particular stereotype of the Indian— that of the Native American as a 'child-like savage.' "[29]

What follows are, of course, pictures of fathers and children, though unlike those showing women, these men appear only with sons. The pictures appear, in

order, from the United States (a white father holding a blanketed infant), Bechuanaland (a near-naked father shows his naked son how to throw a spear at an-
telopes), Jamaica (a father bends over to caress a resting child), and five more from
the United States. The final picture shows a pair from Austria, a father and young
son playing music.

The next Indian epigraph is Sioux, but just as reassuring about universality as
were the Pueblo and Kwakiutl words: "With all beings and all things we shall be
as relatives." Next to this claim is a picture suggesting the extent to which Steichen
misunderstood the Lakota speaker. It is another family—of European peasants sitting on their farm wagon. The father holds a whip and reins, the mother, the infant child. More peasant families follow: from Sicily, Japan, Bechuanaland (more
"savage" nudity), and the United States (again, all white). Presumably, Steichen assumed that "relatives" meant family members, and "as relatives" referred to things
of the earth, with which farming people, as tillers of the soil and keepers of live-
stock, are "naturally" well-acquainted. Here, the Western European belief that *using* the land and *using* animals (demonstrating a Biblical dominion over the beasts
of the fields, and so on) is what a Lakota speaker meant by "as relatives." But, as
is obvious to any tribal person, this is quite mistaken. Lakota tradition (like most
Native American tradition) demands that individual Native people behave toward
the whole world as though everything in it—a tree, a rock, a cloud—is a "relative,"
living, growing, existing as humans exist, following its/her/his path through life.
As every tribal person recognizes, the difference between us and Euro-America is,
in Duane Niatum's words "precisely this sense of coming from the land and not
to it."[30] But here, as with all the pictures and quotations, the contextual meaning
of these words is lost. They are reified into slogans, deployed in turn as abstract
thematic "logos."

A Navajo voice is next, its English version an awkward "chant" in a non-chant-
ing language that effectively blunts and distorts all Navajo meaning into something
very like "Tonto-talk":

> Before me peaceful,
> Behind me peaceful,
> Under me peaceful,
> Over me peaceful,
> All around me peaceful.

As was the case with the Sioux text, these Navajo words illustrate scenes entirely
inimical to the prayer's original meaning: manual labor involving trees—logging,

ground-clearing, house-building—from the United States, New Zealand, Kenya, Bechuanaland, the Soviet Union. All but the African portraits show white subjects. The last intervention by an Indian voice in this text comes near the end. Again, it is dehistoricized; again, it is Sioux. "Behold this and always love it! It is very sacred, and you must treat it as such." Improbably, the four photographs below these words show voters in France, Japan, China, and Turkey, placing ballots in boxes.

Despite a relatively heavy reliance on Indian "wisdom"—or at least on the sort of "meaningful" slogans attributed to the generic "Indian" in American popular culture—few photographs suggest that *real* Indians (and certainly none from the book's present) belong to this "family of man." In fact, in the whole text there are only five representations of North American indigenous people, among them three from "Arctic" (all female), and another of a Pueblo couple (captioned "American Indian," and part of the series "We Two Form a Multitude" near the end of the book). There is another picture from the Pueblos, a portrait of Kachina dancers, so tiny here that they are barely recognizable, though their dramatic setting, against what appears to be fire, but what is more likely a New Mexico sunset, removes them from the quotidian realm. These are, curiously but significantly, not grouped with the photographs showing religious practice, but rather with those showing all kinds of "dancing." There are two tiny portraits of children whose racial identity is ambiguous: both children could be "full" or "mixed-blood" Indians. But other than these scattered pictures, there are no visual representations to give life to the verbal ones. Generic Indians may intone wise sayings, but only a few are actual, living members of Sandburg's and Steichen's "Family." Indeed, in this Family, America's Natives are much less apparent than African-Americans or Asian-Americans. And this despite the fact that Native Americans have historically comprised the most photographed of all American racial/ethnic groups!

A second subtext purveys a clear message about gender: adult women appear as mothers, wives, or domestic workers, primarily employed in the "work" determined as "women's work" by Western European mores and almost always accompanied by children; young women and girls are presented as the objects of male sexual attentions. Here again, the "Family of Man" has "universalized" values and practices actually specific to a single—albeit dominant—culture, and done so in a manner wholly reassuring to a white, ruling-class audience.

The overriding perniciousness of the work—and other similar works of the era—was not, however, merely due to its implication that Western European behaviors were "universal." What was more dangerous was its erasure both of history itself and of those differences that historically have provided the motives for dramatic changes in systems of class, race, and gender. The lineup of visual "similarities" drawn from the book's present and from all over the globe implies that a sacred dance at Zuni is exactly the same as a social dance of tipsy Brazilian nightclubbers or a midwestern barn dance, where the dancers are prosperous white farmers. Work is similarly blended into a meaningless mush. The labor of an adult American male coal miner is equated to that of a little boy in Wales, or—even more absurdly—of an African miner in the notoriously exploitative mines of the Belgian Congo. Voting, in this photographic vision of the world, is exactly the same in (black) South Africa as it is in Japan, in Czechoslovakia, or in China! Motherhood and marriage are the most "universal" of "universals," static and unchanging, they are identical in the Arctic, in middle America, in peasant India, in war-ruined Germany. Moreover, the book suggests, people's relationships to power are both ahistorical and really just the same everywhere, however superficially disparate: tribespeople in Bechuanaland, listening to a tribal storyteller, are just like rows and rows of young university students, taking notes in a lecture room in Czechoslovakia. These latter, in turn, are just like a handful of men and women students at the University of California, sitting in a Berkeley seminar room listening to a male professor. They *all* have mothers; they all suffer fear; everyone dies. As Daniel Bell and others of his 1950s ilk had it, ideology (not to mention rebellion) was dead.[31]

Why? Fritz Scholder put it this way: "When the Negro demanded equality, the response of white Americans was to deny that differences exist between Black and White Americans. You have heard this business about people being basically the same. In doing so, you really are denying that a valid issue exists."[32]

Had we been listening hard as we paged through our copies of *The Family of Man*, we might have heard many sounds counterpointing the universalizing, dulcet tones of America's white, middle-class, liberal, male intelligentsia. The most ominous of these, however, was soon audible to everyone, though at first we scarcely recognized it. (One boy from my sister's high-school class defied local expectations and joined the Navy. He, we learned one afternoon in 1960, had been shipped out to someplace called Laos.) It was the sound of young men's feet, marching again, or, more accurately, slogging, into the jungles and paddies of places we knew only from *National Geographic* (or indeed, from *The Family of Man*), places we had named "French Indochina" on our junior-high geography homework.

Of course, the feet were not the feet of most of our friends: Palo Alto's rich kids went to college, not to war, and liberal Cubberley High School's kids were, almost without exception, antiwar anyway. That they *were* the feet of our *other* people however, the brown, red, and working-class white feet of those from whom we came, I would not learn, and indeed, in my antiwar frenzy, could not readily accept, until that contradiction, too, confronted me many years later, after the war had been lost and my generation found itself faced with itself and with its contradictions: gender to gender, race to race, class to class.

At the same time, consistent with the perplexingly contradictory nature of intellectual life in that era, we grew political amid the Berkeley heyday of the rigidly anti-political, ahistorical New Criticism. Cheerful modernists all, our English professors launched our indoctrination into the beauties of formal perfection with a stern enthusiasm that soon captivated—though not without pain—those of us from Palo Alto's golden land who considered ourselves budding literary geniuses.

> A few Native Americans of my generation, mostly poets, were finding a way not to convert entirely but rather to draw the European-American poetic darlings of the New Critics into their tribal worlds, borrowing only what was useful. Duane Niatum, for example, wrote "Lines for Roethke Twenty Years after His Death." Ray Young Bear's contribution to this part of my (re)education is "Emily Dickinson, Bismarck and the Roadrunner's Inquiry." There are other poems in this hybrid genre, all moving between the worlds with an ease which I still have not mastered.[33]

So there we were: on the one hand (in history classes, in countless reading groups, in political clubs and organizations) learning, with sorrow and horror on my part, the lies our teachers had so smugly, so self-righteously taught us from early childhood; while on the other hand (in English classes, in intense discussions of poetry, both "theirs"—in translation—and ours), learning awe for the interior lives of literary works, the perfectly chosen word, the strikingly apt metaphor, the construction of order out of the chaos of everyday, modern life. Indeed, interpretation of any but formal considerations was severely proscribed. "The POEM," they insisted, "does not MEAN; it IS."

This learning, then, joined the poetry that had lived in my head from childhood, and line after line, stanza after stanza, poetry began to form a thick shield between me and the often bewildering, still wholly white, solidly middle-class university world. Perhaps it was high modernism's privileging of isolation, loneliness, self-absorption ("I wake to sleep, and take my waking slow," "To me, one silly task is like another / I bare the shambling tricks of lust and pride," "There never was a world for her, except the one she sang . . .") together with its political (though New Critics shunned the term) cynicism ("Buffalo Bill's Defunct," "What rough beast, its hour come 'round at last / slouches toward Bethlehem to be born?" "The guns spell money's ultimate reason / In letters of lead on the spring hillside") that drew me? Or was the lure the existentialist credo to which we wholeheartedly (and readily, given its semi-congruence with Native belief) subscribed? With youthful sincerity we intoned: *"Existence precedes essence"*; "What humans fear most is freedom."

Erich Fromm visited the campus in the spring of 1962. Hearing him, in the midst of a vast crowd of students gathered in the plaza outside Dwinelle Hall, I and my friends underwent a youthful epiphany: all of us determined to engage, though we did not quite realize yet with what. We read, and discussed, the existentialists fashionable in the '60s: Camus, Sartre, and, for the women among us, de Beauvoir, as well as Kazantzakis and Kierkegaard, Unamuno and Dostoevsky. In no case, however, did we understand the political context of the philosophy's postwar proponents. New Criticism effectively blocked any understanding of the *collective*, historical context of, say, Camus's *La Peste*. We thus pursued political *engagement* (it had to be in French) as a path to the authenticity we craved. Each individual who followed our code believed earnestly that although she acted alone in the face of an indifferent universe, she nevertheless acted in behalf of everyone else. Shriven of history these acts became hard gems, singular, glowing defiances of the meaninglessness that hovered over every life and its end. Only by grasping this responsibility and accepting the pointlessness and absurdity of death did we believe we could hope to create a genuine self.[34]

 My assimilation of a version of this French existentialism—that which had to do with taking responsibility for all one's actions was also overdetermined. As descendants of the Nez Perce band that resisted theft of tribal land by officials bearing treaty gifts, we had always been taught to view the life given us by the creator as a heavy personal burden. Every action, Chief Joseph had taught, no matter how apparently trivial, had consequences. For members of the Wallowa band, this meant avoidance of all gestures—including the offer of blankets or food, or more particularly the offer of friendship. Joseph knew what Camus learned a century later, that plagues lurk everywhere and must be guarded against always.

> At the conclusion of Albert Camus's novel about resistance, the narrator, Rieux, muses as he listens to the crowd celebrating the end of their occupation by the plague: "And indeed, as he listened to the cries of joy rising from the town, Rieux remembered that

such joy is always imperiled. He knew what those jubilant crowds did not know but could have learned from books: that the plague bacillus never dies or disappears for good; that it can lie dormant for years and years in furniture and linen chests; that it bides its time in bedrooms, cellars, trunks, and bookshelves; and that perhaps the day would come when, for the bane and the enlightening of men, it would rouse up its rats again and send them forth to die in a happy city." [35]

At the same time, however, some aspects of this bourgeois idea of freedom contrasted sharply with traditional Native America. First of all, its origins lay in the European past. As Bill Brandon noted in 1970, this "freedom" had emerged from the (imperialist) European world of the sixteenth and seventeenth centuries, when it was explored in popular tales of "fantastic voyages and the stories of the new world." "All this idea of freedom," he noted, "came from the description of the new world as far as I can determine. In Dante you do not find the term 'freedom' mentioned once. Loyalty, however, is all through Dante. Freedom is not there."[36]

Alfonso Ortiz examined the differences between European ideas of individual freedom—sacrosanct "right" of bourgeois society—and those held by Pueblo people and by certain Sioux. His words are worth quoting at length:

There is very little need for children to ask "May I?" In every Pueblo language, these words are irrelevant. They have no point because all Pueblo people have . . . the Indian belief that freedom is not theirs to give. There is also a striking passage in the writings of Standing Bear, a Sioux, to the effect that when he was 11 years old, recruiters came to his reservation from the Carlisle School. . . . He decided to apply. He went by himself without telling anyone and without asking anyone. The recruiter, of course, would not accept his application because he didn't get permission from his parents. So they called his father, and his father said permission is not for me to give. "He is an individual. If he wants to go he can go."[37]

In the lexicon of postwar French existentialism this casual, unremarked assumption that each individual (of any age) is free meant terror to most Europeans because it implied *total* responsibility for each act. There was no one else to blame; no personal past carried excuses. Traditional Native Americans, however, grew up accepting this "unbearable" freedom.

Chief Oren Lyons explained how traditionals taught an acceptance of individual responsibility in the face of the "mainstream" culture's avoidance of it:

I am a member of one of the Six Nations Confederacy. The question that arose here about how do you teach your children is very real to us. We are a very traditional people.

And yet, at the same time, we have managed to coexist. We go out and we come back. The thing that we have had to be very careful of was the dominance of this larger society which has a great deal of pressure and power so that it can bring to bear the way of the dollar bill, and its values. . . . And how we teach is by example: You set an example and they will learn. You can't tell somebody what to do. If you don't do it yourself, they are not going to listen to you. So you teach by example.[38]

Although here again I hesitate to reaffirm romantic generalizations about "traditional Indians," it does seem to me at least that this abiding sense that every life carries a responsibility to find and then to walk its own path provides some of the explanation for a phenomenon that often baffles white—and black—observers. That is, Native people tend to avoid the kind of confrontations that make demands through guilt-eliciting accusations about the past. Since the very earliest contacts between Europeans and indigenous people in the Americas, the former—and their descendants—have repeatedly remarked what they perceived either as an almost unbelievable forgivingness or the pitiful resignation (and hopelessness) of "savages" confronted by more "civilized" people, their inevitable masters. Because of this characteristic "passivity," tribal people often find themselves the focus of advice-giving non-Indians. "I think," one young white man from New Jersey told a Lakota filmmaker recently, "that you should be much angrier in your film about what whites have done to you. You should use much stronger language to tell them [!] how badly they've treated Indians." The filmmaker, Harriett Skye, responded, politely, in a characteristically "Indian" way: "This is my film," she told him. "If you want to make your film, go ahead." On another occasion, an African-American student interrupted a lecture I was giving to say, "Why didn't they just get guns and kill the whites. That's what we've learned to do!"

Movie-Indian stereotypes notwithstanding, this has never been the traditional Indian way. Here, for example, is Chief Joseph's speech (at the 1904 Carlisle Indian School graduation) where he was a guest along with the man who was personally and morally responsible for the slaughter of Nez Perces and other tribal people:

We are both old men, still we live and I am glad. We both fought in many wars and we are both still alive. Ever since the war I have made up my mind to be friendly to the whites and to everybody. I wish you, my friends, would believe me as I believe myself in my heart what I say. . . .

I have lost many friends and many men, women, and children, but I have no grievance against any of the white people, General Howard, or anyone. If General Howard dies first, of course I will be sorry."[39]

 We, too, learned these ways from Grandfather's life, his words. Both aggressive, accusing confrontations and recitations of a personal—or collective—"victim" history, replete with excuses for moral failings, are anathema (making life in the contemporary United States very, very difficult).

Only once did Grandfather make public an exception he found in his rules, insisting that we *should* accept something from white people. The occasion arose when officials of the Great Society announced an "affirmative action program" to direct special scholarship monies toward members of previously excluded groups, including Indians. (The definition of "Indian" for the purposes of these grants was possession of a one-eighth blood quantum and occasionally "recognition by an Indian community.") All of us, my brother, sister, and I and our two cousins were gathered at our grandparents' house arguing about about whether or not we Penns, urban bred, mixed blood, had the right to claim such money. My position was then what it remains: we (with the possible exception of my sister) had none of us suffered any of the discrimination for which such programs were meant to compensate. None of us grew up on a reservation: none of us looked sufficiently Indian to have drawn more than a few public insults or the private prejudgments of bigots. Both my brother and my male cousin disagreed, and the argument grew more and more heated. On my side, I kept insisting that we had never "paid our dues." Finally, my normally silent grandfather interrupted: "You take every penny the white government gives you," he insisted loudly, "*I* paid!" "Anyway," he added in a softer voice, "that's what I think."

"That's what I think." Such remarks, familiar to all Native Americans, are an important strategy for translating the unequivocal dualisms of "protestant" English-speaking culture into the much more complex, far more nuanced moral world of Native America. I am, more often than not when acting my "white," professorial half, guilty of forgetting the more subtle dictates of my internal "other" half, as my Japanese colleague Shigehisa Kuriyama repeatedly notes. Once, after I made a particularly sanctimonious speech to graduate students, Hisa chided me gently: "You couldn't say such unequivocally judgmental things if you came from a Buddhist culture, such as that of Japan." Of course my other half understood his point instantly, as he knew "it" would. I later showed him some examples of the "that's my opinion, anyway" reaction to controversy which I found in the minutes of the first national conference of Native American scholars. A wonderfully typical series of exchanges occurred during the discussion of Alfonso Ortiz's talk, "American Indian Philosophy and Its Relation to the Modern World." Regardless of the strength of their positions, every Indian respondant concluded with a traditional equivocating statement. The only undiluted polemics came from non-tribal speakers, especially from young non-Indian male students who felt free to intervene at will, both to tell the Indians what they should think and do, and to explain in detail all about their personal lives. The most egregious of these speakers was one "Mr. Venters," introduced with wry "tribal" humor by a gracious Alfonso Ortiz: "We have one young white radical here, who has been saving up a mouthful." Needless to say, Venters did not take the understated hint, and proceeded to talk at length about his plans for Indians and himself. At one point Herb Blatchford tried again to suggest that the young man was a little out of order, concluding by challenging him, gently, "Is that burden of understanding upon us, to have you understand it? Or is the burden upon you to expand yourself to where you can understand?" Venters remained oblivious: "The burden is for me not to get arrested in the attempt. In terms of what I can do, you see, I have different problems with the United States government. I don't want to go to Viet Nam. I don't want to be busted for smoking pot or dancing in the streets. I want to kind of shiver in the corner in a way, because I want to have peace, freedom, beauty." Thus the *Family of Man* generation.[40]

 Throughout those Berkeley years, I continued to live white (even when I was with Jim Mott), in almost the same way as I was playing "honorary male."

It was not until I read Sheila Rowbotham's Woman's Consciousness, Man's World[41] *that I realized how many of us "intellectual" women had internalized men's contempt for our sisters. By virtue of our brains—which made us superior versions of the mirrors Virginia Woolf had long since described, mirrors which reflect men back "at twice their natural size"—we were admitted, albeit as auxiliaries, to the male club so that they could enjoy our willingness to listen, hour after hour, day after day, to their brilliance. Most of us didn't even know how to join in their conversations. They certainly never asked us to utter more than the words that would assure them that they were, indeed, just as clever as they had thought themselves to be all along. If we were attractive to them, we could find ourselves the objects of a confusion of intellectual and sexual desire as well.*

I was politically somewhere to the right of Mario Savio and the other student movement leaders (I never could seriously entertain violence as a tactic, for example), but far to the left (as I was to learn upon leaving Berkeley) of America. I was in favor of civil rights, Kentucky's miners, Cuba's revolution, revisionist history (Michael Harrington's *Other America* hit much closer to my home than to the homes of most Berkeley undergraduates), the Republican side of the Spanish Civil War. Like everyone else I knew in my generation, I was solidly against the Vietnam War.

I marched, I sat in, I demonstrated, I went (once, terrified) to jail. I wrote letters and polemics; I picketed, made coffee, painted signs. I sang and played my guitar. I dressed in black and peace signs. I pierced my ears. I dragged my books around in a green canvas Harvard book bag. I discovered the fashion benefits of "Indian hair": no need to iron my hair straight and flat and fine. My blue eyes, once a barrier separating my racial halves, now seemed to work together with my California air of good health to prevent both mistreatment by police or sheriff's deputies, and (more frustratingly) my achievement of a politically authentic decadence. I never really fit: not a Sally Sorority, I was also never a red-diaper baby. Not sufficiently white, I was also not anything else.

In those days, the only visible minorities on Berkeley's campus were Asian-American students, most of whom seemed to commute from across the Bay. The most visible social restrictions were those placed on Jews, who were, until my final year, forbidden entry into WASP fraternities and sororities. There were thus exclusively Jewish equivalents. There was also, at least by 1964, a black sorority, but I never knew anything about it. The lily-whiteness of the institution is underlined by the fact that I can recall knowing only one African-American student. Except for a few Asian and Asian-American scientists, there were only whites—and white males at that—on the enormous Berkeley faculty. Only in the course of civil-rights politics did Berkeley's students meet large numbers of people of color. Through most of that decade, the university remained a place of almost total white—male—privilege.

Despite my "passing," I never doubted that my life's destiny was to "go home" to "my people" to help make changes. If anything, that determination was constantly fortified by my grandfather, who, during my Berkeley years, was suddenly more accessible than he had been during my time in high school. Two events from this time are unforgettable.

BOARDING SCHOOL LEGACIES[42]

I wrote to my grandparents every week. Usually I simply babbled innocuously about my life—my classes, my social activities, my various political efforts. My grandmother always answered immediately. In her turn, she told of their daily

Robert Penn in uniform.

lives, and sometimes reminisced a bit about her childhood days in St. Louis, our years in Los Angeles, or—she loved to tell of these exploits—our uncle's years in the Army Air Corps during the war. She also wrote of the doings of that same uncle who, with my aunt and two cousins lived next door in Napa. My cousin Bobby in those years was living a difficult adolescence. Increasingly involved in the same politics that were consuming my life, he was far more radical in a very conservative small town. Trouble was inevitable. (He would ultimately also attend Berkeley, but only until he fled the United States after a conviction for "defacing the flag," part of which he had defiantly stitched onto his jeans to symbolize his protest against the war.)

One week, in place of Grandmother's familiar "Spencer-script," I found a letter written in Grandfather's hand. It was written on a torn, ragged piece of bright gold paper. The letter explained that Grams had been called to Missouri to the funeral of one of her sisters. She expected to be away for a week, and Gramps didn't want me to be distressed at not hearing from them. He was well, he wrote, and looking forward to my next visit. He signed it: "With love, from your Gramps." Scrawled along the bottom of the page was a chilling postscript: "forgive the paper, the handwriting, and your stupid old Gramps."

This paper, folded and refolded into a tiny, asymmetrical shape, became the first piece in my medicine bundle.

One weekend I went to stay in my grandparents' tiny house. Two things reinforced my dawning realization of the extent to which Grandfather was handing on his ancestral burden. The first evening Gramps hurried us through supper, uncharacteristically insistent that we watch a particular show on television. As Grams and I washed the dishes, he went into the living room to tune it in. "Every week he watches College Bowl," Grams told me, softly. "He always thinks you should be on it because he thinks that you are much smarter than all the other college kids they choose." "Oh, *no!*" I thought. "He's going to expect me to call out the answers!"

And sure enough, he did. "You know all this stuff, don't you?" he asked proudly. To spare him total disillusionment, I tried to explain that I wasn't very good at science or math, that I might know a few of the literature or history questions, but then again, I might not. "I'm only a sophomore," I said desperately. As the show unfolded, and every time I *did* know an answer, he called out "I knew it!" I don't recall how many answers I knew, but to my vast relief I knew just enough to pass his uncritical muster. (On the other hand, I resolved to time future visits to avoid another test.)

The next day I was doing some homework in the living room while my grandmother worked in the kitchen and grandfather rocked on the front porch. I heard the postman approach. "How are you, Mr. Penn?" he called out. "Oh I'm fine today," Gramps replied. "We've got our Patsy visiting. She's the smart one, you know, the one who goes to Berkeley. She knows just about *everything.*"

"You must be so proud," the postman said as I groveled inside, horrified, scared, overwhelmed. "No," I wanted to cry to him, "*you* know everything. I am only that

Grandfather in his backyard in Napa, California.

same little girl whose blue tricycle you made, who tried to shoot a straight arrow, to ride bareback without falling, who listened for your drumming and who is still grieving about what they did to you at Haskell." I couldn't say these things, any more than I could show him how I felt about the gold letter. But the next day, as I left, I let him drive ahead of me—slowly, slowly—in his splendid shiny old car showing me the way from his house to my freeway on-ramp, so that I wouldn't get lost again, as I had done on a previous visit.

Even had I wanted them, my grandfather left me no hiding places. He knew who I was, what he wanted me to be. And so did I.

Although sadly ignorant of its effects in Indian Country in those years, I finished Berkeley a recruit for the War on Poverty.

 It was the era when "Cultural Deprivation" provided a handy euphemism for "poverty," "oppression," "exploitation," "racism." In 1970, a Catholic priest, speaking, he claimed, "for the Blackfeet," told a group of scholars that when some BIA "experts" decided "that children in all the schools on the reservation were culturally deprived," they gave the districts "funds to bus

the children into Great Falls or to see a circus, to hear a symphony, or one thing or another. What it meant," concluded Father Brown, "was that they were deprived of the experiences of the middle class Anglo-Saxons."[43]

As part of a University of California–sponsored effort to fill this putative cultural void (albeit an effort based on a rather different interpretation of "deprivation"), the summer of 1965 found me solely responsible for forty-five youths, all African-American, all but two male, and all on parole from the California Youth Authority. It was the best of times: not only were my students clever and enthusiastic, but I knew just enough about the "new history" (which, at the end of the 1950s, had begun to reconsider America's past from points of view other than that of the victors) to begin a mutual reeducation. It was this experience of teaching African-American history (as well as what I knew of Indian-white history) to young people who had been taught their collective insignificance in the broad sweep of America's heroic past, that made me begin to understand how essential historical knowledge was. Because it destroyed almost every comfortable, self-serving version of European-America's past, such knowledge had been carefully denied those who had lost in the struggle for the United States. Together, my students and I began to relearn U.S. history, discovering that their ancestors, like mine, had—despite historical arguments to the contrary—rebelled against slavery, not only with violence, but also with the skills of "survivance," cultural strategies that protected memory from forgetting and that shielded them from being recreated in a European image of servitude. As we explored what was beginning to be called "Black History," their excitement, and mine, grew. (How thoroughly hegemonical was the dead upper-class guys' version of American history became evident the day I asked them to tell me what they knew of Harriet Tubman. None had heard of her. "Well, what about the Underground Railroad?" I asked forty-five black youths. Again, silence. "Frederick Douglass?" I ventured. But still no reply. "Why don't you just *tell* us?" Conrad Fox said, annoyed. And, equipped with lecture notes from Lawrence Levine's American history class at Berkeley, I did.)[44]

There were many ridiculous events in that summer, as some in our naïve, "save the world," Berkeley group took seriously their mission to replace deprivation with "culture" (though *all* of us were challenging the prevalent Eurocentric definition of culture). One woman, who was herself European-American but married to an African-American and the mother of a mixed-race child, determined to teach her students what she considered to be their "African heritage." She was teaching in an adjoining building, so I was unaware of her efforts until one day when my class was interrupted by a group of her students, near hysteria. "Miss Penn, Miss

Penn, come quickly: something *bad* is going on in Mrs. X's class!" In that school, patrolled by armed policemen, such summonses were heeded, so I rapidly put a student in charge of my class and ran down the corridor to Mrs. X's classroom. As we approached, I heard loud African drumming. Looking through the glass insert in her door I was stunned to see my colleague barefoot, clothed in a black leotard, writhing around, first on the desk then on the floor, watched by a visibly horrified group of mostly male students. *She* was demonstrating African dancing: *they* were seeing the behavior of a white whore.[45] I intervened, to her intense anger. Despite the undoubted sincerity of her intentions, her evident inability to respect—indeed, even to know—her students meant that these well-meaning but impossibly stupid efforts brought an abrupt end to her career in the War on Poverty.

Lest I sound too smug, another event reveals the extent of my own naïveté (though not, I hope, condescension). One day I began to hear considerable noise in the corridor outside my classroom. Soon, the school's Chicano janitor summoned me to the door where he whispered, "There's a knife fight going on out here. I'm locking you in so your students can't get involved. Don't let them find out, though. Use the emergency buzzer on your wall to call for help."

Shaken, I continued my lesson, gradually working my way around the walls of the classroom, heading for the emergency button inconveniently located half way down the rear wall. When I reached the back, I leaned casually against the wall, pressing the (silent) buzzer with a hand held behind my back. I continued (quite coolly, I thought) to talk on and on about that day's lesson. The noise outside grew louder; the thudding of bodies flung against the classroom wall increased; no help came. I kept pressing and talking, despite the fact that my position at the back of the room grew more and more bizarre. Finally, Conrad Fox, always the class leader, raised his hand. "Miss Penn," he said kindly, as though hesitant to add to the progressive destruction of my innocence, "you might as well stop pressing that button. It don't work."

That was the last time I pretended with them, though I waited until the final day to confess to them that I wasn't really twenty-six years old. Needless to say, they already knew that, too. They had considerately allowed me to believe that this little fiction, too, had been successful.

I spent the next several years immersed in teaching—continuing to believe, in the face of every kind of evidence, that inner city public schools could be transformed into truly educative institutions. In the midst of these years, I heeded the call of several black leaders to take my teaching where active racism had its origins, the white lower–middle-class suburbs of the San Francisco Bay Area. What next followed were terrible years: in one white school district, an area occupied mainly by the know-nothing denizens of America's despised white petite bourgeoisie, I was attacked by the local John Birch Society: my classes were taped, my car followed. They telephoned, anonymously and invariably late at night. ("You hippie-commie" was this imagination-deprived group's favorite epithet, but not the only one.) There, and in schools in similar neighborhoods, I learned that most parents feared the education of their children. What they wanted was a thoroughgoing reinforcement (at the lowest cost possible) of all those lovely myths satirized by Tom Paxton in "What Did You Learn In School?": "I learned that Washington never told a lie / I learned that soldiers seldom die / I learned that murderers die for their crimes / Even if we make a mistake sometimes / And that's what I learned in school today / That's what I learned in school."

Still, I was slowly becoming less isolated. Though I had felt far less alien in the African-American "inner city," the white suburbs held a handful of Indians. We found each other because the California state curriculum included Theodora Kroeber's *Ishi in Two Worlds* as a set text for the ninth grade. Though I taught this white anthropologist's version of Ishi's story many times, I never found it other than terribly painful. Like most Native people, I cannot now write much about the insupportably painful narrative of the final years in the life of this man they called "Ishi." I leave the task to more talented pens than mine. But the one good thing that came out of this experience was contact with Indian students, alerted to my presence because I identified myself as a distant relation of the book's subject, and added to lessons on the text a considerable additional curriculum about America's genocidal past and present. It was my intention to demonstrate that Ishi may have been the "last of his tribe," as the book proclaimed over and over again, but he was most assuredly not the last Indian, whatever the school board might have wanted students to believe.

One day, an Indian student whom I did not know came to see me in some distress. He ran track, and the track coach (alas, the athletic coaches at that school were uniformly right-wing and moronic) had told him that he could no longer belong to the school team unless he agreed to cut his "hippie," "fairy" hair. He had tried—in nonconfrontational Indian style—to explain that his culture demanded his hair style. (He wore his hair Hopi-style, above shoulder length and held by a head band.) But the track coach, a troglodyte with butch haircut and minimal neck, continued to call him names and threaten him with dismissal from the team. (Needless to say, the man's critical vocabulary depended heavily on homophobic terms which he used freely on Greg Valdez.)

I went to see this coach, hoping to explain Greg's desire to continue to run track and his need to remain part of his culture. I needn't have bothered. The man viewed me with even more suspicion than he aimed at Greg. Now I was not only a "hippie-commie-pinko" English teacher (too much reading of books was widely believed to signal dangerous political subversion), but I was also an Indian.

As was common in those politically fraught days, the incident rapidly grew into "us against them"—a handful of progressive teachers, concentrated in the English department, most commuting from Berkeley, against the overwhelming majority of extreme right-wingers, all perfectly at home in the neighborhood. Social-studies teachers weighed in, assigning reading and research papers aimed at showing how Europeans had brought the benefits of "civilization" to Indians (as, we English teachers were quick to point out, "we" were still doing, and with similar methods, to the people of Vietnam).

Students chose up sides as well. Greg and a small handful of others resigned from the track team and began to organize for an "alternative school" which could exist within the larger school structure. I—frustrated, feeling helpless to get anyone, even my friends, to understand what was actually at issue—wrote a poem about giving grades for "social studies" research on Indians and placed a copy in every teachers' mailbox.

I got more anonymous phone calls. *Ishi* continued to be taught. The students and I got the alternative school.

 Toward the end of my public school teaching years, a sad occasion prompted Gramps to teach me what became his most extensive lesson about being Indian. In 1971, when he was very old, he fell and broke his hip. Taken to Napa's Queen of the Valley hospital, he refused any "extraordinary measures"—in his case including hip surgery—to prolong his life.

So Gramps was visibly in pain and very, very ill when I arrived at his side. He took my hand: "Don't be afraid about this death," he began. "I won't die today. I'll die in two weeks, on Christmas. I want to tell you about death so you won't be afraid for me and you won't cry for me when I have passed over."

We spoke together for a long time. Some of his words are too personal to relate. But generally what he told me were details of his spiritual beliefs, those taught originally by the prophet Smoholla, whose practices are usually called "dreaming," and whose followers had been known since the late nineteenth century as "dreamers."

Like all traditional Native Americans, Gramps was not afraid of death. Death, to him, was merely transition, a going home, as he put it, "to the earth." His mark on this world had been made; he had kept his way as best he could; he had passed it on in stories and in acts. As a Dreamer, he reminded me, every act, no matter how seemingly insignificant, made part of a life. He reminded me again to take care in every part of my daily life. A person's heart, he told me for the last time, was visible in everything she did.

We each had time to say our goodbyes to Gramps. He died, two weeks after his fall, on Christmas day.

There was another affirmation of my identity during these years. At one of the dozens of "War on Poverty" conferences I was assigned to attend, I found myself part of a "discussion circle" that included a Native American man about my age. Both of us were much too shy to do much talking in this group of much older people. At the break, however, the group leader insisted that we all introduce ourselves to the person designated (Berkeley-style) as our "partner." The young man and I turned tentatively toward each other. I began, "I'm Pat." "I'm Jesse," he replied. Then we both paused, simultaneously embarrassed as we realized that we were both wearing enormous name tags. They used the first name only—after all it was California. JESSE," his read. He tried again. "I'm Indian." "Oh yeah?" I said. I paused a long time. "So am I." Another silence as he looked me over. I assumed he was noticing the blue eyes and brown hair, thinking, perhaps, that I was about to confess to a Cherokee princess in my past. I had the first of what became a familiar thought: that I should show him my teeth and point out the shape of my face and my ears, the texture of my hair. He said only, "I'm Nez Perce. Do you know who they are?" "Yes," I said, and then, still more hesitantly, "I'm Nez Perce too. Or at least some." Then I began babbling: "My grandfather's mother was called Mary Blue. She was part of the band that was sent to Indian Territory, Chief Joseph's band. She never went home, though. She stayed and married an Indian man in Kansas." Jesse didn't laugh at me, as I feared. "I know who you are," he said.

We spent the rest of the conference together, Jesse telling me of the problems at home on the Nez Perce reservation, problems of poverty, homelessness, alcohol. I told him, in turn, about my family, though he was perplexed that I knew none of my grandfather's brothers and sisters, or even where and if they lived. Jesse's description of life at Lapwai and Kamiah did not weaken my resolve to take my battle closer to Indian Country when I got the chance. But I was overwhelmed by what I interpreted as his sense of the near-hopelessness of the task. Of course

I had never been to the Nez Perce reservation: Gramps disdained "treaty Indians," and those with allotments in Idaho were all, in his mind, descendants of that group. But both Jesse and I were of the generation that wanted the future to include a reawakened traditional culture, the tribal sovereignty necessary to sustain it, *and* an end to the terrible poverty that plagued reservations. Neither of us knew how to accomplish what seemed to us—as it seemed to many—to be antithetical ends.

One commentator has described other young Indian activists' frustrations, these a group working in the Nez Perce Community Action Agency, established under the auspices of the Office of Economic Opportunity in 1965:

Occasionally bitter from the frustrations of a daily struggle to make a dent in almost total unemployment, bad housing, limited health care, and inadequate educational opportunities, the young adults who work for the Nez Perce CAA believe it may be too late for them to achieve the role in society that is open to the children they want to help.[46]

Had we but known it, those struggling in universities in these years creating programs in what were then called American Indian Studies were encountering similar problems, much closer up. One event, the Indian occupation of the former federal penitentiary at Alcatraz Island, brought to a head some of the most important, and baffling, contradictions inherent in university and college level programs in Indian, or Native American Studies. Roger Buffalohead, Director of the American Indian Program at UCLA, described the Indian faculty's dilemma: "we got the students very much involved indeed, as you probably know. The students all departed for Alcatraz. Here then another question was raised. If you are going to teach students to be involved and to be activists, as was done at California, can you then draw a line and say to them: You've got to come back from Alcatraz and learn your lessons? Those of us who had approved this involvement at Alcatraz were caught in a fix. What could we say? The only argument that we could make when the administration told us to get the students off of Alcatraz, was that the administration would then have to call in ALL of its activists in their involvements with the white world." Beatrice Medicine's students at San Francisco State included many whose decisions to participate marked the end of their university careers. "Many of the people who went to Alcatraz didn't keep up their studies," Medicine recalled. "Others stayed on campus and made the Dean's List."[47]

Some Indian scholars felt much clearer about the place of university educations in Indian lives. Scott Momaday, for one, described universities as "the enemy camp" where Indians students could learn about both opportunities available in the European-American world and about ways Indians could avoid America's efforts to keep them "frozen in time," still-vanishing Indians of familiar American stereotype. Combining the enemy's knowledge with their Indian ways, young people could choose for themselves where and how they moved through the contemporary world. Others suggested a third way: rather than viewing this venture into the world as a one-way street, traveled by Indian students from the reservation into the European-American university, Indian Americans should begin to think of themselves as white people's universities—tiny educational institutions carried on every Indian back. It was their knowledge, drawn from their identity, their culture, their ways that the modern white world needed, and needed desperately, to save itself and the whole world from destruction.[48] (It would be some years before America began to accept this view of Native America. And then, as we shall see below, these "Indian universities" were often little more than spiritual trinkets for sale to soulless tourists.)

Other battles loomed. Not only did the war against the war continue, but women, prompted by myriad examples of rebellion, began, so slowly it seems in retrospect, to awaken to their own situations of oppression. And at the same time as I was becoming aware of what was then a multifaceted women's struggle, I was learning what I else I had missed, the struggles of Indian people against the historical and cultural forgetting that had plagued all of us for so long. Soon after I took a "leave of absence" from the War on Poverty and spent a year regrouping in a peasant village in Greece. When I returned, to Davis, California, I found myself once again embattled, this time on two major fronts, one in the race war, one in the gender war.

Every year, most of the traditional tribes are beginning to stir. You can hear the drums; you can almost see the fires.
Don Wanatee, 1970[49]

For Indians, as for other groups excluded from rights and privileges enjoyed by most white males in the United States, the 1960s proved a watershed, replete with the politics of group identification. (These built, of course, on the efforts and work of several key forebears.) Several activist movements and organizations emerged into the public spotlight: the Pan-Indian Movement with its organizations; the National Congress of American Indians; the National Indian Youth Council (which grew out of a caucus of Indian young people meeting at the American Indian Conference at the University of Chicago in 1961[50]); a more militant "Red Power" group, the Red Panthers, self-consciously modeled on the Black Panther Party; the organization best known by the United States public, the American Indian Movement, or AIM, targeted by the FBI for an extended, internal war; and, following hard on the heels of the birth of the United States feminist movement within Students for a Democratic Society, the Women of All Red Nations, or WARN.

These developments were not always received with unmixed pleasure in Indian Country, however. Although Gramps loved AIM, regretting often that he was "too old" to go join militants in their many California activities, lots of tribal people didn't share his reaction, leaving many militants frustrated. At a 1971 conference of Indian scholars the clash of contrary views was heard in many speeches. Some remarked that the "Red Power" movement's unfortunate choice of name put off lots of patriotic reservation people who linked "red" with communism. Others noted that confrontational political styles flew in the face of tribal traditions. Of course such recalcitrance frustrated many younger Indians, anxious for change. Dick Wilson spoke for this group: "We don't live in the middle of cities, what kind of clout can we muster, what kind of impetus does the United States government feel to keep the treaty we signed? A moral right, a moral urging? These last only until the dollar sign appears." Thus, in his view, militance offered the only path: "Most of the time, too many Indian leaders sound like somebody running for office on a law and order ticket, or someone trying for the Little-Brown-Brother award for that particular year." Another speaker, Joe Sando, added, "They want to be a white man but they can't, because American people are very conscious of color. I don't care how much education you have. If your skin is brown or non-white you are never going to be a white man."[51]

Now, when I teach these years I try to keep an eye on all the sides involved, all points of view. This, combined with the knowledge of a generalized Indian repugnance for the kind of activist politics characteristic of what are now cozily referred to as "the Sixties" makes such teaching a difficult high wire act. Most non-Native students enrolled in courses about Native America *want* to see issues in the clear binaries deployed to explain most American social problems. I like to use the following story, told by Gerald Wilkinson and published in Kenneth Philp's useful collection, *Indian Self-Rule*, to counter both students' simpleminded lust for one right and one wrong side in every issue as well as their heavily romanticized ideas about life on reservations. It tells about one effort by young Indian militants to use surveys in a well-meaning attempt to understand grass-roots needs in the Navajo nation. What they discovered was that their issues were not necessarily the people's issues.

We assumed that the people at Crown Point, for the most part, were concerned about being exploited by the big energy companies and about combating racism from the white ranchers in the area. We also assumed that they agreed with tribal leaders about the need to expand the medical clinic and refurbish the high school.

In our survey, we discovered that those things were not really on many people's minds. The most important issue at Crown Point was dogs. On the Navajo Reservation, ten thousand people a year are treated by the Public Health Service for dog bites.[52]

Once learned, that story quickly becomes a useful short-hand warning from older Indians to younger would-be militants (or to historians, teaching the recent past): "Don't forget about the Navajo dogs."

Although now romanticized, vilified, or in other ways distorted beyond recognition, the actions of that messy decade transformed much of American life. Students and activists joined the Great Society's many "wars," on poverty, on discrimination, on war itself. The new Office of Economic Opportunity (for which I worked on and off from 1965 to 1977) provided alternatives to the politically very suspect Bureau of Indian Affairs (the hated "BIA," which not only militants described as being full of "hang around the fort Indians"). OEO, as it was familiarly known, encouraged grass-roots participation in the various programs and policies dealing with tribal people who began to build their own programs outside those government controlled structures of the BIA. So many were the activities and events of this decade, that it is impossible even to attempt to be exhaustive here. There were, however, several key events following that 1961 initiative at Chicago of which I became aware and which affected both my politics and my activities.

In 1969 (a year marked outside Indian Country by the invasion of Cambodia), Scott Momaday, a Kiowa writer, won the Pulitzer Prize for his 1968 novel, *House Made of Dawn*. Not only was this an event of great pride to those of us previously (and how sadly!) ignorant of John Joseph Mathews, Mourning Dove, D'Arcy McNickle, Ella Deloria (or for that matter, William Apess and many others), but it also signaled the birth of a new fashion for "Indians" throughout "middlebrow" America. (As Momaday himself put it in 1970, "Berkeley is a prime example. I have students in my classes who would give their left arm to be Indian. To be an Indian on the Berkeley campus now, is to be *somebody*."[53] Hippies, like Momaday's students, often modeled themselves, their dress, their beliefs, and so on, on a movie version of Native America.)

The year witnessed growing militance. Vine Deloria, Jr., published the illuminating and witty *Custer Died for Your Sins: An Indian Manifesto*. A group calling itself the Indians of All Tribes seized Alcatraz Island, claiming a defunct federal prison in San Francisco Bay for a vast Indian cultural center.[54] These and other activist texts and campaigns increased both the support Indian initiatives got from the youthful left and the intensity with which the FBI and other government surveillance efforts followed Indians.[55]

Militance continued into the '70s. The American Indian Youth Council played an increasingly important role in arousing young tribal people to political consciousness. Elders, organized into the National Congress of American Indians, supported most of the initiatives of the youth, adding many of their own.[56] Then in 1971, a polemic by a non-Indian, which claimed to be "an Indian view of history," raised consciousness all across non-Indian America. This was Dee Brown's *Bury My Heart at Wounded Knee*. One San Francisco writer, Jerry Mander, recalled his first encounter with the book in his recent neo-hippie reprise of that era, *In the Absence of the Sacred*: "That book impressed me tremendously. . . . In one sense it was a masterful work, detailing in excruciating fashion U.S. double dealing and brutality against Indians." At the same time, *Bury My Heart*, like *Ramona* and dozens of other popular condemnations of the historical treatment of Indians, passed on a troubling message:

Brown did the Indian cause a disservice by seeming to suggest that they were all wiped out, and that now there is nothing to be done. The book put the reader through an emotional catharsis: having read it, it was as if one had already paid one's dues. Combined with the popular imagery from television and films, the book helped remand Indian issues to the past.[57]

In that same year, another "relic" from the past reappeared. *Black Elk Speaks*, the "autobiography" of a Lakota medicine man told to (and, it turns out, "translated" by) John Neihardt, became, along with the *Tibetan Book of the Dead* and the *I Ching*, a manual for hippie living. Here too, however, amid the semimystical pronouncements of an impossibly wise, impossibly gentle, impossibly consistent

Black Elk, lurked a familiar refrain, quoted, interestingly, as the final epigraph in *Bury My Heart:*

I did not know then [at Wounded Knee] how much was ended. When I look back now from this high hill of my old age, I can still see the butchered women and children lying heaped and scattered all along the crooked gulch as plain as when I saw them with eyes still young. And I can see that something else died there in the bloody mud, and was buried in the blizzard. A people's dream died there. It was a beautiful dream. . . . The nation's hoop is broken and scattered. There is no center any longer and the sacred tree is dead.[58]

It is, perhaps, fitting that it should be discovered (as Shari Huhndorf first informed me) that those lines were never uttered by Black Elk, but were, rather, the utterance of one of history's best-known Indian lovers, John Neihardt!

> The "fake" industry, which raises numerous knotty questions about "authenticity," continues to thrive, however. The Education of Little Tree, written by an ex-official of the Alabama Ku Klux Klan called Asa—or Forrest—Carter, remains a best-selling "non-fiction" autobiography, despite the fact that it is made up out of whole cloth by a singularly unpleasant Southern bigot. Chief Seattle's prescient warning about killing the earth is also captured in dozens of recent texts—including one splashy and expensive coffee-table book cherished, no doubt, by ecologists everywhere.[59]

In 1972 AIM and other groups organized a vast march to Washington, a journey known as "the Trail of Broken Treaties." Upon arriving in Washington, the young marchers seized the Bureau of Indian Affairs, where they remained encamped for several days under heavy FBI surveillance. Meanwhile, back at the Pine Ridge Sioux Reservation, a struggle was going on between young militants—many in AIM—and the tribal chairman, Dick Wilson. People were regularly killed by the tribal police force, known as "Wilson's Goon Squad." Some young militants and older "traditionals" called in AIM, and in 1973 that group seized the town of Wounded Knee.[60] This event, more than any other, became the emblem of the new "red power" movement. It also marked the point at which the FBI openly declared war, a war whose "final" moment also occurred at Pine Ridge a couple of years later, when two FBI agents and two young Indian men were killed in a shootout. The only young man convicted of the killings was Leonard Peltier, whose corrupt arrest and trial is the subject of a sadly flawed and unfortunately unpersuasive documentary, Michael Apted's *Incident at Oglala,* as well as of Peter Matthiessen's far more carefully argued *In the Spirit of Crazy Horse.*[61] (Peltier, one of a handful of political prisoners left from the 1960s, remains in Leavenworth.)

Of the dozens of books and articles (not to mention films) published about what has come to be called "Wounded Knee II," one is particularly intriguing because it so candidly and ingenuously reveals both the extent of the FBI's war against Indian militance and a typical government official's attitude toward Indians, and especially toward the young urban activists of AIM and their "traditional" ("blanket," in BIA terms) Indian allies at Pine Ridge. This book is Stanley David Lyman's posthumously published diary of those months as he—then BIA superintendent at Pine Ridge—lived them.[62]

Lyman's background had prepared him well for his role. A native of South Dakota (and, like Richard Nixon, a "bad Quaker"), he had spent World War II working in a program to bring Mexican workers (temporarily legalized) "to work in the fields while 'our boys' were overseas." He then worked in the infamous Relocation Program (directed by another World War II patriot, Dillon Myer, who had learned *his* relocation skills rounding up Japanese-Americans for America's concentration camps) until he was chosen as superintendent at a variety of Indian reservations in the West.[63] As the book reveals, Lyman was a quintessential government "suit"; not only was he utterly unable to grasp the extent of government perfidy, or the Indian militants' point of view, but he had a little boy's fascination with the "covert" operations of the FBI as they illegally stalked AIM and other "suspect" Native people. Every "secret" he learned delighted him, *especially* if he recognized that it had been obtained in some illegal FBI action. The book's opening includes the first of many such incidents:

I spoke with U.S. Marshal Reese Kash, who told me that AIM was definitely coming today. I questioned him about his source, as to whether or not it was reliable. He made a curious remark, something to the effect that "Well, [nudge, nudge] I can't tell you that it is from wiretapping because that is illegal. Let me just say that it is from a very reliable source." Naturally, this made me wonder how the FBI and the U.S. Marshal Service manage to get some of the information they get. They, of course, would not reveal this, but they *must* have wiretaps and they *must* have undercover people because otherwise there would be no way of knowing some of the things they know.[64]

So caught up does Lyman become in the "Boys' Own" reprise of the traditional American cowboys versus the Indians that he is led to break the law himself, this time stealing cases of government C-rations and having them delivered daily to the Goon Squad, manning the anti-AIM tribal roadblock.[65] More seriously, and despite his frequent claims to "fairness," he sees only the government point of view.

A friend who was there, and who is no admirer of the BIA superintendent, interjects the voice of the tribal trickster once again: "Lyman had to act that way," she writes in reaction to my unequivocal condemnation. "If he hadn't, the FBI would have shot him just like they shot all those others." But here is still more of Lyman's "John Wayne" version of events:

Look at the situation: AIM is up against a disciplined force, firing coolly and purposefully and only on command. The men in the government bunkers are well-trained riflemen with high-powered weapons. Under these conditions, although there is sure to be a mar-shal or two hurt, it is obvious that the folks taking the aggressive action (!) within the peri-meter are the ones who are going to be really hurt. That is what happened this morning.

(At 5:30 A.M., five AIM people were shot by government officials, one "critically." This young man, later identified as Frank Clearwater, a Cherokee, had been shot in the head "and had suffered massive brain damage.")[66]

Lyman expresses still more awe at the efficiency of the feds' war against those American citizens they defined as "unwanted":

The FBI, it seems, has watched these groups as they started out from their various loca-tions all over the country. I don't know how they manage it, but they seem to know who is who and where they all are.[67]

Throughout the diary, Lyman shows himself to have been closely allied with Dick Wilson and those on his tribal council who supported him. Indeed, he joined Wil-son even against the federal government, which uncharacteristically (consider the massacres of Black Panthers) chose to attempt to negotiate an end to the occu-pation, despite the "trigger happiness" of many of the local federal marshals and FBI agents. ("It was good to see Russell Means in handcuffs, finally, after all this time, submitting to arrest," Lyman wrote. "I couldn't keep back the hatred and the glee when I saw that man finally submitting." In another context, he noted, "I looked out through the open door and saw one of the AIM-type people coming across the airport parking lot. . . . Just seeing him made the resentment well up inside me. This is a strange, strange thing that has happened in the business of In-dian affairs. Time was when I would never have had that kind of reaction toward an Indian—any Indian—and here I felt resentment toward this individual because he was dressed in the way AIM members dress, which [says this grey-suited, crew-cut white male] almost amounts to a uniform."[68])

Too, because officials coming from Washington rarely, if ever, consulted him (except when the FBI let him in on their "secrets"), thus wounding his deep-seated *amour propre*, the diary is riddled with tidbits demonstrating his superior knowl-edge of "Indian ways," each deployed to demonstrate that he, the BIA superintendent, knew more about Indians than anyone else. Needless to say, perhaps, most of this secret knowledge replicated widely held stereotypes. When at one point his Indian secretary, Jo Cornelius—"Pretty, chic, enthusiastic . . . Jo is really a brilliant secretary"[69]—refuses to tell him something, he writes, "All I got . . . was the 'buckskin curtain.' . . . The 'buckskin curtain' is what we [!] jokingly call it when Indians just quit talking. It can be because you quiz them too much, or because they don't trust you, or just because you are not an Indian."[70]

To explain the intertribal hostilities that led to Wounded Knee, he employs an interesting dichotomy, pitting "mixed blood" (Dick Wilson and his Goons, though by no means all of the mixed-blood tribal leaders were anti-AIM[71]) against "pure blood" (or "traditionals," whom he views with a typical BIA disdain). It is a distinction also made by Alvin Josephy, in his introduction to the work:

One of the problems to afflict the tribal council was a split between those of mixed-blood Sioux ancestry and those who were full-bloods. The full-bloods felt that those of mixed ancestry were too close to the white establishment and that basic Sioux interests and culture were compromised. The mixed bloods were often viewed as far more articulate in dealing with the outside world, and they, in turn often thought of the full-bloods as less able to accommodate to a rapidly changing society.[72]

As to those who came from outside Pine Ridge to offer support and supplies to the occupiers, Lyman minimized their participation by categorizing them as representatives of those stereotypes familiar to the far right throughout the 1960s and early 1970s. "Angela Davis was here and was run off by the tribal police. Also here was Hank Adams, who was the chief negotiator for AIM in their takeover of the BIA building in Washington last fall. He was run off, again by tribal police. . . . Rev. John Adams has been here with about twenty-five members of the National Council of Churches. They were run off, but the reverend is still here. Numerous hippie types were run off. Numerous members of the press were excluded because they had connections with underground papers."[73] When, from a considerable distance, The Young Men and Young Women's Hebrew Association of Miami tried to help AIM, sending canned goods to Wounded Knee, Lyman quickly halted distribution of the food, convincing a reporter from the *Miami Herald* that the situation was sufficiently complex that the canned goods should not go to the besieged AIM militants. "I don't know where the ten thousand cans of food will end up," Lyman wrote with satisfaction.[74]

Even those planes that managed to avoid FAA and tribal proscriptions were flown by "duped outsiders." "There are rumors," Lyman wrote, "that the planes sneaking into Wounded Knee are flown by Canadian bush pilots. One plane that landed the other day was reported to be of foreign, specifically Canadian, registration."[75]

Stanley Lyman's straightforward anti-AIM attitudes were widely shared, of course. And not only anti-AIM attitudes. In the minds of most Americans of that era, all the political efforts of students, members of minority groups, and, by the end of the '60s, women, were subversive of what they held most dear, and they acknowledged this in countless right-wing polemics and marches supported by constant police and FBI harassment.

But at first, to some of us at least, it looked as though "they" might lose at least some of their iron control of American society. The war ended—ignominiously—and some civil rights activities led to important and positive changes. Watergate drove Richard Nixon and his sleazy friends from the White House. A new era, of honesty, openness, equality seemed, briefly, to be dawning in America.

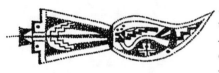 . . . The old coalition that had set up the original programs in the first place —between Blacks, Mexican-Americans, Oriental and Indian students—was fine so long as everybody was confronted with the common enemy, that is the white administration. But once you got problems going . . . the coalition fell apart.
Roger Buffalohead[76]

Some of us can go back and forth between reservations and the white society and be effective in this way with nothing more than a blown mind now and then, and other people just can't do that.
Buffy Sainte-Marie[77]

It was during this halcyon period that I reentered the Indian world, this time working in an OEO "support services" program at the University of California at Davis. At the Learning Assistance Center, I created and codirected a tutoring program aimed at keeping in college those minority students (including Indian) who had been admitted as "special action students." In the summers, I taught in Davis's highly successful Upward Bound program.[78]

This reentry was not easy; I carried a heavy sense that I, mixed-blood, urban, and now Palo Alto and Berkeley educated, was an intruder in the lives of the young reservation Indian women and men who were the focus of OEO initiatives. Feeling at least somewhat illegitimate, I took care to apply for work without mentioning my Indian blood at all. Thus I was hired on the basis of my War on Poverty experience, ironically because I appeared to be (and, to some extent was, of course) familiar with the African-American and Latino communities whose children also populated Upward Bound and the many support programs offered at the center.

In addition to a fine sensitivity about my (visible) blood quantum, a feeling exacerbated by the proliferation of "wannabes" through the first half of the 1970s, I bore a second burden. I was female, and I was a feminist. Both were to prove problematic.

•5•

BLOOD WARS

 Native American students came to the University of California in Davis primarily from Hoopa Valley, but also from the Navajo nation, from several Apache reservations, from the pueblos, and from cities and towns all over state. Several California nations were also represented: Pit River, Miwok, Pomo, and others.[1] Responsible for academic support services for these students, we in the Special Action Tutoring Program undertook a complicated (and often frustrating) effort to help them confront what we were learning to describe as cultural schizophrenia.[2] When young people from tightly knit reservation communities encountered the university, they faced a myriad of perplexing contradictions not unlike those that had awaited their grandparents at boarding school. Native students, whose scholarly survival skills had been sharply honed at substandard reservation schools, were strikingly adept at academic work. Most, for example, startled their stereotype-laden professors with their ability to grasp the principles of modern physics, the most metaphysical philosophers, and the forms of modernist poetry. At the same time, few found it easy to cope with the extracurricular culture of the university. Many, in fact, were driven—quite literally—mad. The absence of face-to-face contact—the "village" behavior familiar to most Indians, whatever their tribal background—the prevalence of what they understood as lying,[3] their inability to understand non-Native acquaintances (to read the external signs of dress, gesture, intonation, facial expression, and social status that hold meaning for non-Native students), their puzzlement at the strict exigencies of scheduling that underpin university life, all posed serious—and often insurmountable—problems. Add to these difficulties the fact that some had been "prepped" back home by militant traditionalists who warned them of unremitting white hostility (against which they sometimes "guarded" them with cere-

monies that could be frighteningly unfamiliar), and the eventual collapse of many students was overdetermined. Several students arrived in the small farm town of Davis prepared to read hostility in every non-Indian face—in spite of the fact that most of the town's inhabitants, whatever their race or nationality, had never knowingly seen an Indian, except in the movies. (This is not to say that there was no racial prejudice in Davis. Like most agricultural centers, Davis housed a transient population of migrant farmworkers, most Chicano or Mexican. Though the presence of the university ensured that open expressions of racism were much rarer than among the less educated populations of nearby Woodland, Dixon, or Winters, any objective observer would quickly have noticed that "Mexicans" were less than warmly welcome in Davis.) When people's reactions met their expectations of prejudice (fostered by their experience of non-tribal people back home or encouraged by young campus militants anxious for recruits), some found it impossible to continue to endure the pressures of academic life at all.[4] These young people followed one of two paths: they fell into madness or returned home.

One student's dilemma was particularly intractable. She was seventeen, born a Navajo but reared almost entirely in San José, California, by a Chicano foster family. She had a Latina name and spoke fluent Mexican Spanish as her first language. She knew—or remembered—not a single word of Navajo.

I met her when she arrived for student orientation, and agreed, at her request, to become her primary advisor. We settled on her classes and picked tutors for those she thought she might find difficult.[5] During the first two weeks of class I kept in close touch with her. She had found her way to the Tecumseh Center, and although she did not make friends with those her own age, had been welcomed by older militant students. She had formed a particularly close bond with two older women students, both of whom had young children, and who shared an apartment in the married student housing complex.

One very early morning in the third week of the semester I got a telephone call. Maria[6] needed me; could I come right away to her friends' apartment, she asked, where, I learned, she had been staying for several days. Groggily, I found my bike and set out in the cool Central Valley dawn. When I arrived at the address, I was startled to find a greeter, a very large Lakota militant, whose reputation I knew but whom I had not met. Deliberately posed like a movie Sioux, chin forward, arms crossed across his chest, he looked me over and said, angrily, "What do you want, white woman?" I explained that I had been called for Maria. He reluctantly moved aside so that I could slip my shrinking self through the door, but he con-

Teaching Upward Bound at the University of California, Davis, in 1975.

tinued to glare at what he took to be my unsuitable "whiteness." Frightened and intimidated, I went inside.

I found Maria in a state of almost complete delirium. Her older women friends, visibly exhausted after several hours of trying to help her, told me that the only understandable thing she was saying was my name. Maria grabbed me as though she were drowning, and she held on. Many hours passed as we clung together, Maria talking and talking (in a mixture of Spanish and English), I desperately trying to figure out what she was telling me and how I might stop, or at least lessen, her audible and visible torment. In the background, as the strange morning wore on, a chorus of normality accompanied Maria's desperate, incoherent ramblings. Maria's two friends made coffee and prepared breakfast, roused their children, sent them to school. Finally, they set off on their bikes for class. From time to time the self-appointed Lakota identity cop stuck his head in the front door to mutter more racial imprecations.

Slowly, I began to sort something out. Maria had two main narratives threading through her misery. One had to do with an incident at a store in Davis, where she had encountered what she perceived as racial hostility. (The clerk, who was a white student, had asked her if she was Indian.) Because Maria had had no experience of white-Indian racism (her sole experience of racism was that between two groups to which she did not belong, Anglos and Latinos), and because this event supported the stories militant students had been recounting this shy young woman had become terrified. She believed that she would not be able to stay in a racist Davis; all her dreams of college had been destroyed.

The second narrative was harder to comprehend, though after five or six hours of incoherent repetition I began to grab on to some of it. It seemed that when Maria was admitted to the university, her foster parents had notified the Navajo nation. Her family there (or perhaps tribal officials) had decided to invite her back to Arizona for ceremonies that would both honor her achievements and protect her as she went off to Davis. Unfortunately, this was a child whose life had been utterly devoid of Navajo ceremonies, or, indeed, of Navajo culture, a child reared in the Catholic Church by deeply believing adults. Moreover, she had had no experience of the people in her family or clan. Thus when she found herself the object of what were to her incomprehensible, and in fact frightening, rituals, undertaken in a language she did not understand and among people she did not know, something inside her apparently began to shatter. She knew, on the one hand, that these were the people to whom she belonged, by blood, by heritage. But she had been reared in an "Anglo"/Chicano religious world where Navajo rituals were either entirely unknown, or, if encountered, relegated to the much-denigrated, European-defined world of savage, primitive superstition.[7]

I don't know what the particular ceremonies were that distressed her so utterly, and it is none of my business. But Maria's version of them was terrifying: she had been "captured" by strong men she did not know, who hurt her in their effort to teach her that, in her words, she was a "weak woman" and "no good." At the same time, she believed that she had been told that the whole Navajo nation was resting its hopes on her. They were giving her medicine to make her powerful and strong, and she must accept it because she was Navajo.

Of course, one doesn't have to be an advocate of psychoanalysis to understand that in Maria's mental fragmentation, many discourses were linking themselves together willy-nilly. I recognized in her troubled, panicky efforts to explain her baffling experience some of the language of feminism (language she had doubtless picked up from the Native American feminists with whom she was staying), as well as bits of the languages of racism, and of what is now called "Eurocentrism."

But however muddled her efforts, and indeed however detached her interpretations of events from their actuality, it was clear that both the Navajo ceremonies and the unfamiliar political militance of some Davis Indian students had combined to overwhelm Maria's young mind.[8]

After several hours I convinced her to come home with me, where I remained mostly by her side for another day and night while she repeated her tales over and over and over. She refused food and panicked whenever I left the room. Finally, after telephoning everyone I could think of, I got help from a university counselor, a warm and kind British woman, who found Maria a bed at the student health center. She remained there, attending classes when she felt able, for several weeks.[9] In the end, although she managed to complete a semester, Maria went home—not to Navajoland, but to San José. Although she soon vanished from sight, I like to think this very clever young woman ultimately found a way to make peace with her Navajo self.[10]

Maria's experience, however, together with mine (was I "white woman," to be shunned by Lakota militants? and if so, should I have answered Maria's call?) posed problems I found I could not solve in my own mind, problems about identity, about blood, and indeed, about gender. Needless to say, I felt far more confidently militant about my place in the latter struggle: whatever question I might feel about my blood quantum, there was no question about my sex.

There were some students, of course, who did cope (more often than not with the tireless and selfless help of David Risling and his staff) by finding ways to continue their tribal life, returning home for important ceremonies or other tribal or family events. These necessary journeys at the same time provided those of us in the support staff with challenges. Because many Native American students rejected the tight demands of university schedules, none ever provided any warning of departures for home. Sometimes, in the case of well-known ceremonies or regularly scheduled powwows, we were able to anticipate the event and to intervene with professors so that they could accommodate the students. More often, I arrived at my office to find panicky messages from faculty that so and so was about to fail because he/she had not shown up for a midterm, final, or. . . .

That most Native American students were among the best in every class they took meant that their teachers were even more distressed about their unexplained absence than they might have been in the case of less able students. As was not the case for other minority students, most teachers also shared America's curious love affair with "Indians," a love they extended to what many saw as their wonderfully "exotic" students. These two factors, the students' excellence and their stereotypical identity, made interventions easier than they might have been, but no less frequent.[11]

Such administrative problems were not the only difficulties. Before Davis, I had never had to travel back and forth between cultures: Indian had been L.A., white was Palo Alto and Berkeley. Thus this daily crossing from Indian to white was, though I don't want to exaggerate, exhausting. I was, moreover, enrolled as a graduate student in a very traditional history department at the same time I was directing a very untraditional program. The two worlds clashed constantly. Just accepting the unmarked passage of communal time without the constant harassment of my "western" sense of clock time, a process necessary for my life with Native students, meant that when I "returned" to my academic life, my mind felt fractured. Usually, mental reassembly (there are no adequate words) required some period of time. Too, the intense sense of community among Indian people demanded that I relinquish my "western" sense of individual privacy—as well as my attachments to "private property." My house and its contents were open—always.

Even the most subtle expression of admiration for a possession—a piece of jewelry or clothing, for example—posed a problem. In every tribal culture, good behavior would require the immediate giving of the admired object to the admirer. In "western" culture, such behavior would be both utterly unexpected and completely "over the top," as the British would say. It is always interesting to watch what tribal people do when they are confronted by this situation in a completely foreign context, such as a primarily white university, where there are both tribal people and non-Indians present. At the very least, or so I have observed, there is a visible *frisson* of confusion before the owner of some object decides which behavior to follow.[12]

Another anecdote from this time—among the least painful ones—might help suggest the totality of this cultural split. One day I was away from my house from early in the morning until very late that evening. Upon my return, the houseful of "hippies" next door, sitting pleasantly stoned on their front porch, called out that I had missed a visitor. I walked over to get the details. It turned out that a young woman, whom they described as heavy-set, with black hair (interestingly, not as "Indian"), had arrived at about ten that morning. Discovering I wasn't home, she had sat down on the porch. At one or two in the afternoon one of the neighbors, feeling the oddity of her unusually long, silent presence, went over to find out if she needed anything and to warn her that I might not be back for several more hours. The young woman responded politely: she needed nothing, she knew I wasn't home. She was waiting. As several more hours passed, all the neighbors began to emerge from their marijuana haze to note that this unusual young woman continued to sit, quite still, on the porch. Thus they all noticed when she suddenly stood up and left, at about nine o'clock.

Their "western" assumptions ("time is money") suggested that anyone waiting that long—and especially without a book or (to their minds, especially) other stimulant—had a problem that must have been enormous and immediate. Thus they awaited my return with as much attention as a cluster of mellowed out Californians sitting in warm spring sunshine smoking dope could muster in order to tell me about what was to them a curious, perplexing, event. But in fact they had completely misread the situation. Billie Wilson, a Hoopa student from the Trinity Forest in northern California, had simply wanted to see me, and had come round to my house. When I wasn't home, she had waited. When I didn't return, she left. There was no problem, nothing special to discuss. That was all. For Billie Wilson, I was simply someone always accessible, who belonged to her because I belonged to her. Period.

Although such ways were less incomprehensible for me than for my neighbors, coping with such things remained far from simple. Often, I cycled slowly home from hours first at the Learning Assistance Center then in a graduate history seminar repeating, over and over, "Who *am* I?" Sometimes I found myself staring for many minutes at my mental picture of Gramps, listening, as I frequently do, to his voice across time. In fact, throughout my years at Davis, I remained torn, inside by the problems of trying to inhabit two cultures, outside by my constant concern that I not act in any way to usurp the rightful place of a person "more Indian than I." I chose to stay silent about my mixed blood, unless asked (as Maria had, for example). Thus I hoped to distance myself from any untoward affirmative action benefits that I believed were not mine.

This silence, too, finally proved untenable. After I had been directing the tutoring program for some months, I was visited in my office by a group of Native American student tutors. We greeted one another, and they all sat down around me, on chairs, table tops, window sills. Following custom, I did not ask the reason for their visit, though I was desperately curious. They too followed custom, assuming the posture of "potted plants." I hid my growing anxiety by continuing to work—making phone calls, shuffling papers, marking student essays, and so on. About two hours passed in near-complete silence, only one of us squirming uncomfortably, if (I hoped) invisibly. Finally, one of the men cleared his throat. Relieved, I turned toward him. In very serious and slightly angry tones Gerald told me, "You shouldn't be ashamed." "What?" Still solemn and more formal, he repeated, "You should not be ashamed."

Despite desperate efforts to guess the subject of this conversation, I was completely baffled. As I had long since learned to do in such situations, I awkwardly confessed that I had no idea what he was talking about. He looked skeptical. "Oh, yeah?" "Really," I insisted more vehemently, "it's true. I really don't know what you're talking about. I'm sorry. Please tell me." After much silent thought and some looks exchanged with his companions he said, "We've just found out that you're Indian. Why didn't you tell us? You should be proud of it, not ashamed. If you are ashamed, you'll teach shame to everyone else."

What irony! I had been so concerned to avoid stealing the benefits and compensations more legitimately due, I believed, to others that I had unwittingly overlooked two more important elements of the dilemma (thereby effectively hurting those for whom I cared most). First, I had forgotten that it was not Native America that divided itself by appearance or even by daily experience of reservation life (the Lakota "identity police" militant's actions notwithstanding), but rather European America that drew such careful distinctions. To most Native people in those years, being Native had more to do with a deliberately ambiguous "accountability" to an Indian community than it had to do with the precise dose of Indian blood flowing in one's veins (and still less with the presence of agreed-upon physical markers of race). Second, in that era of rising political consciousness, when hope for a long-withheld justice was rife, it was essential that Indian people be able to see around them those who could guide or open doors in the world to which they aspired. When the possibility of attending graduate school was a distant dream for most Native kids arriving at the university, my presence in school (like that of all the Native American tutors) offered an important embodiment of possibility. My meticulous care not to grasp "victim" status unfairly, or to pretend to have grown up on the "rez" (or to call it "the rez"), or to speak with an assumed "Indian" accent (e.g., dropping the "a" in "Indi'n"), I had, I believed, painstakingly chosen the existentially correct position, bearing the burden of the bones— Quaker and Indian—silently. And then this! After much talking, I managed to convince my friends that far from being ashamed, my Indianness was an essential part of my identity. It was, after all, what had driven my life since I first signed up for the War on Poverty in 1965, and what kept me working in EOP through the 1970s, despite the proliferation of distressing and discouraging sectarian quarrels, and despite the spread of an oppressive sexism through much of the student politics of minority America.

It was some time that afternoon before everyone accepted my explanation of what had seemed to them to be disgraceful behavior. The sharing of a clearly cherished—and extremely rare—photograph of my grandfather napping in his rocker shortly before his death, carried, together with a handful of other such personal items, in my wallet, helped evoke his very strong spirit in my defense. Finally, to my relief, everyone declared their acceptance of my explanation about my care never to walk a mile uninvited in someone else's moccasins.

Of course, I did not realize then that my confusion about my right to a place in the burgeoning politics of identity was not widely shared among militants. Those most visible were, in fact, mixed bloods, and from urban families like mine. Many even possessed considerably less than the federally required one-eighth blood quantum. Many, moreover, evoked mixed feelings from reservation communities. "To some," recalls Gerald Vizenor, these city-bred militants were "the heroes of contemporary history—but to others they [were] the freebooters of racism."[13]

But unlike prominent (male) militants, I remained confused through those years, unable to decide—about them, about myself. I could not resolve the dilemmas posed by the conflicts between urban politicals who were only slightly Indian and the young reservation people I dealt with, daily confronted by the stark contrasts between their previous experience and life in the university. Moreover, I could not understand my role in this historic confrontation between tribal life and the demands (and rewards) of university success. If we strove for academic success in the European-American curriculum, were we not, I wondered constantly, continuing the process of assimilation begun by boarding schools? Were our goals the eventual destruction of traditional tribal life? Were we *un*-fitting Native American youth for life among tribal people? The problems encountered by one of D'Arcy McNickle's fictional protagonists, Archilde, when he visited his family after moving away from tribal life, suggested that this had been part of McNickle's own experience of university success. In *The Surrounded*, Archilde muses, "These efforts to bring peace and order into the lives of his relatives before he left them forever did not please him greatly. Whatever he did, he felt that he remained on the outside of their problems. He had grown away from them, and even when he succeeded in approaching them in sympathy, he remained an outsider—only a little better than a professor come to study their curious ways of life. He saw no way of changing it."[14]

But, on the other hand, what arrogance, what elitism, prompted such questions from those of us who were products of our forebears' decision to abandon that same tribal life? How could we make decisions for other people? Was it possible to offer the university as a choice rather than a goal?

And most perplexing of all, where did I fit in all this? How Indian *was* I?

A SHORT HISTORY OF BLOOD

With the politicization of Indian identity in the course of the late 1960s and early '70s, blood quantum reemerged from several decades of neglect as an issue of paramount importance. And as was always the case in Indian Country, opinions varied, often wildly. Jeannette Henry, speaking at a gathering of American Indian scholars in 1970, put it thus: "According to the Bureau of Indian Affairs, an Indian is one who is enrolled on a federal roll of Indians, in some cases of one quarter quantum. In other cases, such as that of California, the Bureau accepts one-two hundred and forty-sixths degree of Indian blood. . . . Native Americans," she continued, "have been assimilated and any other ideas are foolish. The bloods are mixed so much, and inter-mixed again and again, so that the full bloods can be counted in the mere few hundreds."[15] And almost everyone recognizes the person described at the same conference by Steve McLemore. In his youth, there was "a kid in school [whom] we used to call . . . 'Spec' and he was red-headed and freckle-faced. But he was on the rolls as a Cherokee Indian. . . . He was, to all intents and purposes, white. But spiritually he wasn't. His mother wasn't white, obviously, because he was one of the most stubborn Cherokees and he wouldn't speak anything but Cherokee. . . . This boy was accepted by the whole run of the school as a Cherokee. . . . This mother had raised a red-headed, freckle-faced kid . . . an INDIAN kid. So it's the culture rather than the blood quantum."[16]

Of course, McLemore's point was much more complicated than his words suggested. "Spec" *had* the blood quantum, and it was that, together with his culture, rather than his red hair and freckles, that made him Cherokee.

Ironically, but characteristically, this 1970 scholarly gathering was full of "less-than-full-bloods," many as troubled about their identity as I was. Marigold Linton announced, "I look around here, and the thing that strikes me is that I thought I would be a freak here because I am so white. It's very clear that I'm not the only one who has a non-Indian parent. . . . If you ask whether we need to be concerned about this . . . of course . . . because none of us is the Indian that we're talking about who existed somewhere in our past."[17] Even sufficient blood did not necessarily "an Indian make," as Frank La Peña lamented. "I talk to fifth and sixth graders who visit the school on a special program, and I ask, 'How many of you are Indian.' Six hands came up and to four of them I said, 'What is your tribe?' And they didn't know their tribe."[18]

This theme, more than almost any other, ran through the speeches and writings of Native American activists, scholars, writers, and artists. Whatever their tribe, whatever their politics, almost all—like the majority of Native American people in the United States today—were "mixed blood"; most were easily set to brooding over the meaning of that condition.

Wendy Rose explored her reactions to the problem in an early collection of poems, *Half-Breed Chronicles*. Gerald Vizenor chose to reject the implications of "mixed blood" in favor of the term "crossblood," also the title of one of his early books. And Linda Hogan revealed her awareness of "cross-blood" status in a short autobiographical piece:

I am aware of the fact that as a light-skinned Indian person I am seen as a person of be-tweens, as a person of divided directions. Non-Indians are more comfortable with me than they are with my darker sisters and brothers, for they assume that I am similar to them, or somehow not as real as other Indian people. This preference for light skin is true of other minorities also; the light ones, the mixed ones, are seen as closer, in many ways, to the dominant culture.

Whatever our station on this white-constructed continuum of race, then, all of us can hear echoes of Duane Niatum's words: "I was born here of two worlds, the Native American's and the white man's. For better or worse I must live in them both. I have no choice."[19]

BEWARE THE DREADED WANNABE

One curious element intrinsic to the world of Native Americans differentiates it from the situations of all other minorities in the United States. Native Americans are familiar with the strange fact that lots of people—including, indeed, members of other minority groups—long to be Indian. In the 1960s, as Scott Momaday noted,[20] this longing enveloped the student movement; thousands donned beads and turquoise and flocked to newly opened Indian centers. Once there, many were evidently overwhelmed, and driven by an uncontrollable longing, they abruptly discovered a relationship to some Native person, usually a "Cherokee grandmother."[21]

Almost no young political militant attempted to pass for black in the '60s and

'70s, yet hundreds—especially young men—grew ponytails, darkened their skins and tried to pass for Indian.[22] Louis Owens's novel *Wolfsong* recaptures these days, when this flood of would-be Indians had an equally bizarre effect on young mixed bloods:

> There was a contest among the urban mixed bloods to see who could be more Indian. The skin cream called "Tanfastic" helped, and there was a lot of unnaturally black hair. . . . McBride always liked to point out the white hobbyists who'd be at the dances, out on the floor doing a high plains traditional or fancy dance with outfits that were more au-thentic and impressive than the real Indians who'd come all the way from North Dakota or Oklahoma. "You know," McBride said once with a grin, "in Switzerland there are hobbyists who speak Lakota and do beadwork that museums can't tell from the real thing. They're really screwing up Indian collectors, messing up the commodity."[23]

Warnings from Native America to wannabes proliferated. Buffy Sainte-Marie's "Now That the Buffalo's Gone" condemned the "radical chic" of those who boasted of In-dian ancestry at cocktail parties while doing nothing to involve themselves with the legacy of European-Americans' perfidy. It was the "J'accuse" of our day:

> Can you remember the times
> That you have held your head high
> And told all your friends of your Indian claim
> Proud, good lady, and proud, good man
> Your great-great-grandfather from Indian blood sprang,
> And you feel in your heart for these ones . . .
> Oh it's all in the past you can say
> But it's still going on here today . . .
> It's here and it's now you must help us dear man
> Now that the buffalo's gone.

Floyd Westerman joined his voice to the criticism of wannabe hypocrisy: "Now you claim to be / Part Sioux or Cherokee / But where were you when / We needed you my friend?"[24] To that important question, I, along with many others of my generation, tried to live our feelings of responsibility to the tribal world. But despite repeated assertions from Native people that "Indianness" was not mea-sured solely by blood quantum, much less by physical markers of race, I remained embarrassed by my skin and eye color, and terrified lest Indian friends mistake me for a dreaded wannabe. Mixed blood, however red, carried a heavy burden, and one that had its origins not in the Indian fashioning 1960s, but rather in the first days of the European conquest.

Like most Indian-White problems, the dilemma of people with mixed, Native-

European blood stemmed from years of nurturing by successive colonial and United States government officials. From the first, "mixed bloods" were favored in North America because it was widely believed—or so ideologues proclaimed— that "mixing" red (!) blood with white (!) was conducive to the "assimilation"— into civilized's society—of the primitive indigènes. Such beliefs about "blood" appeared very early in accounts of the encounters between Europeans and Native people.[25] But for the purposes of this exegesis, I shall take up a more limited story, beginning with the final century of the military conquest, the nineteenth.

In 1803, Thomas Jefferson offered blood mixing as a solution to what was then the vexed and frequently lamented "Indian Problem":

> In truth, the ultimate point of rest and happiness for them is to let our settlements and theirs meet and blend together, to intermix, and become one people. Incorporating themselves with us as citizens of the United States, this is what the natural progress of things will, of course, bring on, and it will be better to promote than to retard it.[26]

At first, such race mixing promised to recreate the red race in the (preferred) image of the white. In 1854, the anthropologist J. C. Nott published a work explaining the beneficial effects of white-red blood mixing on Indians:

> It has been falsely asserted that the *Choctaw* and *Cherokee* Indians have made great progress in civilization. I assert positively, after the most ample investigation of the facts, that the pure-blooded Indians are everywhere unchanged in their habits. Many white persons, settling among the above tribes, have intermarried with them; and all such trumpeted progress exists among these whites and their mixed breeds alone. The pure-blooded savage still skulks untamed through the forest, or gallops athwart the prairie. Can any one call the name of a single pure Indian of the *Barbarous* tribes who—except in death, like a wild cat—has done anything worthy of remembrance?"[27]

The most influential American in these debates was another anthropologist, Lewis Henry Morgan, who began his study of "Indians" with the Iroquois in the 1850s. Soon after, he moved his research to tribes living in the middle west. The title of his 1877 book reveals his underlying program: *Ancient Society or Researches in the Lines of Human Progress from Savagery Through Barbarism to Civilization*. Because he agreed with other anthropologists that the pinnacle of human development was represented by the white "race," Morgan approved intermarriage as a means of advancing Indians. On one visit to Kansas and Nebraska, he observed with approbation what he saw as the degree of mixing: "The color of the Indian women is quite uniform, and is light. It shows that white blood infused into them in the East has been well diffused throughout. The next cross will make a pretty white child." He noted further that such intermarriages carried distinct economic benefits for white men: "[They] marry Indian wives and get adopted into the tribes and thus some few have gained farms, or the possession at least of valuable land." Furthermore, these farmers would produce children who "will intermarry respectably with our white people and thus the children will become respectable and, if educated, in the second and third generations will become beautiful and attractive. This is to be the end of the Indian absorption of a small portion, which will improve and toughen our race, and the residue [will be] run out or forced into the regions of the mountains."[28]

According to Robert E. Beider, blood was "no mere metaphorical device for Morgan. To him, it became the controlling or limiting factor in the transmission of culture."[29] In fact, by the 1870s Morgan was arguing that acquired ideas and behaviors could be stored and then transmitted, via a "channel of transmission," the blood.[30] Soon these convictions led Morgan to decide that blood mixing was not altogether beneficial. He detailed a dangerous behavior modification likely to result from too much mingling of blood:

The Indian and European are at opposite poles in their physiological conditions. In the former there is very little animal passion, which with the latter is superabundant. A pure-blooded Indian has very little animal passion, but in the half blood it is sensibly augmented; and when the second generation is reached with a cross giving three-fourths white blood, it becomes excessive, and tends to indiscriminate licentiousness. . . . Whether this abnormal or disturbed state of the animal passions will finally subside into a proper equilibrium, is one of the questions involved.[31]

For whites, there was a positive side to this: for those enamored of what was already a heavily romanticized "Indian" personae, mingling blood with an Indian suggested the possibility of gaining some, at least, of the heroic qualities carried in "red" blood. Thus in the wildly popular fin-de-siècle novels of the German writer Karl May, his young German hero (improbably nicknamed "Old Shatterhand" because of his European-style boxing skill) learns that he has, at last, overcome his "greenhorn" status in the reified Wild West of the 1890s when, after having undertaken labors much more difficult than those the gods demanded of Hercules, he is invited to "mingle blood" (in this case by drinking) with the Apache hero Winnetou. "So this was to be a blood brotherhood, a real, true, blood brotherhood of which I had so often read," thinks the hero. Upon drinking each other's blood, he and Winnetou are told by the chief: "The soul lives in the blood. The souls of these two young warriors shall pass into each other so that they form one.

Forthwith, what Old Shatterhand thinks shall also be Winnetou's thought, and what Winnetou wants shall also be Old Shatterhand's will."[32] (This whole episode is, of course, redolent of concepts the twentieth century has come to associate with the darker aspects of German history. Its most horrible reiteration is found in *Mein Kampf,* where Hitler insists that Jews were spreading their racial contagion via injections of their tainted blood into "Aryan" women.)

Such popular and "scientific" ideas soon found expression in government policies—which, like the intermarriages approved by anthropologists, coincidentally offered white people the opportunity to seize even more Indian land, albeit in this case "legally" rather than by murder or fraud. Although the details of thousands of transactions between the U.S. government and the people of hundreds of tribes are complicated and confusing, two acts laid the groundwork for such "legal" land theft in the twentieth century: the 1887 Dawes Severalty Act, also known as the General Allotment Act, and the 1890 law establishing the National Indian School System.

The Dawes Act, ostensibly aimed at teaching Indians the character-building wonders of owning private property, provided that all reservation land—held in common by the tribe, in keeping with traditional practices—be "allotted," divided up into parcels of property.[33] Heads of families (always males) received the most land, with single people getting smaller bits and pieces. (Married women were usually excluded—and thus the phallocentric property relations of European-America were imposed on Native people.) All reservation land not allotted was "freed" for outsiders—and the result is that no present-day reservation is wholly owned by tribal members. Furthermore, the act provided that full-blooded Indians could not sell or lease their land for twenty-five years. (Mixed bloods were often exempt from this paternalism.) Full-blood allotees were required to "work" their land (work usually being defined as farming) to the satisfaction of corrupt (white) Indian agents, who were allowed to seize any land they decided was unworked or underworked. This the agents either kept for themselves or sold to other outsiders. When even this did not satisfy the insatiable hunger for Indian land, the act was amended, in 1891, so that any agent or government official could lease any land not being used as he saw fit to any outsiders of his choice. Again, full-blooded land owners were the victims, though mixed-blood owners now fell as well under the control of almost universally corrupt agents or government officials. As a result of the various provisions of this act, the 138 million acres of reservation land in 1887 had shrunk to only 48 million acres in 1934: of these, 20 million acres were "arid."[34]

The education act had equally deleterious effects, some of which have been described above. It was aimed specifically at assimilating Indian children, who were seized (sometimes in chains) from their families and taken to government boarding schools—often located across the continent. Carlisle Indian School, in Pennsylvania, was the largest "home" for children from western tribes. My own grandfather was more fortunate than thousands of Indian children sent far from home. From his home near Leavenworth, Kansas, he and his brothers and sisters were sent to Haskell Indian Institute, in nearby Lawrence. (Despite this troublesome history, the town of Lawrence continues to glory in its historic relationship to Indians. One local artist, Stan Heard, demonstrates this affection by "growing" Indian heads—"braves" and "chiefs"—in wheat fields. His works of art can be seen only from the air.[35])

Needless to say, these schools, all of which adopted the motto of Carlisle's founder, General Richard Henry Pratt—"Kill the Indian and save the man"—drove thousands of Indian children mad. Thousands more tried to run away. Most were quickly tracked by bounty hunters and brought back to school where they were viciously punished ("for their own sakes"). Louise Erdrich's poem "Indian Boarding School: The Runaways" describes some would-be escapees. Its lines tell a common story:

> Home's the place we head for in our sleep
> Boxcars stumbling north in dreams
> don't wait for us. We catch them on the run . . .
>
> The lame guard strikes a match and makes the dark
> less tolerant. We watch through cracks in boards
> as the land starts rolling, rolling till it hurts
> to be here, cold in regulation clothes.
> We know the sheriff's waiting at midrun
> to take us back. His car is dumb and warm . . .
>
> All runaways wear dresses, long green ones,
> the color you would think shame was. We scrub
> the sidewalks down because it's shameful work.[36]

When we saw Grandfather's school transcript we discovered two things: that his teachers found him "brilliant but incorrigible," and that he successfully escaped from Haskell. This event is marked with a date and the single word, "Desertion."

The result of these two acts (and other government policies) was that Indians became "wards" of the government. It was a permanent colonial status, reinforced by practices familiar to "colonial" people all over the European empire: native languages were forbidden (punished by beatings and other physical tortures), cultural practices systematically stifled.

One example: because most tribal people traditionally work together, for the good of the group, five-year-old Indian children, newly arrived at the school, responded collectively to "tests" and other school work. This behavior, so antithetical to the competitive individualism which underpins the capitalist economic system of the United States, was against school rules and mercilessly punished. Children caught sharing answers to questions were called "cheats"—an anathema to Indian children for whom honesty was among the highest virtues.

After many years of such forced deculturation, many children were no longer able to exist comfortably within the tribal structures. Indeed, some could not easily exist anywhere. Linda Hogan's novel *Mean Spirit* includes a scene in which a group of traditional, non-boarding school Lakota youths meet an Osage graduate of Indian school:

After the ceremony, the younger men from South Dakota went home to stay with Cal Severance, but they kept their distance from him and remained silent. They didn't like his drinking. They couldn't and didn't blame him, but they were traditional, and they felt uncomfortable with the other men their own age who had gone to school and returned with lives full of holes. Cal took out two blankets, using only his palms and four fingers, and he unfolded them for his guests. "What happened to your hands?" asked one of them. Cal looked at his hands. "It's my thumbs," he said, "They broke them at school."[37]

(Cal Severance must not have been one of the majority of Osages who were mixed blood, who, according to an inspector for the Indian Office, "act like white people, well-educated and intelligent."[38])

The fashion for "Indians" that swept through the 1960s shifted the focus of would-be educators of Indian children. Reacting against the body and mind-deforming practices of earlier eras, teachers, prophets of "self-esteem" *avant la lettre*, sought instead to highlight Indian "traditions." These efforts sometimes took bizarre forms. One such project was aimed at keeping Oglala children in school by highlighting what a group of "experts" described as their "essential warrior heritage." Vine Deloria was driven to protest,

What, I ask, would a school board in Moline, Illinois, or Skokie, even, do if the scholarly community tried to reorient their educational system to conform with outmoded ideas of Sweden in the glory days of Gustavus Adolphus? Would they be expected to sing "Ein Feste Burg" and charge out of the mists at the Roman Catholics to save the Reformation every morning as school began? or the Irish? Would they submit to a group of Indians coming to Boston and telling them what a modern Irishman was like? Expecting them to dress in green and hunt leprechauns so as to live on the leprechauns' hidden gold would hardly provide a meaningful path for the future.[39]

Not surprisingly, those Indians who were able to negotiate successfully with the all-pervasive United States were often either those who acculturated successfully at boarding schools (the "Ariels" of Roberto Fernandez Retamar's analysis[40]) or those whose mixed blood gave them an advantage. (That it was their "white" appearance that mattered was underscored by dozens of examples. Charles Lummis's biographer offers one: "The more an Indian looked like a white man," he noted, "the better Lummis liked him." This attitude—the reverse of that prevalent in the 1960s and after—was widespread throughout the era of "assimilation.") In the case of both mixed bloods and boarding school successes, their facility with the white world often allowed them to become dominant in tribes—especially after the 1934 Indian Reorganization Act imposed U.S.-style elected governments on most tribal groups.[41]

In the period from 1910 to 1920, the "wardship" attitudes of the government began to change—again in favor of those with whom European-American officials believed they could "get along." Those designated "competent Indians" were released from the provisions of the Dawes Act which limited their use of their own property; at the same time, they were also freed of "trustee" status. But how was competency defined? There were two criteria: graduation from an Indian boarding school or white blood.

That the numbers of people identifying themselves as "Indian" on official records—birth, marriage and death certificates, military papers, census forms— kept dropping year by year is explained in part at least by the government's continual rewarding of those with white blood. My family is probably typical: children with one "full-blooded Indian" parent are described as "white" on all such records. And tribal identification disappeared even earlier. Rather than "Nez Perce" or "Blackfoot," early nineteenth-century records read merely "Indian," usually with the designation "full blooded." From the period following World War I (after which Indian veterans were granted U.S. citizenship) those of mixed blood (so long as it was mixed Indian and white) continued to enjoy benefits withheld from full bloods. When, for example, oil was discovered in Indian Territory (then the state of Oklahoma), hundreds of Native people found themselves declared "incompetent" so that their land could be seized by greedy white men. *Mean Spirit* narrates the process that alienated so much oil land from Osage people during the 1920s and '30s. But in this case, blood and lack of blood was used craftily by the government to make sure few Indians—full-blood or mixed—enjoyed the vast oil riches. In one incident in Hogan's novel, government payments—the treaty payments that allowed many Indians to refuse oil drilling on their land—are altered according to blood. "That spring," Hogan writes, "nearly all of the full-blood Indians were deemed incompetent by the court's competency commission. Mixed-bloods, who were considered to be competent, were already disqualified from receiving full payments because of their white blood."[42]

From 1945 to the 1960s, the government undertook three more policies: relocation, termination, and "compensation"—payments for land stolen from Native people. In each—relocating Indian people to cities as a cheap labor force, terminating designated tribes from tribal status, and paying legally identified groups of Indians for land assessed at the rate prevalent at the time of the treaty signings—blood quantum mattered. And again, it was mixed-blood, often already urbanized Indian people who often managed to profit.

> Whatever the government's policy, Hollywood's mixed-blood Indian, like Twain's Injun Joe, remained an altogether unsavory character in these years. John Ford spoke about this group in an interview discussing his westerns: "Traditionally the half-breed is a villain. . . . For many decades he has been a renegade combining the worst features of both races. He drinks. He is treacherous."[43]

As I have already noted, once the 1960s began to see federal programs and policies directed at rectifying some of the wrongs, blood quantum reemerged as an essential factor in most federal guideline definitions of Indianness. Although Walter Echohawk, director of the Native American Rights fund, has calculated that there are currently *eighty* different definitions of what it is to be Indian, most federal programs of that period required one-eighth Indian blood for those claiming affirmative-action benefits of various kinds.

Because blood quantum, rather than some less clearly definable quality of "Indianness," became the significant factor in sorting out who among the non-enrolled, non-reservation Indians was or was not eligible for federal actions of various kinds, families like mine found themselves mired in arguments, divided among those who joined the Indian politics of the 1960s and proudly claimed their "blood," those who joined such activities but kept silent on the question of identity, and those—most of the parent-generation—who scorned what they saw as a regression to a cultural and racial state they had proudly "overcome." (Many who began to try to reclaim traditional cultural practices recall being accused by parents and others of "returning to the blanket.")

The continued proliferation of Great Society benefits for those with certain blood quanta kept the issue alive through the 1970s. As the situation became more and more fraught (the government had no designation that divided "reservation" people from "urban" communities, for example, or completely assimilated people, especially academics, from those "left behind"), I retreated into a very Indian reaction: silence. Ironically, in those days my choice was far from common among mixed bloods—or wannabes. And the numbers of these latter continued to grow. Unlike those white Americans who are, according to Adrian Piper, usually offended by being told that they appear to have African blood, most (then and now) glitter with joy if one "guesses" that they are part Indian. Indeed, many (a majority of undergraduates in my classes on Native American politics and culture, for example) believe, quite sincerely, that they possess a Cherokee grandmother. Those for whom such ancestry is just too improbable, Europeans, say, or the children of European immigrants—often claim the ancestry by reincarnation. (A recent attack on such identity collectors is tellingly titled, "For all those who were Indian in a former life."[44]) A twist on this claim is that of certain New Age feminists, who argue that Native American spiritual practices embody something called "the feminine," thus legitimating *their* claims to be "Indian." These so-called feminist ideas are deployed, to the considerable profit of the "absolute fake" authors, in such bestselling books as *Jaguar Woman,* by Lynn Andrews (published, where else! in my poor native state), or *Women Who Run With the Wolves* by the Jungian analyst Clarissa Pinkola Estés.[45] (It's hard to imagine who could read either of these works and keep her dinner down, but. . . .)

Whatever the emotional yearnings of such "wannabes," the federal government—as usual—continues to dictate the grounds for claiming Indian identity. And from the 1960s, the grounds have been based on a single biological marker, blood.

Blood wars continued to rage throughout the 1970s and early '80s, dying out only as Native America once again went out of fashion with the election of the movie western actor Ronald Reagan (as abysmally ignorant of Native America as he was of almost everything else) and his Indian-hating cabinet officials, many of whom represented western interests in the continued theft of tribal lands. For a while, then, controversies of blood quanta disappeared from public view—or at least from the view one had from abroad, whence I removed myself once again in 1977. For me, the battle lines had shifted, from the war over Native rights and blood quantum to the wider and even more problematic war over gender equality.

.6.
DE-COLONIZING THE
(WOMEN'S) MIND

The ideological construction and consolidation of white
masculinity as normative and the corresponding racializa-
tion and sexualization of colonized peoples . . . [means that]
white men in colonial service *embodied* rule by literally and
symbolically representing the power of the Empire.
Chandra Mohanty[1]

I quickly discovered that the struggle over blood, like most other social and political problems, was further vexed by the fact that it was—and remains—heavily
gendered. Explanations for this gendering of Native America lie both in the past—
grounded in the historical relations between the European invaders and indigenous people, in which the conquerors' patriarchal social relations often overwhelmed those already in existence in native societies—and in the present, a
near-constant subtextual message in almost all the artifacts of American popular
culture.

Relations between two groups with which I have been associated—European-
American, mostly bourgeois, mostly academic feminists, and Native American
women—are deeply vexed. Although this is not the place to disentangle all the elements that complicate such relations, I should like my own position—which is
itself far from stable, far from certain, sometimes changing day to day, and always
circumstance to circumstance—to be as open as possible. I write, that is to say,
only from my own position, not that more legitimately claimed by others. It is,
therefore, my view that the "mainstream" feminist movement in the United States
has diminished its credibility among those from groups other than theirs by a long
history of selfishness, ignorance, and patronization. Conference after conference,
meeting after meeting, middle-class white women have taken to podiums to inform "others" not only of the extent of their oppression, but also of what these
white experts think Indians ought to do about it. (Feminist grant-giving bodies,

founded and staffed by white, middle-class feminists, ensure that this advice will be followed by the recipients of the largesse.)

Native American women in the public eye—as filmmakers, writers, artists, professors, and so on—always incur this helpful attitude from non-Native feminists when they appear on panels or at conferences. One of my friends is invariably asked why she didn't discuss "women's oppression" in her film. Others are asked why they made films about male leaders. And on and on. I had a curious experience at a UNESCO-sponsored conference in the Netherlands in fall 1992. I had been asked to write a paper describing how I perceived the state of white, bourgeois feminism in the United States and England in the waning years of the twentieth century. The paper I circulated before the conference was, admittedly, quite pessimistic, and I was prepared for some disagreement from the other woman invited to speak about feminism to about thirty-five Dutch and British men and two Dutch women. What I was not prepared for, however, was the aggressive positioning of this speaker, someone called Rosi Braidotti, a director of a women's studies program at the University of Utrecht. She, startlingly, assumed the place of a "third world woman" and attacked what she described as my "typically American ethnocentrism," which, she claimed, overlooked the vast strides being made by Africans—men, mainly—toward gender equality. She shouted at me for some forty minutes, allowing no space for response. Then she swept her manicured and painted fingers through her carefully styled hair, gathered her vast wool shawl about her suited shoulders, and, glaring one final time at my blue-jeaned "Americanness," rushed from the room muttering about an appointment in Copenhagen. A potted plant could not have been more amazed.[2]

At the same time such feminists avidly report on the oppression and degradation (or, in Braidotti's case, strides toward equality) of women in other cultures they pay almost no attention to the much nearer "first world" struggles of their working-class sisters (of all races). Not surprisingly the hostility often directed by Native women at such self-indulgent European-American feminists is echoed over and over in women's union meetings. I heard it again and again for example at the annual conference of women coal miners—sponsored by the national Coal Employment Project—held in Harlan County, Kentucky, in 1987. Indeed, with only a few changes, these words of Lorelei DeCora Means could have come from the pen of a militant women underground coal miner: "We are *American Indian* women, in that order. We are oppressed, first and foremost, as American Indians, as peoples colonized by the United States of America, *not* as women."[3]

At the same time, there are feminists—albeit with carefully nuanced positions—in Indian Country. Grass-roots efforts against sex oppression, against child and wife abuse, against discriminatory practices in tribes or other Indian organizations, and so on, can be found everywhere, with varying levels of militance and grounded in varied analyses. One remarkable collective feminist voice, heard now for nearly twenty years, is that of the pioneering Native women's troupe, Spiderwoman Theater, based in New York. One of its founding members, Gloria Miguel, remembers the group's first public production in 1976: "We were doing work that was avant-garde at that time. People were impressed with us because we were very controversial—all women, all ages, sizes, and backgrounds, and we were addressing issues of child abuse, domestic violence, and abuse against women."[4] (The group continues to delight, instruct, and challenge, often joined these days by two more remarkable actress sisters, Hortensia and Elvira Colorado.)

Community-based efforts, in keeping with Native tradition, are marked by their willingness to hear various points of view—from women in tribes where traditions differ considerably as well as from women from indigenous communities all over the globe. At a recent panel discussion, held at Cornell University and chaired by Katsi Cook, titled "Seeking the Balance: A Native Women's Dialogue," a characteristically wide range of views was expressed by women from all over indigenous America. There was a description of Native women's traditionally powerful roles in the nations of the Iroquois Confederacy by Cook herself. Other women, such as Elsa Guevera from Bolivia, raged against the patriarchy that constricts the lives of some nations' Indian women. Her language was very close to that used in the discourse of many radical European and European-American feminists.[5] Others took pains to differentiate themselves from that same discourse. Whatever the points of view expressed, however, there was no *overt* disagreement, no hostile recriminations such as would inevitably have broken out at most feminist conferences. Ola Casadora Davis concluded the speeches describing women's place in her Apache community:

You know, being a woman is a heavenly gift for all of us. Bringing the kids into this world, you look at your kid, how it grows, what you have to say to them, where the food's coming from the next time they eat. You really, really have a big job right there for us women. You know, if it wasn't for us, I don't think there would be anybody here in this world today. It is wonderful to be a mother, it is wonderful to be a grandmother. A grandmother is a special person. My grandkids are very special to me. . . . I have quite a bit of grandkids. I'm a great-grandma and I'm so proud of my grandkids and my great-grandkids. And then they all intermarried to different tribes. I have a United Nations at home when Thanksgiving comes. Different tribes—Mexican, White, Hopi, Navajo, Papago, and California Indians. These are the kind of in-laws I have!

She closed with the traditional modesty:

So, this is all about me and myself and what I'm doing. I open it to you what it's like to be a mother, and thank you.[6]

"Feminism," at least that which represents the mainstream, has traveled a rocky road through Indian Country. Not only have middle-class feminists themselves in-dulged in the most blatant Eurocentrism, but Indian women have frequently cho-sen different paths of struggle, some through women's organizations and efforts, some through the mixed-sex but, in its early days, deeply sexist, militant urban wing of AIM. Here, as in virtually every struggle facing Native people, all kinds of opinions and efforts are accommodated—usually without the kind of sectar-ian friction that has divided other movements of oppressed peoples. (Given AIM's current frenzy of self-destruction, it should be pointed out that the argument these days is not based on gender differences. Instead, the issue is "identity," grounded once again in "blood," the relative absence of which can, in turn, be overcome by "tribal enrollment.")

One of the explanations for Native American women's more inclusive feminism may arise from their widespread awareness that certain gender relations were brought across the ocean from Europe and imposed on unwilling Native popula-tions both through overt government policies that *always* excluded women from decisionmaking processes whatever their traditional roles, and through the privi-leging of those Indian males (or, more accurately, stereotypes of some Indian males) who seemed to embody the most aggressive, "macho" aspects of Ameri-can masculinity. America's popular culture industry, then as now, concentrated on male High Plains warriors to the near complete exclusion of women of these cul-tures and men and women of less militaristic (sometimes this meant only "un-mounted") behavior.

Invaders, in fact, once they had slaughtered, sold into the slave trade, or im-prisoned Native populations on the east coast, quickly began glorifying and ro-manticizing those "enemies" who remained "out of reach," denizens of the "empty continent," symbols of the Wild West. These were a single group of In-dians—those from High Plains tribes, commonly depicted riding against a wide western sky (though of course the horse was a Spanish introduction which created this rather recent mythical hunter/warrior figure), chasing buffalo or wagon trains. Because most such mounted hunters and warriors were male (or at least so ran the stereotype[7]), and because gender relations privileging these kinds of male activities were prevalent in an extremely patriarchal "Christian" Europe, the extension of European assumptions about the relative status of the sexes to Native America was easily accomplished. The very first accounts of contact began the process of "taming"—and often infantilizing—indigenous women, whose "best" representatives made a name for themselves by rescuing white men. (Pocahontas was the first in what became a long line of such females.[8]) And as Native warriors demonstrated their talents for war—ignominiously defeating countless better-equipped cavalry battalions—the European-American popular mind soon raised Indian men to a revered status as the most "macho" of America's minorities. Too, the braver the "warriors," the more noble in their defeat, the greater the military honor for those who were slaughtering them. (Congressional Medals of Honor were given out by the handful to the mass murderers of Wounded Knee.) Had the "victors" admitted to themselves that their victims included many females (or indeed, as was often the case, women, children, and old people), the conquerors' self-celebrations, as well as public admiration might have been somewhat muted by the image of "helpless," and therefore "unworthy" opponents, especially, in the Western war pantheon, mere women. The self-conscious elevation of Native opponents to maleness and to heroism proceeded even more rapidly once it was clear that these disingenuously admired "warriors" no longer posed a threat, that most were imprisoned in Indian Territory, locked up on reservations, or dead. By the close of the nineteenth century, in fact, white American males celebrated their victory all over the landscape, in statue after statue of noble, but utterly defeated, "savage warriors."

Even earlier, of course, some prominent intellectuals, most notably indefatigably self-congratulatory anthropologists, went so far as to appoint themselves personal repositories of "vanishing" Indian culture. Lewis Henry Morgan, representing white males of America's Northeastern establishment, had this to say to a friend in 1844 after he had been elected to something called "The Grand Order of the Iroquois": "We now hope to enlist the interest and aid of those literary Gentlemen of our Republic who have distinguished themselves in the field of Indian history and literature. . . . We need somewhere in our Republic an Indian Order which should aim to become the vast repository of all that remains to *us* [emphasis added] of the Indians—their antiquities—their customs—eloquence—history—literature, indeed, every thing pertaining to them which can be rescued from the oblivion to which it is rapidly hastening."[9] Needless to say, Morgan had no interest in preserving *people*—nor, of course, in including females among either his preservationists or his artifacts. His "grand orders" were boys' clubs, organizations for superannuated Boy Scouts who longed for their childhood days camping out in their back gardens and playing "Red Men."

This silliness continues. Geary Hobson's analysis of a contemporary phenomenon, "White Shamanism," includes attacks on a number of white men who claim an identity with a stereotype of the "noble redman." In most cases, they claim to embody medicine men—and, of course, those are always men. When Indians complain about such cultural theft, some "shamans" reveal an arrogance that is typical of white "New Agers." Gene Fowler, who wrote a song cycle called "Shaman Songs" that drew the ire of the Northern Cheyenne people whose culture he was "borrowing," replied with offensive flippancy:

Every one of us is part Indian yuh know. Some can trace that through a grandmother or grandfather to the Amerindian. Others across Europe to the Phoenicians (red men). In my case, it goes back to the owl in FOWLer. Magician in the workshop, as it were, hidden there, the skeleton of the shop.

As Hobson points out, this kind of attitude does "nothing to endear him to Indians, and certainly creates no sense of relationship with Indian people whatsoever."[10]

The Spanish conquest, where the geographical roots of my own past lie, brought a rather different, Catholic, concept of gender, one which shaped the so-called mission system that tore asunder Indian tribal cultures all over the American Southwest. Feminist scholarship has begun the process of retrieving this terrible history. Several historians have detailed the total subjugation of female tribal people in the mission system, an oppression that included imprisonment along with the involuntary servitude which they shared with males of their tribes. According to one historian,

In an effort to preserve purity, a large concourse of unmarried women and girls were kept segregated and carefully guarded from white contact. The "Monjerio" in which these *unmated* [emphasis added] women were quartered was locked on the outside at nightfall and was never opened until broad daylight, and then by one of the Padres.

One satisfied Padre insisted smugly that "These women . . . seldom die, unless it be one of those who are given to running away."[11]

Edward D. Castillo, in a recent article, offers many more details of the "civilizing" influence of the padres on Indian women. Here is a description of the methods by which females—in this case Kumi vit women—were captured like animals. Castillo quotes that hero of our elementary school textbooks, Junipero Serra:

In the morning, six or more soldiers would set out together . . . on horse back, and go to the far distant rancherias, even many leagues away. When both men and women at sight of them took to their heels—and this account comes from the father, who learned of it from the many declarations and complaints of the gentiles—the soldiers, clever as they are at lassoing cows and mules, would catch Indian women with their lassos to become prey for their unbridled lust. At times some Indian men would try to defend their wives, only to be shot down with bullets.[12]

These women, as Castillo notes, were then taken into a strictly guarded captivity in "harems" from which there were but two means of escape: marriage or death. The men (or at least those who survived capture) were, by contrast, allowed "occasional freedom" from their slavery, though they, too, "abused" it by repeatedly attempting to run away. Recapture, for them as for the females, meant severe punishment and often death.

Interestingly, one historian, writing in 1929 for the Santa Barbara Museum of Natural History (where bones and artifacts of California's tribal people abound), justified such treatment in terms very similar to those used by the Padres themselves. He, too, was evidently unaware that women—even those who behaved "like men" by running away—were equally deserving of his solicitude:

In spite of what may at first appear to have been arduous restrictions, these regulations were undoubtedly made with the express purpose of uplifting the savages. As Fr. Engelhardt earnestly says: "the missionary rule was a mild one; no army, labor-union or school, grants such liberties [as were allowed to the men]."[13]

Men and women were equal in two important respects: in the punishment meted out to runaways (or, more accurately, escapees) in which men and women—and children of both sexes—shared stocks, shackles, lashings; and in the results produced by the alcohol they were given. In the latter case, violence, not surprisingly, was the inevitable effect: "Nor were these tendencies toward violence confined to the male sex. Of the few remaining females, all now strangers to moral rectitude, several were held in great dread by the townspeople. One, known far and wide as "La Chola," lived alone in a hut near the mouth of Mission Creek. She, on more than one occasion, when in her cups, caused wide consternation by recourse to her "ever ready knife."[14] One James Ohio Pattie, a fur trapper by trade who was recruited to help vaccinate Indians against smallpox at Mission San Luis Rey in 1828, remarked a similar situation of virtual slavery, worsened in women's case by sexist Catholic assumptions about female sexuality. Thus the priests, in whose hands was placed "all the income of the Mission," were "the self-constituted guardians of the female part of the mission, shutting up under lock and key, one hour after supper, all those whose husbands are absent, and all young women and girls above nine years of age. During the day, they are entrusted to the care of the matrons." Of course rebellion was rife. ("Never mess with Indian women," was the warning repeated throughout Betty Louise Bell's Cherokee childhood.[15]) Pattie's testimony continued, "I saw women in irons for misconduct."[16]

The "Anglos" brought their own version of "civilization." Every Saturday night they captured Natives (gathered in a corner of town known as "Nigger Alley") drunk on the liquid wages paid by employers. After a night in a guarded pen, the now-sober Native people were sold as what one eyewitness described as "slaves for a week." And when they were once again paid with aguardiente, the routine began all over again. Its consequences were grave: "Those thousands of honest, useful people were absolutely destroyed in this way." Thus, a critical Horace Bell (one of the "good white guys") added sarcastically, "the conquering Saxon came with his boasted perfection of laws and his much-vaunted *advanced civilization*. . . . Surely, we civilized the race of Mission Indians with a refinement known to no other people under the sun."[17]

Soon, "civilization" ensured the spread of a stereotype of California's tribal people, hopelessly primitive "Diggers." Judge Benjamin Hayes wrote approvingly of California Natives' passivity in 1853: "A Man who has never mixed with these Indians can have no idea of the utter difference between them and those of the Great Plains."[18] Such degraded people still prompted more of the curious phenomenon of wannabes, however. When Los Angeles celebrated its (Anglo) self in 1876, paraders included not only the usual lineup of ridiculous white men's sophomoric "secret organizations"—the Knights of Pythias, the Independent Order of (aptly named) Odd Fellows—but also the "Improvident Order of Red Men," none of whom was, needless to say, "Red."[19] Parade organizers (like their descendants who organized similar parades in my childhood years) also encouraged wannabes to dress up as "representatives of the noble red man of the forest." So secure were they in their victory over the models for their efforts that one man even dressed up as the recently slaughtered Modoc hero, Captain Jack. An eyewitness noted that these costumed European-American fellows "contributed not a little to the hilarity of the occasion."[20]

When Anglo-Americans arrived in California beginning at mid-century, they added their twist to the Spanish-created stereotype of what became the universally despised "Digger Indian." Because California's Native population was by then very sparse, their social organization destroyed, their culture nearly lost, the incomers readily found them wanting, especially by comparison to the other tribal groups whose conquest was far less certain. "The Yankees," wrote one observer, "fresh from contact with the natives of the plains who were prone to fight to the death in defense of their lives, treated with contempt the quiet, unresentful slaves of the Spaniards, in derision dubbing them 'diggers,' in common with all other coastal tribes." And even those few who continued their rebellious ways soon met their Yankee comeuppance: "Woe to the hapless native who, under the influence of liquor, attempted the terrorism that had been the dread of the 'paisano.' If he tried his violence upon one of the newly-arrived Anglo-Saxon lords, the chances were very slight of his ever again appearing before an accredited judge for sentence."[21]

Through the second half of the nineteenth century, as the conquest of western Native America proceeded with bloody haste, the government's representatives, most military officers, continued to impose—by force—European-American standards of sexual conduct, including the transformation of Native women into objects for soldiers' rapacious sexual appetites. It is not necessary to reiterate the well-known horrors of the sexual subjugation of Indian women and girls here. But what is less recognized is the extent to which the entire conquest was remembered in a gendered language that effectively obscured this history. Those victorious generals (Howard, Miles, Sheridan) who left "memoirs" almost never mentioned female Natives. Throughout these "eyewitness" accounts, male Indians are the focus of attention. Even the mysterious "vanished" Mound Builders of the Mississippi River Valley, whom Miles described as a "non-Indian race," were primarily male: "We also know," he wrote confidently, "that the [generic] mound builder included in his activities those of the farmer, the hunter, and the warrior." So blinded was he by what must have been a constant state of testosterone overflow that Miles never even saw females doing the work that most whites considered genetically part of a woman's value: "I hope before I am through . . . I shall be able to show that much that is good may be said of the Indian. . . . I shall . . . describe his industries, his games, his music and his art, for there is much of art in the Indian's decorations, his blending of colors, his pottery, his feather work and his bead, basket, and blanket work." Needless to add, in stark contrast to Miles's ubiquitous and near-invisible "squaws," his white women were eternal, flowerlike victims. "After the Custer massacre," he wrote, the widows of Custer's troops traveled through the Dakotas "in sadness and loneliness, including the widow of the brave Custer. Such a scene could not fail to touch every heart, while it nerved them all to fortitude for the future." So fortified did Miles himself feel at the sight of all that drooping, grieving white womankind that he resolved: "I would clear the Indians out of that country by spring."[22]

By the early years of the twentieth century, the stereotype of the stoic, vanishing male brave, accompanied by his possessions, *his* children and *his* silent, industrious, forebearing "squaw" was sufficiently embedded in the mainstream psyche that descriptions like the following, taken from a 1904 U.S. history, were commonplace and unremarkable:

Sometimes . . . [the "brave"] would sit for hours in absolute silence and gaze on the ground, not giving the slightest attention to the gambols of his children about him or to his squaw by his side busy with her bead work or in the dressing of skins.[23]

At the same time, however, the somewhat positive stereotype of the hard-working Indian woman was in the process of transformation, as this same historian suggested (in terms hinting that his male *amour propre* had not been unaffected by the suffrage movement roiling all around him in those years): "Another popular error is the belief that the Indian squaw is a slave to her husband, [that she] did all the work." In the writer's view, that was far from the truth; the Indian man was the real hero in all this: "Her husband engages in the more arduous duties of following the war trail and slaying the wild beast. His toil is less constant, but far more perilous and fatiguing than hers." Moreover, this model brave was wonderfully tolerant when "his squaw" failed to live up to this historian's measure of good housewifery:

The man does not abuse his wife; she manages her home as seems best in her own eyes and if she has nothing to set before him when hungry, he does not chide her for being improvident or for not raising more corn or gathering more rice and berries; he bears it in silence and without murmuring.[24]

These words betrayed a stupefying ignorance of Native America. His 1904 "Indians," riding the plains hunting buffalo, taking to the "war trail," existed nowhere but in imagination. His "squaws" could not possibly have been "improvident" (in the manner widely believed to explain the poverty of Philadelphia's immigrant working poor, for example), given the fact that most were living imprisoned on squalid, infertile reservations, ignored by the perfidious American public, whose treaties had all long since been broken.[25]

Once defeat was ensured by the close of the nineteenth century, "education," mostly in boarding schools, strove to "acculturate" the newly captured savage boys and girls by inculcating "American values." Primary among these continued to be those that shaped gender relations. America's white educators were, in fact, so anxious to recreate Indian children in their own sex-determined images (the boys in metal- and wood-shop classes, the girls in sewing and cooking) that fully one-half of the prescribed boarding-school curriculum was devoted to the teaching of gender roles![26]

In the 1940s and '50s it was still "manly" for white youths to imitate Indian icons of masculinity such as Straight Arrow or even Tonto. It was *not* manly, on the other hand, to imitate Stepandfetchit, Rochester, or Amos and Andy. No white Boy Scouts dressed up as butlers or took up tap dancing. But both Boy Scouts and that organization's dozens of imitators (the Woodcraft Rangers, for example) spent long hours "making men" by practicing "Indian."

Perhaps because of childhoods spent learning "Indian" from a popular culture that was almost exclusively male, the 1960s world of urban, mixed-blood politics was primarily a masculine one. Indeed, except as sexual objects, tokens of victory for male competitors in this internal race war, urban-raised, mixed-blood women appeared only rarely as writers of polemics and position papers, givers of speeches, leaders of marches and demonstrations, or convenors of conferences.[27] One anthropologist's description of the "pan-Indian" politics of this period suggests the extent to which they were grounded almost entirely in European—and, though she does not note this, patriarchal—stereotypes:

Pan-Indianism is fostered and shaped by the non-Indian's stereotype of the High Plains warrior as the embodiment of all things Indian. Weekly Saturday night pow-wows, film and television depictions of 19th century Indian life, and bumper stickers fore-warning others that "Custer Died For Your Sins" all invoke Plains Indian cultural styles as models for contemporary Indian identity. Importantly, the Plains Indian ethos serves as an icon for both the non-Indian general public and a considerable number of urban Indians who are not Plains Indians. Its invocation by those Indians who wish to create and sustain an over-arching mythic commonality supports a sense of shared ethnicity cum community.[28]

And as was also the case in exclusively white political organizations, those few women who were heard from time to time (until the founding of Women of All

Red Nations, at least) were usually heard only because of their personal relations with key male leaders.

Only when feminism arose among some Native women did they—we—began to elicit serious male attention. And often in those early days, or so it seemed to me, it was primarily negative. Like our African-American, Latina, and European-American working-class sisters, Native feminists in my circle were frequently told that the women's movement was white and middle class, useless for the struggles of Indian women. Moreover, some male militants added (hopefully?), Indian women's roles (usually as subordinates, unpaid servants to males) were prescribed by "honored tradition." And if these two arguments failed to move Indian feminists from their claims for traditional equality, they were warned that a separate Indian women's movement would, in racist America, seriously weaken the larger—and by implication, more important—(men's) struggles.

Thus the silencing of many of us mixed bloods was a result not only of our own consciences, which recognized our privileged relationship to our diluted Indianness, but also of the identity sexism which glorified militant males and relegated females to the background. In other words, the reflection many of us women saw in others' eyes, fixed "in the sense in which a chemical solution is fixed by a dye" (to borrow from Frantz Fanon), showed not only light skin and blue eyes, but also a disregarded gender.

BURY MY (WOMAN'S) HEART . . .

A recent memoir of the occupation of Wounded Knee by AIM militants and their supporters suggests the extent to which a very European-style male chauvinism shaped both events as they were happening in the early 1970s and also their more recent interpretation by "eyewitnesses." (Stanley David Lyman's book mentions only his "pretty" secretaries or the fearsome Angela Davis. Otherwise, no women mar his very macho account of events at Wounded Knee.) Mary Crow Dog's autobiography, *Lakota Woman*, narrates an awakening women's consciousness and— in a buried subtext—the extent to which it was twisted and reinterpreted both by the Lakota militants with whom she worked and by her "coauthor," the European-born Indian enthusiast Richard Erdoes. The book, though often attacked as lacking authenticity,[29] is replete with the contradictions and confusions inherent in the struggles of those years. Mary Crow Dog details—often harrowingly—the exploitation of women in the movement almost without remark, as though such women's problems are, in some sense, "usual." In one lengthy passage, for example, she offers readers a glimpse into her daily life with the Lakota medicine man, Leonard Crow Dog:

Sioux always drop in on each other and stay over—a day or a week, as the spirit moves them. People eat at all times, whenever they are hungry. . . . So the women are continuously busy cooking. . . . Indian women work usually without indoor plumbing, cook on old, wood-burning kitchen ranges, wash . . . laundry in tubs with the help of old-fashioned washboards. Instead of toilets we have out-houses. Water is fetched in buckets from the river.

As if this were not enough to complicate a typical woman's life,

Leonard is a medicine man as well as a civil rights leader. This means that we have ten times more guests than the usual Sioux household. . . . When I moved in, the place was a mess. Nobody tried to clean up or help out. They all came to eat, eat, eat, expecting a clean bed and maybe to have their shirts and socks washed. I spent a good many years feeding people and cleaning up after them. It is mostly men who stop by at the house, and only very few women, and you cannot tell men to do anything, especially Sioux men.

Evidently, beyond her occasional usefulness as a sex partner, no one paid her much attention. "I even sometimes moved my bed outside the house into the open to get some sleep, because the men stay up all night, talking politics, drinking coffee, and gossiping. Sioux men," Crow Dog added, "are the worst gossips in the world. I would wash dishes for the last time at midnight, go to bed, and in the morning all the dishes would be dirty again."

Throughout this tale of domestic exploitation, her listener, Richard Erdoes, remained silent. In the end she drew her own ironic conclusions: "Leonard is much admired for his old-style Sioux generosity. At the Sun Dance of 1977 they put the war bonnet on him and made him a chief. They call him a wicasha wakan—a holy man—but confidentially, it can be hell on a woman to be married to such a holy one."[30]

Part of the appeal of this book lies in the detailed depictions of these traditional Sun Dances, once forbidden by a fearful government and now symbols both of a defiant return to tradition and, in some cases at least, of a rampant masculinity. So appealing are these annual dances that they attract numbers of Native men from tribes in which such rituals were never practiced as well as many non-Indian males who feel (as their grandfathers clearly felt when practicing the rituals of "The Ancient Order of Red Men" and such) that participation in the prayers, fasting, sweating, and piercing of the event makes them "honorary Sioux."[31]

Such tales of Mary Crow Dog's problems elicited no reaction from Erdoes, though he obviously felt quite free to interject remarks and questions when his interest was piqued. The concluding section, which might at least have led the coauthor to mute his otherwise uncritically adoring tone, is reproduced without comment. In it, we learn that Mary Crow Dog ultimately tired of her life of unremitting, and unrewarded domestic drudgery. (Time spent in New York City, working for Leonard Crow Dog's release from prison and living in the radical and chic Erdoes household, gave a young Mary Crow Dog a chance to see that not every woman lived as she did back home on the rez.) She fled life with Leonard, hiding far from the Dakotas for a year. "After I had been away for almost a year," she admitted,

it no longer seemed quite so normal to me that so many Sioux men habitually beat their wives. My sister Barb came to cry on my shoulder. She was living with a boy at Porcupine. "When that boy is sober," she told me, "he's good, a right guy, but when he's drunk he becomes a monster. He beat me up. He was off drinking last weekend. He came home and vomited all over me. I told him I was going for some clean clothes for myself. He said, 'No, you're not going anywhere'. . . . He ripped off a two-by-four from the fence and used it on me. He started beating me with this chunk of wood and messed up a couple of my ribs. So I left him for good." I grinned and told Barb, "For a little thing like that, most Sioux women wouldn't leave their men." My sister said, "Indian women are stronger than the men because they have to put up with all that shit, but I've had it." I answered her: "Barb, we've been away for too long. We don't see things the way we used to."[32]

How Mary Crow Dog has dealt with this persistent dilemma remains a mystery. We never learn whether or not she returned permanently to life with a medicine man.[33]

This passage, and several like it, including vague references to Leonard Crow Dog's "problems" with Native feminism, provoke no analysis from Mary Crow Dog's "coauthor." Instead, there are optimistic Dylanisms, "times are changing" and such, strewn around as though to mitigate the darkness presented by such details of daily life. As a result, readers are left to comfort themselves that those movie stereotypes they have long cherished are real. The reaction of film director Oliver Stone is probably typical. On the book's cover, Stone concludes that the book is "a piercing look into the ancient yet modern mind of a Sioux woman." (Dances With Wolves goes on.) That Mary Crow Dog is, in fact, mixed blood, and therefore presumably only half "ancient," to use Stone's curious essentialism, has clearly escaped both him and no doubt most of the blurb writers who celebrate the work on the book's jacket.

It is not clear whether the film of *Lakota Woman*, made by the Turner Television Network, will reproduce the ugly details of Crow Dog's daily life. Given the sentiments expressed by its executive producer, Lois Bonfiglio, I imagine it will not. Bonfiglio's version is a much more glamorous, and much less taxing, narrative of struggle and victory, good against evil. Moreover, she believes that Mary Crow Dog's is a life worthy of emulation by other non-Native women: "What's interesting to me is that it's a woman's story," the producer told a reporter. "And a Native American woman at that. . . . Mary is a very strong, brave woman. It's very gratifying to me as a producer, and as a woman to make a film like this." Bonfiglio believes the film will offer "authenticity." She and her co-producer, Hanay Geiogamah, insist that "the film is very faithful to the book." Furthermore, "No Caucasians will play Native parts."[34] Well, we'll see. Authenticity is already a problem if the central actor is not half Lakota and half European-American. And if none of the horror of Mary Crow Dog's domestic and sexual servitude is portrayed, then. . . .

But it is interesting to note, too, that it is this book, rather than any of dozens of other more complicated—in Beatrice Medicine's words, "more authentic"[35]— Native autobiographies which Atlanta Braves–owning, "tomahawk chopping" Ted Turner chose to film as part of his exculpatory series of movies about Indians. Mary Crow Dog and her story, absent evidence of sexism, clearly embody most of the romantic essentials required for another movie take on Native America.

Richard Erdoes and Ted Turner are not the only ones whose profitable use of gender—and Indians—is less than honest, of course. In 1992 the Latino historian Ramón Gutiérrez won a raft of professional prizes with his purported history of the impact of the Spanish invasion on Pueblo culture, trendily titled *When Jesus Came, the Corn Mothers Went Away: Marriage, Sexuality, and Power in New Mexico, 1500–1846.*[36]

> When I was in graduate school in the mid-1970s, a group of us who called ourselves, jokingly, the "Socialist Humor Party" [our motto, "First to Flee," our aesthetically inclined subgroup "L'Histoire pour L'Histoire] decided that our future academic success would depend upon whether or not we could find a way to put "Sex" and/or "Torture" into our dissertation titles. Alas for our brilliant careers, we all failed. Gutiérrez, on the other hand, at least managed to find a place for sex—and that juxtaposed with both Indian and Christian deities!

This work—by a *minority* author, and thus fashionably garbed in political correctness, has aroused abundant hostility from Pueblo people themselves and from Indian scholars all over North America. Not only does the work depend upon a dubious evidentiary apparatus (primarily the self-serving accounts of the invaders themselves), but it also offers an outrageously sexist portrait of Pueblo women (this portrait too, as reviewers have noted, also drawn from the public statements of Spanish soldiers!). One of the book's most infamous passages, which bolsters Gutiérrez's "left-wing" argument that Pueblo women used their sexuality to "resist" the Spaniards, aroused the particular ire of reviewer David Harris: "Gutiérrez recounts the Spanish narratives of lustful Pueblo women, taunting the righteous Spanish soldiers," and, in Gutiérrez's own words, "cool[ing] the passion of the fierce fire-brandishing Spanish katsina through intercourse."[37] (I have no doubt whatsoever that if this kind of thing were said about, e.g., Belgian women coal miners and mine owners, howls would go up from labor historians everywhere. But these are Indians, and their historian is Latino, so the American Historical Association's prize givers accepted the portrait of sex-crazed Pueblo women without a murmur.)

At the same time, it must be said that times *are* changing, as anyone listening to John Trudell or other '60s generation male activists, or reading the work of male Native historians and scholars as they tell all of our story, or listening to younger male filmmakers and writers, knows. Tomson Highway, a young First Nations playwright, in language utterly foreign to most Indian militants of the 1960s and early '70s, announced recently, "I'm really heavily into the whole gender issue, the male/female dichotomy, the sexual hierarchy, which is an area that knows no racial boundaries."[38]

The contemporary American Indian press, in its turn, is replete with militant statements from women of many nations, all of whom expect to be heard by readers of the Native press. Recently, for example, *Indian Country Today* headlined a letter from Karen Artichoker, Melissa Makes Room, and Grace Menard, "Sexism Isn't Traditional." The letter, written by three women who "sing with the Kiukanpi drum from Rosebud," complained that their drum, "Marty Makes Room's drum," was excluded from the 4th of July Powwow at Sisseton because the "rules stated that no women were allowed at the drum—out of respect for the drum and Dakota tradition." When Marty Makes Room protested, he was told "that it was not a woman's 'place' to sit at the drum and that it would make other (men) singers feel 'bad' if they got beat out by women." The three correspondents then pointed out—again in language virtually unheard a couple of decades ago—that "excluding women from the singing contest had nothing to do with respect for tradition and culture. What it does have to do with is ego, sexism, and the power to impose a sexist and discriminatory belief." They continued, "What is 'traditional' about a singing contest for money, use of public address systems and a cement arbor? Culture changes and adapts to meet the needs of the people. Our ability to change and adapt is what has kept us alive as a people." And more importantly, in stark contrast to many 1970s militants' assertions, they argued that discrimination was never a Dakota tradition. "At a pow wow in Sisseton this past winter, women veterans were honored. A man stood up and talked about how Dakota women were always warriors. . . . He cited battles from our ancestors' time that women fought in." Moreover, they pointed out, they had been winning contests at other powwows where men didn't discriminate against them. "We resent the implication that we are being disrespectful to our culture and traditions," they concluded. "If men in your community want to maintain culture and tradition, might we suggest that they get involved with stopping child abuse, rape, woman beating, and the exploitation of women and children. We see those 'traditional' men at pow wows, sitting at the drum at that."[39]

Their campaign for equal treatment, like that of other Native women (including, for example, Rayna Green, Elizabeth Cook-Lynn, Winona LaDuke, LaDonna Harris, Wilma Mankiller, Paula Gunn Allen, Clara Sue Kidwell, the women of the Indigenous Women's Network, the Spiderwomen, the Colorado Sisters, and many others) has male supporters and participants. Campaigns in favor of respect and equality take many forms. As the same newspaper reported more recently, Dr. Arthur Zimiga, Oglala Lakota, has "undertaken a campaign to get the names of Squaw Creek and Squaw Butte . . . and . . . two creeks . . . Little Squaw and Big Squaw . . . changed." Again, he employs very contemporary language. "If I do not pursue such actions, I feel I am contributing to this type of gender misrepresentation." He continues, "'There is a creek on Pine Ridge Reservation called 'Squaw Humper' which has not only been an embarrassment to Lakota people but also reinforces stereotypes about Native American women."[40]

But as the reluctance of officialdom to rename the hundreds (possibly thousands) of places called "squaw" suggests, the struggle is not easily won. As I shall suggest in the next chapter, popular culture continues to rely on European gender stereotypes to depict Indian people and their varied cultures. Moreover, the backlash against mainstream feminism, felt throughout the United States in the 1980s, has its counterpart in Indian Country, though perhaps there it has been less effective because of the barriers provided both by traditional customs of gender equality and lingering suspicions of outsiders' prescriptions of all kinds.

Although not fakes or wannabes, then, we were neither sufficiently Indian *nor* male to avoid being mistaken for one of those two despised groups.[41] (Nor, I should add, was I willing then, or now, to dye my brown hair black or don headbands or tie my hair back into the ponytail adopted by so many mixed-blood men.) The result was a perplexing dilemma of identity. On the one hand, in our heads we were able to inhabit cultures (albeit those mixed and muddied by distance from tribal life) that challenged the dominant American culture. But because of our looks (and sex), outsiders—even those willing to try to accommodate cultural difference—were rarely prepared to understand that our behaviors were not those of aberrant whites, (or temperamental white women) but were, rather, those learned primarily from our Indian side of the family, from another tradition that potentially subverted almost every aspect of our other "side," the European culture that controlled the political, intellectual, and social life of the United States. Thus we lived in a continually confusing half-world. To most outsiders, we were white. To Indians who knew us, we were Indian "mixed bloods." To those who did not, we were often mistaken for disreputable wannabes.

BUT THEN CAME GREED

The story of Indian militance and increasing self-determination continued through the bleak post-Watergate years. Relations between Native America and the colonial government of the United States reached a nadir in the Reagan-Bush years. But all the governments after Richard Nixon (whose relations with tribal people were often startlingly positive[42]) posed problems to continued Native efforts to achieve full control over their lives and territories. In fact, many legal battles won earlier (for land, fishing rights, control of water and mineral resources, education, and so on) were fought all over again and this time, often lost. Perhaps the worst moments came under Reagan's notorious Secretary of the Interior, James Watt, whose attitude was summed up in his description of Indians as "social misfits" and Indian tribes as "socialism's failure." Money for the many tribal colleges launched in the mid-1970s disappeared—and at the crucial moment in most of their histories. (Despite this problem, many tribal colleges thrive and more are founded each year. This in spite of government indifference, which leaves many of these institutions heavily dependent on private donations for their survival.) Affirmative action programs, aimed at recruiting and keeping young Native students in universities (including, for example, Upward Bound) found their resources diminishing. Many dwindled and died.

I became discouraged quite early on in this process, and in 1977, thoroughly depressed by what I saw all around me, I once more fled the country and its moribund social experiments, this time for the privileged, sequestered world of King's College, Cambridge. I had not abandoned politics altogether: I went to Cambridge to research the origins of problems I saw in the contemporary socialist feminist movement by examining their roots in relations between France's women industrial workers and the organized socialist movement of the late nineteenth century. But, driven both by dismay at the moral failures of my compatriots and by an exhaustion familiar to those of us who travel back and forth between cultural worlds, I was choosing to inhabit—temporarily, at least—my European identity.

CAMBRIDGE-PARIS-BRUSSELS

If Palo Alto had been a cultural shock of some magnitude, Cambridge was the Big Earthquake. Amazed by evidence of luxury and privilege I had never imagined, stunned by most of my teachers' and student colleagues' smug certainty that all who were not British (by which they meant English) struggled through life with the most terrible handicap ("Wogs," I learned, "begin at Calais"), I again went under water. Everyone I came to know was aware that I was something less than an almost-acceptable American version of One of Them: I had this exotic blood mixed in with a more or less acceptable Dutch and English inheritance and less acceptable female genes.

It was not immediately clear to me which was worse, "colored blood," or femaleness. King's had just "gone mixed," accepting its first female students a year before I arrived. The "old Etonian" senior tutor, coping manfully with his horror at the sight of women in the "class of 1977," reassured all us "first years" that "whatever your sex, huh, huh, huh, you are still all Kingsmen."

A common reaction to my Indianness was the helpful suggestion that I might like to repair immediately to the University Museum of Anthropology to view the spoils of their victory. I never went. I could not explain then—or the year I was in Oxford, where the Pitt-Rivers Museum was the focus of similar efforts—that I carried a relationship to the things lying restively in those museum display case. How could I say to the uniformly white, uniformly rational dons of Oxbridge that I bore a responsibility to such things that I could see no way of fulfilling, not there in Cambridge, not, a few years later, in Oxford?

My cultural reticence, my personal shyness, and their near-total ignorance of American Indians ensured that I slipped through those years without much discussion of race (though much vitriolic discussion of gender). Because the British intelligentsia, particularly that of the political left, despised *all* Americans indiscriminately, one's particular place within America's racial scheme of things was a matter of only slight concern.

Such attitudes were shared by Britons born and bred in the ex-Empire. I had one rather interesting encounter with a white South African who, when told that I was mixed blood, launched into a lengthy diatribe against Americans and their "ridiculous attention to ancestry." "Why does it matter?" he cried. He didn't take it well when I pointed out that in his home country it mattered very much; there, I should be listed as "coloured," and my life restricted to the life designed by his people for mine.

Of course, Hollywood's cultural hegemony meant that from time to time some curiosity about my Indian family surfaced. But until *Dances With Wolves* came to Cambridge, that interest was sporadic and desultory.

From Cambridge I went to Paris; from Paris—with sojourns in the United States and England in between—I went to Brussels, Leuven, Amsterdam and, most recently, Provence.

One day, after many years of living and working in Europe and in the United States, my husband and I found ourselves driving through the interior woods and hills of Provence. The southern French landscape evoked all my longing for home: cedars and pines, oaks crouched over dry riverbeds, deer and jackrabbits, crows and jays, and everywhere the Provençal flowers whose perfume scented the world. Suddenly, my husband shouted "Look! There are teepees all over that hillside!" Unable to pull off the road that abruptly, we continued on to the next turn, looking through the densely planted trees at all kinds of strange "Indianesque" constructions. Plaster teepees sat beside corrals; western saloons squatted along wooden sidewalks, wagons, sagging and rusting in the winter rain, awaited horses and people. Where were we? Soon, we found a gate and a sign: "Bienvenue au Monde des TeePees." (The repetition of this French version of "Welcome to TeePee World" in German and then in Dutch told us who was expected.)

It was an Indian theme park, its "O.K. Corral," its Longbranch Saloon, its myriad teepees sitting quietly, waiting through the winter for summer's inevitable hordes of tourists to ride its rides, drink its drinks, eat its—fry bread?[43]

Stranger still: in the distance, I saw a large, ponytailed man riding through the trees. We followed him. As we got closer, I saw that he was sitting an eastern (English) saddle. This improbability was, in turn, sitting upon a Navajo horse blanket. He was covered in Indian insignia: hair feathers, beads and silver jewelry, a tan, fringed buckskin leather jacket. As we watched, he reached his workplace, "TeePee Land Ranch," where he dismounted. Aha! Here was the wrangler for the dozen or so horses milling around the corral, they, too, awaiting the summer and the German, Dutch, and French children who would come to ride hyper-fake, but "Indian" ponies.

It was, I realized, time to go home.

.7.

INDIAN FASHION

Little Indian, Sioux or Crow,
Little frosty Eskimo,
Little Turk or Japanee,
O! don't you wish that you were me!
Robert Louis Stevenson[1]

Had I been watching with more care, I might have seen "'TeePee Lands'" every-where, all over Britain, in Brussels, in Paris, in all the places I lived and worked dur-ing those years. In both "high" and "low" culture, Indians had long provided Eu-ropeans with intriguing, attracting mirrors. At least by the late 1980s, Europe's New Age, like its American progenitor, was busily re-discovering earlier eras' fas-cination with North America's "Natives."

A few examples: Tintin, boy reporter, Belgian comic-book hero of the 1930s, had initially encountered the "Wild West" in a bloodcurdling (well, for the time) *Tintin among the Indians*. It featured all the usual elements dear to "boys" of all ages: captivity by bloodthirsty savages, torture at the stake, rescue by Tintin's faith-ful terrier, "Snowy." ("Herge," the author of the series, did eventually transform Tintin into a more politically correct adventurer. In *Tintin in America* the bad guys are rich, fat—of course—capitalists who are trying to steal oil-rich land from the Blackfoot tribe. Tintin joins up with the "good guy" Indians to fight these efforts, though he and the Indians fail; the Army soon arrives to drive the Indians away.)

Tintin has never found in the American market the immense popularity the comic enjoys in Europe, so the effects on influential Europeans of the hero's so-journs among "good" Indians in North America are easily underestimated. Re-cently, in fact, Little Man Heavy Runner, a leader of the Montana-based Blackfoot, found a potential ally against an exploratory oil well on sacred ground at Badger Two-Medicine in Tintin's native turf, Brussels! The directors of Petrofina Société

Anonyme, whose U.S. subsidiary, Fina Oil and Chemical Company first received the permit to drill at Badger Two-Medicine, agreed to meet Heavy Runner in an effort to find a solution to the problem. An article in *Indian Country Today* reported that part of the reason for Petrofina S.A.'s interest was their desire to be seen by a critical Belgian public as "Green." But reporters did not explore a more intriguing and more likely possibility: that Tintin's adventures amongst the Blackfoot tribe and his struggles against rapacious oil capitalists, tales that almost certainly resided in the childhood memories of every one of the Belgian company officials, had prepared these Belgian oil executives to lend a much more sympathetic ear than they might otherwise have done.[2]

There are many less positive examples in the European New Age's appropriation of Native America, although some of the self-appointed "guardians" of Native traditions are, in their own minds at least, sympathetic "wannabes." In 1993, Ottmar Lattorf, a German member of something called "Working-circle Hopi, Austria," wrote a warning letter to *Indian Country Today*, describing the growth and spread of "fake" Indian ceremonies for sale all over Europe. He cited the main cause of his distress:

Two years ago I came into contact with a group of people who "go the spiritual way of the Lakota" and have received the name "Two Eagles" in a name-giving ceremony from a "Lakota medicine man," with the last name of High Bear.

The previous . . . authority of this group was Brave Buffalo, another is a Lakota man from Rosebud.

This group has already existed for 10 years . . . and between 150 to 300 people regularly take part in sweat lodge ceremonies. Leading members of this group are so-called "Pipe-carriers" who were, for the most part instructed by the Lakota medicine man mentioned above.

They hold sweat lodge ceremonies and other ceremonies from the Lakota culture free of charge. . . . Sometimes the Pipe carriers travel, when invited, to other places in Germany, and every six months there are large gatherings—"camps."

In May and June 1992 I was a guest at one of these camps. . . .

A Lakota medicine man from Rosebud was present this time with his singer. He performed different ceremonies including healing ceremonies in which I participated. . . .

This medicine man received 100 German marks from each person asking for healing. . . . He himself did not ask for this payment, but rather the "campchief" Manni.

This white "pipe-bearer," Manni, gained credibility with his German clients by describing his frequent participation in "the Sun Dance with Lakota. This," Lattorf wrote, "made a very strong impression on the people in the camp." But there were problems the writer thought "Lakota Elders" should address:

I noticed that although everything had to be done according to Lakota tradition. . . . Very few people knew anything about the history of the Lakota, their present situation, nor about Leonard Peltier. . . .

After I had asked this medicine man about somebody [Leonard Peltier?], it was made drastically clear to me that such questions are not desired.

Then Lattorf added a curious note—albeit in English sufficiently fractured to allow some question about his meaning. "The fact that Brave Buffalo may be on the black list of the Lakota Elders as a betrayer was a disguise of his integrity. This is done to protect Lakota medicine men from pursuit by informers and U.S. law officers."

I take this to mean that "Brave Buffalo," and others, were protecting themselves against possible accusations of fakery by Lakota leaders by claiming that their place on a Lakota list of commercial medicine men was only a means of hiding them from the "danger" purportedly posed by the latter two groups. That Europeans would believe that the United States government—which did, of course, wage an extended COINTEL war against a highly political AIM in the 1970s—would track all the fake medicine men and women purveying their "traditional [apolitical] ceremonies" all over the world suggests the extent of their mildly touching credulity as well as their ready association of "things Indian" with left-wing politics.

This German "wannabe" had even more startling information to pass on:

In a conversation with another Pipe carrier of this group [presumably a white man], I was told that the Lakota Nation is so torn apart from the internal dispute that it doesn't even exist anymore.

In conclusion, a very distressed Lattorf asked,

1) Is there a Lakota Nation or is it a theoretical fiction? 2) What relationship does the Lakota Nation Elders Circle have to the following [white?] people: Brave Buffalo, Martens High Bear, Elmer Running, and a medicine woman named Gloria? 3) Are you aware of the group called Two Eagles which sees itself in Lakota Tradition? 4) Do you know about white men who are Pipe carriers? 5) Are you aware that ceremonies from the Lakota tradition are conducted by white men in Germany? 6) Does my presence at these camps and sweat lodges support the Lakota Nation? 7) Sweat Lodges are an inexpensive and practical opportunity to purify our bodies. What do you think of sweat lodges for physical purification and not as ceremonies?[3]

Although this young would-be Lakota was, it appears, quite sincere in his concerns, he takes his place in a very long line of "wannabes" who believe—doubtless because of the movies—that there exists some "cultural preservation society" among Lakota "elders" to whom people like him can address their desires for reassurance about the "authenticity" of their participation in Native ceremonies. Ottmar Lattorf and thousands of others thus embody the European version of "white shamanism," their protestations to the contrary notwithstanding. (Not surprisingly, given the fact that he addressed himself to no legally constituted tribal council, but rather only to a political non-entity, the "Lakota Nation," there was no one to reply to this earnest European's "warning.")

Clearly it did not occur to him that there is something quite weird about his enthusiasm for the spiritual life (real, or more likely imagined from movies) of distant others. Neither did he consider that he was perfectly free to support the release from prison of Leonard Peltier (or others of America's 1960s era political prisoners, such as Geronimo Pratt) without the imprimatur of "Lakota Elders." Or again that he might readily salve his political conscience by undertaking "sweats" in the traditional European manner known as "saunas."

But then he probably saw nothing odd in the decision of Germany's largest manufacturer of "traditional" wooden nutcrackers to create one in the figure of "Sitting Bull," "dressed proudly in brightly colored head-to-toe feathers and a leather-fringed ceremonial garment. He stands ready," promises the advertisement, "with shield and tomahawk to guard and protect your wigwam and all your treasured wampum." Indeed, "Sitting Bull" will quickly *become* what the writer imagines (incorrectly) "wampum" to be: "As a limited edition of just 8,500, he's sure to become a valued and sought-after collector's item." This carved wooden figure, both aesthetically hideous and culturally insulting in the usual manner of such things, sells for a staggering $189![4]

The European fascination, like that of many white Americans', seems bottomless. In characteristic Dutch fashion (i.e., riddled with collective guilt), a business calling itself "Lakota Stitching" has launched an effort to inform the families of Indian soldiers buried in the Netherlands of the graves' whereabouts. Company executives began by placing a short notice in *Indian Country Today*. This notice makes clear the intensity of research this Nieuwegein [*sic*], Holland company is willing to undertake in behalf of Lakota families. Indeed, it demonstrates its assiduity by offering many details of one Oglala family whose soldier relative, Jacob Herman, Jr., is buried in Holland, only one of many.

Unfortunately, the notice does not describe the nature of the business of the Lakota Stitching Company, though one imagines the Dutch guilt was aroused because the firm manufactures and sells "fake" Lakota clothing and ceremonial items, including, perhaps, pipes and Sun Dance paraphernalia for the Germans? Like Ottmar Lattorf, the owners of this company appear to have consciences that are at least a little troubled by their [post-colonial] practice of profiting from cultural appropriation.[5]

Only once did I experience personally the muddled soup of ignorance, condescension, racism, and guilt represented by these, and hundreds of other, examples. When *Dances With Wolves* arrived in Cambridge, a friend, a member of the British upper classes, owner of his own stately home, denizen of boards of directors all over the City, reader of *The Daily Telegraph,* and a sword- and spurs-equipped functionary of Britain's feudal county-ceremonial structure, asked if my husband and I would like to accompany him and his wife to the movies. "Harry" (a "U" name, but not actually his) knew about my racial identity: in the course of our first conversation I had replied to his offer of pedigree with my own, half Penn (and Mother's Hall, Hotchkiss and Van Sice), half Indian.[6] In an uncomprehending response, Harry had rushed in with his practiced noblesse oblige, assuring me in plummy tones that the fact that I was "Indian" was "quite alright," indeed, something of which I "ought to be proud." (That he felt driven to "reassure" me, that he hadn't realized I *was* proud, only underscored his ambiguous initial reaction.) This proved to be only the first of many such culturally displacing encounters, as my friend—very much to his credit, given his lifetime of significant cultural deprivation—learned to listen to himself and to change. So I quickly agreed to the joint viewing of *Dances;* not only did my husband and I like him very much, but I considered it another opportunity to change some attitudes. Slightly embarrassed, he then passed on the request of his very beautiful, very blonde, very expensive wife that I wear "Indian clothing." Knowing from dozens of previous encounters that she was imagining fringed and beaded deerskin dresses, shell ornaments, and feather tied hair familiar from countless Hollywood films, I asked with faux naïveté if she wanted me to dress "as a contemporary Native American woman might dress to go to the movies?" "Yes, yes," my friend replied enthusiastically. So I washed and ironed my blue denim work shirt and my jeans, and found my abalone earrings and moccasins. (I hoped it would not rain; moccasins and wet city streets do not mix.)

Only a few minutes into the film I realized that I had my pedagogical work cut out for me. It was not a film about Lakota people—then or now. Rather, it was a film about Kevin Costner riding in from the East to offer (his and his woman's) European-American wonderfulness to "hapless" though wise Indians. Like *Mis-*

sissippi Burning, Dances could explore the historical past only by focusing on central characters who were white. Moreover, the film's story was idiotic: far from the relative sophistication of earlier (though admittedly more racist) Hollywood westerns, *Dances* was little more than a series of shallow stereotypes stood on their heads. Thus, where once all Indians had been savage and monstrous—except for a "civilized" hero, sometimes "mixed blood," always friend of whites—here all those of European descent (again, with the exception of the star) were savage and monstrous. As once all perfection lay with manifestly destined settlers of the "virgin land," so now all goodness was the near-exclusive purview of Oglala Lakotas. And yet another similarity: as 1950s-movie white women had been uniformly relegated to domestic silence and willing servitude, so, too, were the Lakota women of this 1990s film. In fact, only one Lakota woman spoke at all. Played by Tantoo Cardinal, this character's role was to provide "lusty" (i.e., "Indian") sex and constant, unwavering emotional support to the wise and good chief (Graham Greene). The white woman had a few more lines (naturally). But she, too, represented a post-'50s, sexually "liberated" Mrs. Cleaver in buckskin. Although cheerfully sexual, she displayed a stunning lack of autonomy. When Kevin Costner (with a nod to 1990s political correctness) conscientiously asks her opinion about his decision to leave the Lakotas to return to the white world, she replies, "Wherever you go, I go" or some variation on the familiar Naomi and Ruth scene. Here too, European-American stereotypes of gender relations dominated a story about Native America.[7]

The film over, we repaired to a nearby pizza parlor. Food in hand, "Fiona" turned her exquisitely madeup face to me: "One thing, Pat, you don't look at *all* like the Indians. If I hadn't known already, I'd *never* have known." "Yes, yes," I replied. "It happens this way in families; one of us looks 'Indian,' one of us doesn't, and so on." "But I'd never, never have known," she repeated, touching my arm. "There's not a single sign that anyone could see." Slightly bemused by her insistence, I caught my husband's horrified expression across the table. I assumed he was bored—he had, after all, sat through dozens of conversations about mixed blood and identity in Indian Country. I thought he wanted to talk about the film. So I changed the subject. For awhile we were all right and the conversation—joined by their young son William—turned to dissecting the movie. But Fiona couldn't let my looks alone; soon, she returned to the issue. "I am sure," she said again, examining my face, "none of my friends would ever know. Do they know in Trinity Hall? Did they know when you were in King's? Does anyone ever talk about it? I shouldn't think they would because you don't look it at all. You could be all white."

Again, I blathered on about genes and physical appearance—even pointing out the shape of my bones and, particularly by comparison with English skin, my color. I told the "shingles story," when a white doctor practicing in the American South had been horrified by the persistence on my skin of one "shingle" even long after I had recovered from the disease. It was only after much muttering and humming (while I imagined that my "shingle" promised horrible possibilities) that the doctor told me why this remaining mark on my skin was odd: Caucasians, she said hesitantly, don't "usually have the problem of one or two staying behind." When I had exclaimed with relief, "But I'm not white!" she was equally relieved—that she was not going to have to explain to what she believed was a white southerner that the shingle signalled what she thought of as "colored" blood!

Fiona, however, still couldn't let it go. Even when I was answering Harry's (tactful) questions about circumstances on most reservations, the poverty, the lack of health care, the absence of decent education, the alcoholism and despair, she continued to remark my whiteness.

But hers was not the only obtuseness that evening. I continued not to "get it," even when she replied to one remark with, "Oh I see; Indians are just like the Abos!" "The who?" I asked. "The Abos. The Australian government gives them all that money and they spend all of it drinking. Then they get in cars and drive until the petrol runs out. Then the government has to go get them and it starts all over again." It was, evidently, no use talking.

When we got home, however, my husband was livid with a quite different reaction. "Racist," he ranted. "How awful you must have felt when Fiona just wouldn't let up with her stupid 'you're almost one of us' junk." "Huh?" I replied. His eyes widened as he realized that I hadn't gotten it, that Fiona's condescending reassurance that I looked just like a white person had completely passed me by. I thought only that she was remarking what was often remarked in my life, the visible signs of my white blood! And I was reacting as I always did—with chagrin that I was a madrone—white on the outside, red on the inside. His Britishness—and that of Fiona's husband—ensured that he could not miss her implications. Hers were classic, and to them recognizable, British Empire attitudes. "Little Indian, Sioux or Crow / Little frosty Eskimo / Little Turk or Japanee / O! don't you wish that you were me!"

 When I was ready to reencounter my more racially mixed and (to me) much more interesting homeland I took the first likely job I saw advertised: teaching in the Graduate Institute of the Liberal Arts at Emory University, in Atlanta. During my interview visit, apprehensive about the South after a youth spent watching blubbery, tiny-eyed white sheriffs sic their slavering German shepherds at black people marching and singing for their rights, I was utterly seduced by what I misperceived as the racial mixing of a city that advertised itself as "The City Too Busy To Hate," a place purportedly transformed by the civil-rights movement. Deprived for so many years of any but European society, I happily embraced the cultural and racial mix I thought I saw all around me.

But how ironic that I did not at first realize that I had taken a job in the only American state where there were almost no Indians! Until I moved to Georgia, I had not realized the efficacy of the Jacksonian Removal which had virtually wiped the state clean of its indigenous population. There were a few Indians in Atlanta; but most were not local. Lakotas and Dakotas, Anishnaabeg, and a few Mohawks, Crees, and Tuscaroras: these were the tribal affiliations of most of the stalwarts of a recently founded Native American Center of Georgia. There were some Cherokees, mostly from the Eastern Band of Cherokees whose reservation lies today in the town of Cherokee, North Carolina. At Emory there was not a single other Indian.

Gradually, despite the isolation of Georgia, I began to discover what had happened to my generation—to Indian and non-Indian students who had been so intensely political in the 1960s and early '70s. With time, many of the latter, once driven to action—marching, singing, writing, sitting-in—had turned toward a more passive, income-yielding politics in academia, where they now wrote book after book that purported to "subvert" something. As the British critic and novelist David Lodge has remarked, these were the many who were "disillusioned by the collapse of the utopian dreams of the 1960s and '70s and the electoral triumphs of neoconservative social and economic policies in the '80s." In self-defense, "they have turned inward and cultivated their own garden—or, rather, dug it up and replanted it, convincing themselves that a radical reform of the curriculum is equivalent to the radical reform of society."[8]

James Clifford is, perhaps, the dean of such self-cultivators. His popularity is such that something must be said about him here—though I shall restrain myself

WHEN NICKELS WERE INDIANS

from launching the full-blown attack the book deserves.[9] His widely acclaimed *The Predicament of Culture: Twentieth-century Ethnography, Literature, and Art,* like two works he admires, Sally Price's *Primitive Art in Civilized Places,* and Barbara Tedlock's *The Beautiful and the Dangerous,* reeks of self-justification. He begins by siting himself in the required post-modernist, [and therefore] fragmented, condition: "This book is a spliced ethnographic object, an incomplete collection." But however partial (another trendy term), the work is evidence of his realization of the importance of "ethnography." This, as fashionably piecemeal as the book itself, is also simultaneously many things, "a hybrid activity," Clifford explains, "writing . . . collecting . . . modernist collage . . . imperial power, [and, most important] . . . *subversive critique*" (emphasis added).[10] Oh yes? subversive? of what? and what is the mechanism of this "subversion"? Obviously blithely unaware that the mere deployment of a "risky" term does not a politics make, Clifford equally obviously considers his work a form of political action.

Like most such academic would-be revolutionaries of our generation, Clifford's language obscures and even denies the existence of wearying, uncompromising facts. Nowhere, for example, does he so much as hint at the existence of staggering barriers to any real "subversion" of Western "hegemony" (or control). He does not mention the pesky problems posed by the distribution of power among and between societies and social groups (and of course he does not mention that discredited term "class"). Even where he does mention "power," such as in the effusive introductory remarks with which he greets one "fragment" of Barbara Tedlock's portrait of her "quaint little Zunis" (her wildly overwritten description of "their" Shalako ceremony is, in his words, "superb"), he employs abstractions as agents, and the passive voice—both linguistic defenses against recognizing the realities of power. He insists, for example, "The relations of power whereby one portion of humanity can select, value, and collect the pure products of others need to be criticized and transformed."[11] So "portions" (*portions?* are we talking class here? or race? as in "the upper white portions of humanity"?) will criticize and "transform"? *How?* We know who will do the criticizing. But who (or what "portion") is going to undertake this transformation? *And what does it mean anyway?* (Maybe he thinks Sally Price's approach, bringing all the quaint little natives, to each of whom she has given a name and a market value, into (her) capitalist relations, will suffice to end all this domination of the "other portion of humanity" [aka the "Third, or developing, World"] by "the upper portion" [aka "us"]?[12]

Clifford and his friends are still at it, even as I write these words. In my mind's eye I see them, computers and recorders in hand, fanning out all across America now that summer's here, flying far from their "home" universities to pass the warm months viewing the "quaint little people of Blank." (Tribal people in the Southwestern United States will once again be bearing the brunt of the invasion: *Everyone* is heading for Santa Fe.)

Soon they will all be back in their various "civilized" eastern cities, metropolitans all. There they will set about writing books and articles and "hybrid pieces" about their encounters with their subjects (objects?), proudly wearing the jewelry and clothing "traditional" in "their" culture.[13] The resulting paper artifacts will soon be showing their peers how busy they have been, collecting once again—for themselves, for museums—and even (if they are intensely radical) criticizing collecting—again, both kinds. The results, in James Clifford's utterly uncomprehending citation of James Fenton's "Pitt-Rivers Museum" in Oxford, will be another "world of fetishes, of intimate encounters with inexplicably fascinating objects," where "[white] visitors find the landscape of their [sic] childhood marked out." He confesses to a personal weakness, though one shared by all of "us": "In the West . . . collecting has long been a strategy for the deployment of a possessive self, culture, and authenticity."[14] Well, o.k., so nutty, object-obsessed white people, their hearts as vacant as their heads, *love* to play childhood games ("Finders Keepers," "Cowboys and Indians," "One Little, Two Little . . . ," "Capture the Flag") in museums full of quaint and curious odds and bits from the exotic Elsewhere. But this shameless absence of understanding (the "objects" are not "inexplicably fascinating" to those whose cultural and spiritual lives they once inhabited) however much it might contribute to a deplorably avaricious "self," does not "authenticity" make.

Thus "anthros" remain, transplanted, perhaps grafted and even "hybridized," and still possibly the most disliked professional group ever to venture into Indian Country. Vine Deloria's 1960s humor captures what remains a widely shared sentiment:

Into each life, it is said, some rain must fall. Some people have bad horoscopes, others take tips on the stock market. McNamara created the TFX and the Edsel. Churches possess the real world. But Indians have been cursed above all other people in history. Indians have anthropologists.[15]

When such egocentric scholars meet equally politically and ego-driven left-wing artists, the results can be stunning. Indeed, the creators of more than one such artifact sometimes appeared to have forgotten the existence of "real" Indians altogether, so anxious were they to reconstruct "authentic"—i.e., politically correct/subversive—versions of the past. A telling example is a recent "middlebrow" miniseries produced with the aid of such non-Indian scholars by French-Canadian Television. A newspaper article describing the series begins:

Rarely has a television production portrayed the utter, pitiless brutality of the European colonisation of North America with as much fervour and compassion as in the new . . . *Shehaweh.* . . . It is a sweeping historical epic which tells the story of an Iroquois girl who is kidnapped, raped, and forcibly Christianized by French settlers at Ville Marie, the semi-religious settlement which was renamed Montréal.

So far, so good, despite the tiresome predictability of rape. But then the article continues: "*Shehaweh* has assembled the best and brightest of French Canadian talent. In the title role is Marina Orsini, 26, who over the last seven years has emerged as Québec's queen of the t.v. mini-series."

What? Was there no Iroquois actress for the role? Evidently not; in fact, the casting suggests that there were no Indian actors available for any of the major parts. Or perhaps no one even considered that Indians ought to be involved in the film—as actors or as anything else. Even the "experts" on Iroquois history include no Native people. In the unself-consciously ethnocentric words of the series writer, Fernand Dansereau:

I wanted to reflect aesthetically as well as historically on the entire period. First, it's a study of the roots of Québec culture and our [sic] initial interaction with the native peoples. Second, it was important to explain how the native peoples fought hard to preserve their [sic] integrity and values. They were as proud of their culture as we were, and that is why I juxtaposed the religious values of the missionaries with the rituals of the Indians.

Of the director, the paper notes, "Dansereau was also keen on maintaining strict historical fidelity. Marcel Trudel, a noted Quebec historian, checked each draft of the screenplay." In the view of the newspaper film critic, Dansereau had achieved his goal, producing a series that was "hard, convincing entertainment that offers an acute perspective on colonialism and cultural identity."[16] But *whose* "cultural identity"? Surely this miniseries has little to do with Iroquois people and everything to do with the cultural problems of Québeçois?

For the higher of brow, the movies offer not only *Dances With Wolves* but also *Black Robe,*[17] *The Last of the Mohicans,* and, for the politically correct, *Thunderheart.* And for the very loftiest brows, the Dance Theater of Harlem presents *A Song for Dead Warriors,* choreographed by Michael Smuin. Anna Kisselgoff's review of the piece in the *New York Times*, "A Harsh Yet Poetic Elegy on Indian Life," offers rich material for satirists such as Wendy Rose, Jimmie Durham, or Vine Deloria, Jr. In her words, the ballet is,

Michael Smuin's raw, poetic and harsh meditation on the plight of the American Indian in urban life. . . . The themes are laid out at the start. Pride is opposed to decline; good battles evil. A prologue recalls the tribal nobility of the past, as an Indian youth is initiated by the braves who represent the spirits of his ancestors. . . . A sheriff and his troopers intrude upon a social dance on a reservation. While he flees into the woods, the protagonist sees his sweetheart being raped by the sheriff. Driven to despair and then beaten in a pool hall, the youth is driven to revenge and scalps the sheriff. The moment is presented with Mr. Smuin's typically unflinching brand of verismo.[18]

This one has it all: the "vanished Indian," the "plight," the rape, even scalping. And, once again, a piece purporting to describe the present exists, instead, in the (vivid) imaginations not of "urban" Indians, but rather of non-Indian Americans. (This tale of thwarted masculinity, needless to say, has much more to do with the dominant discourse of American phallocentrism—in which a man's woman is raped, necessitating his revenge—than it has to do with the "plight of urban [male] Indians.") No tribal person I know, in fact, would recognize *as Indian* a single element of this "elegy"; it cries out instead for the satiric wit of a Sherman Alexie or Tomson Highway.

 Thousands of urban educated tribal people, some adorned with pantribal vestments made of plastic and leather, are withdrawing from civilization and driving back to the reservation to live the way they have projected tribal life to be several hundred years ago. And they are met by thousands of tribal people leaving reservations to attend colleges and find work in metropolitan areas. Neither group is in conflict with the other.[19]

Hundreds of urban Indian militants converted to New Age spirituality and "returned" to reservations to experience tribal life as, they hoped, it is actually lived. Often, as Gerald Vizenor saw, the returnees wore the familiar clothing and symbols of the absolute fake Indian of popular culture. Often, too, they carried in their minds the panoply of "tribal traditions" they, too, often learned not from elders but from the movies. But as a few among them quickly realized, "real life" on the rez *had* changed. Tribal colleges survived and grew, despite Reagan and Bush.

Some tribes (most notably the Menominee of Wisconsin) had succeeded in being de-terminated. (The leader of that movement, Ada Deer, is now the Commissioner of Indian Affairs in the Clinton administration.) In the West, young Native American water and mining engineers, forestry experts, lawyers, doctors, geologists, and ecologists were reclaiming Native rights to tribal resources. Native American academics peopled ethnic-studies programs, which at their best were educating both Native and non-Native students to think outside the Eurocentric vision of previous generations. There were dozens more examples of change.

Those going the *other* direction, leaving the rez, found the "outside" world had grown weirder still.

"WHITE MEN CAN'T DRUM"[20]
On the menu at Al's Oasis in Oacama, South Dakota:
"Bisonburger from the herd that appeared in *Dances With Wolves*"[21]

Native America, they quickly discovered, continued to be for sale—or, at least, the white versions of Native America. Everywhere, highbrows and lowbrows consumed the artifacts of Indian culture—jewelry and deerskin clothing, "dream catchers," smudge sticks, pipe and medicine bundles, and a panoply of spiritual practices including sweat lodges, vision quests, sun dances, and—particularly popular with the "men's movement"—traditional drumming.[22] Reacting to the latter's efforts to appropriate everything "Native," willy-nilly, one of these young tribal people, the writer and poet Sherman Alexie, noted that this era's appropriation—like all its predecessors—is underpinned by, among other things, a serious misapprehension of traditional Native American ideas of masculinity:

A warrior does not necessarily have to scream to release the animal that is supposed to reside inside every man. A warrior does not necessarily have an animal inside him at all. If there happens to be an animal, it can be a parakeet or a mouse just as easily as it can be a bear or a wolf. When a white man adopts an animal, he often chooses the largest animal possible. Whether this is because of possible phallic connotations or a kind of spiritual steroid abuse is debatable.

"Still," Alexie admits, "I have to love the idea of so many white men searching for answers from the same Native traditions that were considered heathen and savage for so long."[23]

Of course, in Indian Country, no tradition is "for sale," whatever the consumer society's myrmidons might think. But in an America where shopping often equals living (or where "consumption equals experience," as Robert Thomas puts it) it is perhaps not surprising that most people believe otherwise.[24] In their collective frenzy to consume the traditions of Native America, whites will, it often seems, buy anything. Jimmie Durham offers a satirical advertisement for himself: "I Am One of Those Indians . . . That fly around witnessing/prophetic novas in burnt-out toasters."[25] My own collection of advertisements for "Native goods," collected by many of my students, includes bookmarks produced by a California company showing Edward Curtis photographs either of familiar luminaries of the Indian pantheon such as Chief Joseph, or displaying types: (e.g., "Nez Perce baby"); jigsaw puzzles (sold in the New York Public Library gift shop) that allow children to assemble "warriors" from representative tribes; coloring books (two of which I found for sale in one local bookstore); and even many objects strangely commemorating the genocide of Native people by Europeans. Some of the latter are critical of this past—for example, a Slave Labor Graphics comic book about the Nez Perce war called *Relentless Pursuit*. Others carry a more baffling message. One "collector's" plate, for example, produced by the ubiquitous Franklin Mint, shows a Plains warrior, seated on his pinto pony half-naked in a misty northwestern forest, holding his sacred prayer stick aloft, his other arm extended in a crucifixion pose. The caption reads, "Great Spirit, Guide Me Today." But what is the guidance for? The plate's title, "Deliverance," tells the story. This brave is praying to the Great Spirit to guide him toward deliverance from those who are in the process of slaughtering his people and whose descendants will ultimately purchase the plate! It is as though a German company produced a "collector's" plate depicting a religiously garbed rabbi praying for deliverance from the Nazis!

But curiouser and curiouser, the picture is not recently painted, but rather a slightly altered reproduction, in miniature, of one of that bizarre group of portraits sculpted and painted of Plains warriors about to ride—together with all their brothers and sisters—into that great western sunset in the sky. These found an enthusiastic welcome during America's smugness-ridden Gilded Age. One of the most frequently reproduced artists is Cyrus E. Dallin, whose favorite subjects were mounted male braves and chiefs. Each of his works gloried in the white victory over the "noble" western tribes. One of his most famous figures, which won a prize at the 1909 Paris Salon, is called "The Appeal to the Great Spirit." Its message mirrors that of "Deliverance." In Dallin's own words, this statue depicts "a despondent Indian whose cause on earth has failed." He "calls upon Powers of the Spirit for deliverance and ultimate sanctuary." Although it is impossible to imagine Helmut Kohl choosing a sculpture of a Jew representing the last handful of Jews left in Germany to decorate his official office, Bill Clinton saw nothing at all dubious in his selection of a tiny version of "Appeal to the Great Spirit" to place in his oval office, directly beneath a painting of "The President's House."[26]

There were, and are, dozens of such works. White America decided that the "Red Man" was doomed quite early on. The "lasts of" began with the Mohicans, whose memorial novel was published in 1826. Hiram Powers sculpted another "last of," this time "Last of the Tribe," which appeared in the 1840s. This figure combined sex with victory by featuring a female subject. One recent historian is critical: "Although she is nude from the waist up and wears a squaw's [sic] skirt, her face seems very much that of a European Caucasian. The 'true' last of her tribe was obviously not available to model in Powers's studio."[27]

More recently, popular culture has provided a counternarrative, this one featuring an expiation of collective guilt. Examples include the sublime and the absurd. Among the latter, as Ariel Dorfman discovered, lies no less a figure than Donald Duck.

It seems that when Donald, his nephews, and Grandma go seeking "adventure in the Wild West," they are immediately—and predictably—attacked by savage Indians. But why? They are not white men, but rather ducks! Alas, it seems that even the birds of the air got in on manifest destiny; one of the Duck ancestors had cheated some Indian ancestors, and (of course) the Indians never forgot. It is up to Donald to "rectify the fraud. . . . Then the races can reach an understanding and there will be a comfortable spot for the outsiders within the prevailing order," as Dorfman puts it. The Ducks make restitution, whereupon "the Indians respond by declaring eternal peace with the ducks and integrating themselves into the modern world which they no longer fear." Peace (albeit with Ducks, and cartoon ducks at that) brings modernity: "a big gas company [that] will create new jobs and pay the tribe handsomely." Capitalism wins! Moreover, "there will be a consortium that will resolve disputes with justice!"[28]

Indians have been the companions of children for a very long time. Almost every white eastern reader (or at least according to those who judge such things at the New Yorker) must have recognized him/herself in Daniel Menaker's deeply offensive "Injun Summer." In this short essay, Menaker adopts a faintly ingenuous tone to describe his children's "Indian theme" summer camp: "Many camps cater to a certain clientele, and for this reason they try to put forward an identity of one kind or another. But not North Wind, as far as I know. . . . Except for the Indian stuff. . . . Every kid in the camp is either a Cherokee or a Mahaiwe." The high point of the week comes at the Thursday night campfire, when, according to this writer, "the Indian atmosphere gets thickest. To the beat of a tomtom, the campers form a circle around the fire:

> The Webelos—teen-age boys, naked to the waist . . . and wearing headdresses of white feathers tipped with red and black—stand in the middle, being serious. The main Webelo has a very long headdress and walks around with a big stick. . . . There are games pitting Cherokee against Mahaiwe. . . . After every event, the head Webelo says something like "for this contest of strength. . . . the tribes of North Wind say"—and here the entire camp joins in—"How!"

Daniel Menaker has not been entirely comatose for the past several decades. He confesses that he knows it is all "politically incorrect." Indeed, he is even smart enough to figure out a little more than that: "This kind of ersatz ritual debases cultural and historical matters of great controversy, I can hear the moralists saying." But, he concludes, "Too bad. I like it." Why? because his own world is so utterly empty of meaning that the "code of conduct" implied, as well as "the [superior] relationship to nature" are "better than no ideal at all." Further, "one cannot help being stirred just by the names of those to whom the ideal is attributed: Abnaki, Mohican[!], Dakota." To these, "the tribes of North Wind and their parents say, 'How!' "[29]

But what's wrong with some other codes and rituals from some nearer cultures? What about, e.g., a Jewish camp theme, where the best and the brightest wear prayer curls and shawls, and become the "Bar Mitzvahers" when they pass through their initiation? Or how about a Plantation theme? The "Jews, Christians, blacks, Amerasians" Menaker lists as populating what he calls this "heartening, unpretentious melting pot," North Wind, might break up into slave groups—house and field—and kapos, and even owners—Dad, Mom, and many lazy rich white kids. Spirituals could be sung by children whose faces are blackened where necessary. When anyone does well, the children could all roll their eyes and cry "lawdy, lawdy," or some such. Watermelon could provide the reward. Or they could do "Wasps," dressing in tiny khakis and loafers or suits, carrying tiny briefcases with small *Wall Street Journals* tucked under their arms. They could all recite stock prices. The boys could earn points playing cutthroat racquetball. The girls, who compete on stair climbers, could win even more advancement by planning the perfectly stunning New York wedding—answering questions like, Should the gown be ecru or white? should a car be rented to take the dress from the reception to its permanent storage, or will it be all right to pack it neatly into the back seat of an already-rented limo? From time to time during this debate, girls who really want to get ahead must successfully interrupt everyone else by using their cellular phones to ring their secretaries (whose response will, in turn, either make or lose more points. If there are no important messages for the would-be bride/lawyer/stockbroker, points are taken off). And as they all win points by lying, all the time about everything, no one need know the truth of the messages, or who climbed the most stairs, or whose ball was actually not out. Indeed, the child who makes it home with everyone else's goods and spending money wins the whole thing! To them, the *real* tribes of Native America say, "Well Done!"

Yuppie advertising is full of Native America, most of it used to illustrate the material girl's version of political correctness. Coach Leather, which manufactures and sells very expensive handbags (a cheap one runs about $100), recently used a photograph of "Sitting Bull's great great great granddaughter, Jacqueline Brown-Smith" to illustrate "her Coach Bucket Bag" ($194). The text reads, "My Lakota name is 'Makpia-Lula-Wia,' Red Cloud Woman, which was given to me by my great grandmother. . . . Sitting Bull," she adds, "did everything he could to uphold the integrity of our people. We're a continuum, often unnoticed, but everpresent and necessary." What connection could possibly exist between Coach leather handbags and Sitting Bull's descendant? The catalog tells us: "We are all part of a heritage that has helped form the great American landscape." "We," in this catalog, include a "great, great, great, great, great, great grandniece of George Washington (with "her Coach Court Bag") and "Daniel Boone's great great great great grandson, William Ingersoll, with his [much more expensive still] Coach Monterey Car Coat." In case you should be feeling left out (*not* because you are one of the many millions of Americans who could not—or would not—spend a small fortune on a handbag), the company asks readers to "write to us and tell us the contributions your ancestors have made, and about how their lives have made an impact on yours." "Us"? It makes more sense to write to a duck.

More straightforward (well, why not just say it?), *Money* magazine, "Where American Dreams still come true," ran an ad in the autumn of 1993 linking the magazine's readers with, pardon the pun, Indian giving. Jodi and John W., it seems, "donate $720 a year [a couple of Coach bags, or Daniel Boone's descendant's Coach coat] to sponsor two Navajo children." Well, good for them. But they aren't pikers: "In 1994," we are assured, "they will spend another $2,600 on what they hope will be the first of many visits to the Arizona reservation." Huh? (or "how?") This couple, the Ws, *give* a measly $720 a year to "sponsor and befriend" two

Navajo children while they *spend* a whopping $2,600—more than three times their gift—on their vacation to "Navajoland."

I must be missing the point. Maybe the marvel is that they choose—like General Miles's troops—to venture far from their leafy eastern suburb to what the ad describes as a "barren" and "desolate" place? Indeed, to some New Jersey commuters, the accompanying photograph showing a neat log hogan still and peaceful under the wide cloudless western sky, the mesas and mountains rising against the distant horizon, may appear horrid and forbidding. Thus, perhaps, the necessity of all that vacation money? The couple doesn't *stay* in a hogan—or indeed, even in the Navajo nation at all. They stay in a hotel in a nearby city, visiting only to receive validation for their marvelous charity.[30]

But for those *Money* readers who can't go on vacation to Navajoland, Saks Fifth Avenue rushes to the rescue, just in time for the gift-giving holidays. "Pure silver from [a] Santa Fe workshop" the store promises, will be the ideal gift for "the man who sports the unexpected." The "bits of wit" on offer? "Indian head money clip, $210, and matching cufflinks, $325."

Poorer souls shouldn't feel left out. Some might want to try to clamber onto the *Money* bandwagon by following the precepts described in Emmett C. Murphy's *The Genius of Sitting Bull: 13 Heroic Strategies for Today's Business Leaders.* (The penultimate "precept" is "Welcome Crisis: Crisis does not signify catastrophe, but a new opportunity for heroism. Facing it squarely frees a leader from pretense and selfishness." In an ironic twist, given Sitting Bull's fate, the final rule reads [sic], "Measure results. They measure the results of their leadership by the challenges faced; evaluate the consequences of their plans" and so on.)[31]

Others might want to buy something with a maternal motif: "In her arms she proudly cradles the newborn chief of the Great Sioux Nation. Presenting . . . White Feather, Princess of the Sioux." White Feather, "a handcrafted porcelain collector doll," involves yet another of Sitting Bull's relatives, "Lady Scarlet Whirlwind . . . great-great-granddaughter of legendary Sioux Chief Sitting Bull," who created the doll's "authentic" costume. (Alas, tiny print explains that the "4,000 beads" are sewn onto "faux buckskin," a petroleum product unavailable in the time of Sitting Bull's "princess" mom.) Though utterly tasteless, White Feather isn't cheap. Her "cascading earrings . . . beaded leggings and moccasins," the "sacred medicine wheel in her hair and a white feather symbolizing the power of the eagle" will together set you back $35 a month for five months—or nearly the cost of the Coach bucket bag cherished by Sitting Bull's *other,* even more distant, granddaughter.[32]

White Feather is a "collector's" doll, not meant to be played with by children. But there is also a new Indian Barbie (a bit of a mess, a bit of what the cultural studies crowd would describe as a "semiotic riot," but at least her dress is *real* buckskin, even though her body and head are "faux porcelain"), or, for the little boys, "Chief Leo," a "Teenage Mutant Ninja Turtle Indian known as the Flame-shooting Feather-topped Foot Fighter."[33]

For those few who think they might actually want to consider history, there are innumerable popular books. From Time-Life Books comes a series, *The First Americans*. A large Edward Curtis portrait gazes out from the advertisement. The text promises, "His eyes have seen what yours could not. Until now . . ." And what is that? "The surprising true history of our continent . . . told in its entirety and without bias." This enlightenment will cost series subscribers a mere $14.95 a volume (*The Way of Beauty, The Spirit World,* and so on).

And if reading (looking, really; the series is full, the advert promises, of pictures) is too taxing, the family vacation can take in a few Indian sights. During 1993, when the Oregon Trail was celebrated all over the West, *Sunset Magazine* produced a special "Making History Again on the Oregon Trail" which suggested taking a ride in the "mule-drawn wagons" which, for a fee, will "give passengers a feel for the Oregon Trail." But it need not be all one-sided: "At Pendleton's Round-Up rodeo grounds, you can get an understanding of what the wagon trains meant to Native Americans at a re-created 1840s Indian village set up by the Conferated Tribes of the Umatilla Indian Reservation." And what "meaning" will tourists learn? No worry, no politics: "You might see weaving demonstrations, mat making, and traditional dances."[34]

Traditions are a shield against the social and spiritual plague of twentieth century consumer culture.
Duane Niatum[35]

The marketplace offers thousands of examples—of an America rapacious in its hunger for (imagined) Indians. And in this, too, the government has intervened. Ostensibly in an effort to "protect" Native artists—though its effects are more likely to "protect" dealers and "investors"—Congress passed the Indian Arts and Crafts Law in 1990. This law makes it an offense punishable by up to fifteen years in federal prison and one million dollars in fines for anyone non-Indian to "offer to display for sale or sell any good that suggests it is Indian produced." And how is an "Indian" artist certified? There are three possible means: proof of one-fourth

Indian blood, tribal membership in a federally recognized tribe, or a birth certificate that lists "race" as "Indian."[36] But here, too, the government's efforts to identify Indians has provoked more problems than it has solved. For one thing, there are many artists of long standing, including Jimmie Durham, who have no tribal membership—although the Cherokee nation of Oklahoma has offered to provide Durham with the necessary papers. Some, although one-half Indian, cannot establish tribal membership because their tribal blood comes from a parent of the "wrong" sex (as would be the case with someone with an Onondaga father and non-Indian mother, for example). Still others belong to tribes that are not federally recognized—the case for Lumbees, as well as for many other smaller Native nations of the eastern United States (whose lack of federal recognition continues to exact a high price for their having lived on the shore nearest Europe). And tribes require varying amounts of blood for membership. Some go along with federal regulations and count one-eighth as sufficient. Others, such as the Eastern Cherokee, allow up to one-thirty-second degree of blood! Still others have no blood count, and rely on community recognition. These latter, ironically perhaps, are actually the most "traditional" in their practice. "Citizenship in Indian nations," observes the Comanche writer Paul Smith, "never had anything to do with blood count until after colonization."[37]

Birth certificates as a means of race identifying are even more problematic. Unless a child is born in an Indian Health Service hospital on a reservation, birth certificates are not automatically filled in with "Native" or "Indian." (Indeed, a friend's birth certificate suggests that race can be assessed solely by skin color: a hospital employee's assessment of his mother's "race" reads "white," his father's "colored." Such meaningless distinctions embody the idiocy of defining people by the tone of their skin—*as perceived by viewers*.) In the days when assimilation was the goal of thousands of people of non-white background, birth certificates often read "white" if hospitals agreed. Parents chose to designate the category which would allow their children to pass safely into white America. (This was particularly a problem in the segregated South, of course, but it happened all over the country.) And what about the majority of Native people, who are "mixed blood"? Many who have long been recognized as Native American artists, most of whom are "mixed blood," have refused to accommodate themselves to this Indian Arts and Crafts Act, although it means exclusion from galleries and shows devoted to Indian work. Jimmie Durham is among the most prominent of this group, most of whom argue that the law is "racist" and divisive, at a time when Indians can ill afford to begin cutting people out of their legally exclusive club. Some political activists have therefore called on all Native people to join this movement against yet another perfidious division of Native America by blood quanta.[38]

What the new tribal world needs is a better puppet to balance the tense distances between reservations and cities, a satirical puppet to modulate the differences between men and women, mixed bloods and others. Not the human varieties of puppets who are invented and manipulated in the white world, but the hand-animated characters with real hollow heads.

Gerald Vizenor, *Earthdivers*

Their author, of Russian-American descent, is internationally recognized as a Chicano writer.

West End Press, advertising Jim Sagel's *Más Que No Love It*

"Real hollow heads" are everywhere in this debate over blood, however, and any would-be head puppet would have to depend on very agile puppet masters indeed. The most recent twist on the dialectic of Indian blood has been documented by Paige St. John in the *Detroit News*. This special report, dated April 12, 1992, is headlined, "American Indians Hurt by College Admissions Abuses." The story begins:

Native American.

Matthew Moore checked that box on his admission application to the University of Michigan two years ago, and got four years of free tuition, worth $15,000, and a coveted student research job in a campus lab.

But until two years ago, Moore considered himself white.

While he was applying for college, he says, his parents searched the family tree and found a great-grandmother who they believe qualified their son for special admission and financial benefits, even though Matthew didn't meet U-M's definition of "Native American" which requires tribal or community recognition.

Even the 18-year old U-M freshman from Farmington Hills admits that his is a loose connection to the American Indian race: "It's hard for me to consider myself a Native American."[39]

But is he? The article continues:

Among 40 U-M Native American students contacted by *The News*, eight were enrolled in a tribe. Another 10 had some tie to a Native American community. Twenty knew little about their American Indian heritage—sometimes not even the name of the tribe or ancestor. Two said they were on the U-M Native American list by mistake. "In my opinion, they wanted to designate me as Native American," said Starr Stricklin of Wayne. "Then they get the required number they needed. And I needed the aid."

She said her great-grandfather was Cherokee but does not know which band.

These may be viewed simply as pathetic examples of a particularly self-aggrandizing and amoral generation of American youth. But other examples collapse into absurdity:

Catherine Carroll, of Bay City, got a work-study job and financial aid after she applied for admission as a quarter Native American. She later discovered the "Bohunk" tribe she thought she was from is slang for Bohemian-Hungarian.[40]

Such fraud is, alas, more than a simple (if ethically disgusting) con played by some white students on universities. Its effects are far-reaching. As this and other reports attest, universities able so easily to fill a "quota" of Native American students are able to avoid trying to address themselves to genuine Native communities—on reservations or in urban centers, where the problems of Indian life are grave and long-standing. And of course every dollar that goes to a fake cannot go to a student with genuine Native American background.

Interestingly, Native Americans sometimes think the situation is easier for those of mixed black and white blood. Sue Hill, president of the U.M. Native American Student Association believes, "There's no other ethnic group that counts one-sixteenth as being a member. . . . If a white person walks in and says they're black, people will question them." But racism is much more complicated than that. As Adrian Piper pointed out, Sue Hill is, in fact, wrong; in the eyes of most white people—as well as in the eyes of government agencies responsible for affirmative action programs of all kinds—the "one-drop" rule, which designates "black" anyone with as little as "one drop" of African blood, continues to apply.

But even this phenomenon of racism does not suffice to complicate life for most people of varying African-American descent. Among some African-Americans, what is known in Indian Country as "MITT" (More Indian Than Thou) has an analog. Those whose physical markers (rather than such determining factors as class, which might, in fact, be far more important in determining an individual's sense of his/her identity) suggest "mixed" rather than "pure" blood often encounter hostility.[41] Not "one of us," such mixed-blood African-Americans are thus also "not one of them." (For Native American people with blood mixed with African as well as European ancestry, the situation is even more complicated, of course.[42])

Whatever the similarities with other racial minorities, Native Americans remain uniquely the target of innumerable "wannabes." Many—perhaps most?—Americans are anxious to *be* Indian, as they are not anxious to be African-American or Asian-American.[43] That this lust to "borrow" someone else's racial identity is not a simple anodyne desire for transcendence of one's own unsatisfactory racial assignment is underscored by Angela Gonzales's observation about fakes on university faculties: "They get paraded around as Indian. . . . They're being placed on committees as the Native American voice. Once again, the Native American voice is being drowned out."[44]

Oh it was Coyote
It must have been Coyote
Oh, Coyote,
Oh, just Coyote.
    Traditional Nez Perce song.

But what about the forty-five-year-old man who suddenly discovers he has one-quarter Mohawk blood, for whom the discovery means not only graduate school financial support, but also a new world of "Indian Culture"? Who becomes an assiduous attender of sweat lodges and powwows, wearer of Indian jewelry (made by Dine, Zuni, Hopi jewelry makers, not by Mohawks), speaker of strangely accented, but heavily "spiritual" language? (Given the breadth of this stereotype of Native people's natural "religiosity," it is not really surprising that those who discover an Indian self begin to experience it. Characterizations stressing the ubiquity of this quality are everywhere, including in a glossy advertising brochure put out by New York Telephone in the summer of 1993. Its "Hidden Treasures," include "delights" scattered throughout New York State, and includes the National Museum of the American Indian. The description of the latter assures readers that "Visitors will come away with a greater understanding of Native Americans' ethic of sharing, their deep spirituality and magnificent art." It is not clear how this understanding is to be achieved.)

This man's blood is quite genuine; he even looks part-Indian. But is he?

And what of us? Because the journalists' exposé provoked a reaction in Michigan's colleges and universities, all minority faculty were offered research funds to document, as completely as possible, their "Indian blood." Thus my brother set out from Michigan State to "fill out" the documentation we already had, which placed our Nez Perce grandfather, William Penn, at Haskell Indian Institute. What he discovered muddles every idea of "identity." The Penns, who lived in our childhood imaginations as pale (they lived in the sunless "back east") white people garbed in somber black hats (we had Quaker oats boxes for a model), were only slightly English, if at all. Rather they, too, were Indians—Osages. This fact, rather than the geographical proximity of his family to tribal headquarters, suddenly explained why my grandfather's records were—and are—held at the Osage agency/tribal headquarters! Moreover, this meant that we were all much more Indian then we had known—a mixture of Osage *and* Nez Perce. Furthermore, some records indicate that the Osage part married a Mexican part as well as an English part at some point. Thus my father's mysterious "Aunt Consuelo" and her children, "Juanita," "Flor." . . .

But who are we then? Osage? Mexican? or are we what we always thought: urban mixed bloods of Nez Perce and European heritage?

And does it matter?

And how does it matter?

Perhaps it's just Coyote.

.8.

'TIL INDIAN VOICES
WAKE US ♦ ♦ ♦

 After months of remembering, the dreams stole my nights as the horror of New York City captured my days. One dream came every night—suitably accompanied by sound effects in the city dark: sirens, small explosions, sounds of windshields shattering, shouting, cries, and the endless wail of car alarms.

A dark-haired evil woman announced that she had located the "remains" of a man in the water of a wide river, just across from where I lived. Although I knew it was Patrick's body—my kind and gentle young husband who, when he could bear the world no longer, committed suicide—she and other white people would not let me claim it, or even identify it. They insisted it was to go into a museum; that they had the right to use it as they wished because it was an "unknown." The dream was a horror of anguished frustration as I tried repeatedly to claim him and they refused.

A terrible dream: memories of Patrick, memories of his terrible death, memories of my helplessness, all prompted by a collective memory of tribal bodies, thousands of them, claimed and stolen by white people for their museums, their collections, their scientific academies. It was a dream of my grief, and a dream of grief shared.

I had to get out. When the semester ended, we rang up Avis, the first step in the rescue.

Early one Sunday morning, we headed for Penn Station, climbing down the stairs to the Long Island Railroad train that would take us to the car rental agency in Westbury. Everywhere, *comme d'habitude,* I told myself, men, black and white, old and young, sprawled on the steps. The smell of urine, scent of all New York, overpowered the constricted space as we climbed carefully down and around body after body. Not sufficiently practised at life in this place, I kept looking carefully:

"Is he dead or alive?" Watching anxiously for a movement, the slightest lifting of a chest. . . . THIS MORNING'S DEAD PERSON: NEW YORK. We got the car. We headed West. Three long days later, I was home under the wide skies. No people. No people smell. Here, in California, I write you a letter; I write the end to this book.

The modernist culture of exile reflects "the radical instability of contemporary experience. . . . [It is] a metaphor for the alienated or marginalized modern consciousness."
Michael Seidel[1]

The culture of exile can be "a rewarding adventure into the unknown, or the melancholy trauma of moral and spiritual abandonment. . . . Modernity is a sensibility which is obsessed with journeys."
Mikos Papastergiadis[2]

Indians were, of course, Baudelaire's inspiration for "the dandy." He saw George Catlin's paintings and those "mask faces" inspired his. [emphasis added]
Richard Sieburth[3]

Thus do "Indians," represented, translated, embodied by George Catlin's paintbrushes (as later by Edward Curtis's camera lenses), become, for this literature professor, agents in one French poet's quest for that which could symbolize his "alienated" modernist identity. Similarly translated from living people into inspirational artifacts, "Indians" seemed no longer to exist at all by Baudelaire's mid-nineteenth century. They were muses, "pathways" into the male artist's soul, caught up in the creations of the industrial world's aesthetic consciousness.

Europe's artistic muses, Native people were America's self-congratulatory symbols—of the wondrous Wild West, of the sorrows of lost innocence. As material culture, "they" offered salve for the [minor] wounds inflicted by history on genteel, fin-de-siècle liberal consciences. "If people could not take cocoa and cookies to Dull Knife's fleeing Cheyenne and piously separate themselves from advocates of Manifest Destiny," Vine Deloria explains, "they could at least mount a Curtis print prominently in their homes and silently proclaim their solidarity with Indians."[4]

From material symbols haunting America's living rooms (landing up, at the close of the twentieth century, in a white president's White House) "Indians" have become the spiritual tourist destinations of thousands of "journeying" self-exiles, carriers of the [contagious?] "marginalized modern consciousness." They—as individuals, as collectivities, as disembodied words and even fashion's accessories— are no longer "souls to be saved," but rather destinations "where [modernist] man," in the words of Johannes Fabian, "was to find nothing but himself."[5] As the century's end nears an apocalyptic religiosity finds increasing numbers of recruits, terrified of their newly minted "post-modern" condition, so disturbingly uncertain that even a single, straightforward "modernist" exile begins to evoke nostalgic yearnings.

As has historically been the case, Native America is once more the destination of souls lost in the "New Age." The tribal world is bracing itself. *They* are coming, fat with their conviction that their experience of their culture's death agonies renders them fit companions for those they name "marginals," those "exiled" from what they all see as "real history"—the long [upward] trajectory from the Enlightenment to the troublingly "fragmented" and uncertain present.

Just as Native America turned a baffled face to the first invasion of European egomaniacs, so now it turns its collective gaze (the old people sigh and shake their heads: "white people are funny") to encounter this incarnation of the Indian scholar, seeking scholarly enlightenment in the names of cultural studies *and* anthropology. Unlike its forebears, this younger generation of culture scholars no longer lusts after intricate diagrams of kinship relations or titillating details of exotic Native sexual practices. Rather, they want tribal people to move over a bit (sometimes quite a lot), so that they can share the cultural space they have defined (from a distance) as this strange condition called "exile."[6]

No tribal person recognizes herself in this state. The closer comes this refugee from urban modernism, arms outstretched for the collegial embrace, the farther backward moves the Indian . . . until, in fact, she vanishes once again, over the shifting post-modernist horizon.

The seeker, however, is untroubled; it was not she he wanted. Rather he wanted what she leaves behind: her shadow, her representation, ready for freezing into the background portraits with which these "exiles" decorate their lives. Thus Natives once again resume their historical destiny: "primitive" yardsticks against which the (post-)modernist subject measures himself.

Soon, the portrait's caption, "Marginality," assumes life, assumes permanence; forever (again!) hung on those vacant walls, coloring the empty lives of the self-described, self-chosen, "post-modernists."

Although representation suggests that they are now really truly vanished, we know Indians are still around. So where are the "real authentick Indians"?

LETTER TO CHRIS

17 July 1994

Davis, California

Dear Chris,

That night at Pane e Cioccolato, you were cross with me. You had just finished reading the first two chapters of "Nickels" and wanted to talk. "Don't worry so much about your blue eyes and your light complexion. Don't talk about it," you said. You don't want me to mention them; you don't want me to be so self-conscious when we go together into company. My attitudes, you told me with an unusual seriousness, were wrong. They cut me off from you. By considering how I look to most white people, I am not just giving in to their racism, I am also suggesting to you that we are not the same, not as related as we feel, one to the other—across generations, across gender, but *not* across race.

And you are right. You and I and Shari and Bill and Waukena and Carol *are* relations: all mixed blood, all condemned to live crossing back and forth across the worlds. (Unlike Harriett, "Standing Rocker" through life, though she, too, is mixed blood, though she, too, feels like my sister. Unlike Dean, who stands on the deep, solid roots of the Crow nation. And unlike Miryam, though she too, is mixed blood, Andean, Quechua-speaking.)

What makes our group of fragments, assembled by pure accident in New York from (reading around the table) Alaska, Oregon, Montana, California, New Jersey, Oklahoma, Bolivia, Peru, Texas, Louisiana, and New Mexico (via Vietnam), and North Dakota (via the world) an "Us"? Dozens of things, whirling around in concentric circles, stars in the constellations of identity, of its community—things white people don't know anything about. The moccasin telegraph hums: "Whom do you know?" telephones connect the "ins," exclude the "never heard ofs." Anagrams from the old days link: "OEO," "EOP," "Upward Bound," "IYC," "NCAI." Or there is AIM, there are Indian Centers, there is Wounded Knee, the Trail of Broken Treaties, Alcatraz, Washington Fish-Ins. There are academic and artistic worlds: historians, writers, artists, scholars, filmmakers. "Do you know?" "Do you know?"

There are relations: my sister or brother, my cousin, my parents.

There are the histories: who are we? where did we come from?

But you are also wrong.

We know it every week, when, after talking circle, we walk together out of the decrepit NYU building where we meet. Inside, around that table, sometimes smudged, sometimes not (our practices are quite random) we are kin. Outside—stopping for coffee in that same restaurant—we are immediately divided by the gazes of passersby. Waukena becomes maybe "African-Something"? or East Indian? or Mexican? or. . . ? Shari and Bill and I become white: that Shari's blue eyes have an obvious Yup'ik shape, that Bill's manner has Apache written all over it, that all our teeth are . . . teeth!??? You, Harriett, and Dean are the "Indians." Miryam is Indian too—but not "North American." The rest of us?

Our external and—consequently—internal selves are implacably divided by the racism that assigns every individual to her/his group by physical markers alone.

And so our "white" experiences of race are always different from yours, from Harriett's and Dean's, from Waukena's and Miryam's.

Take that plane flight from Atlanta: you and Harriett and I, traveling back to New York after doing our "road show" for Emory University's Native America Awareness Month. On the plane, sitting directly in front of us, were three French tourists, one shockingly kitted out in "Indian" vestments: a tee shirt bearing the face of some generic (unrecognizable to us) "chief," a heavily riveted black leather belt, black trousers, beaded headband, choker, Navajo silver bracelet. They spotted . . . you, Chris, not me, not Harriett. Assuming no one around them spoke French, they began, in high excitement, to speculate about what tribe you might be from . . . "un vrai indien," they murmured joyously, sneaking glimpses of you through their armrests.

You, oblivious, continued to nod and drum to the music in your ears—Pearl Jam, you confided later in the car from the airport. Their voices and their gestures grew more obvious. So I intervened, leaning across to tell you in carefully enunciated English, loud enough for them to hear me, to notice the French people in front of us, the European "wannabes" in their ridiculous costumes. You began to watch them back. Soon, you whispered "Wait 'til you see the guy's jacket!" As indeed Harriett and I soon did as he stood to don it before landing. It was magnificently absurd: black leather, hung with large feathers, decorated with intricate bead work. Along the arms, more feathers, these fake, embossed in the leather itself and painted purple. We all laughed; Harriett, Lakota-style, decided to confront the man once we were all off the plane.

At the baggage turnstile, these strange tourists gathered together, as close to us as they could get. Harriett immediately went to engage them—introducing herself with her customary graciousness, and adding, "Standing Rock Lakota." They treated her courteously, but it was soon clear that they wanted something more than a light-skinned, light-eyed, curly haired woman, however "authentic" Lakota. They wanted you, your long black hair, your black eyes, your dark skin. I saw them coming and turned to warn you. You, however, had already "glided away"—into the crowd, safe from their rapacious tourism.

There is another side to this, too. When you go among Native people, you do not have to carry extra credentials. Your looks (and, though to a lesser extent, your sex) alone win you instant acceptance. No one questions your claims. . . . No one asks you to *make* claims. Never for you the experience that happened to me not long ago, when I met a very famous Native performer for the first time. She instantly dragged me into a women's restroom where, looking me up and down, she demanded "Who are you?" It took me a moment to figure out that she wanted my tribal background. I told her. She continued to peer closely (much too closely—but she is New York and I am not) and at great length at my face, my body, my hair. At last she pronounced her verdict: "I see it," she told me, "inside those blue eyes and that light skin I can see it." She took my arm to signal this acceptance, pulling me back outside.

Or when I was visiting a western university a couple of months ago. Some people asked me if I would be interested in teaching there—and when I said yes, suggested that I should meet the faculty's only Native, "Gene Tall Tree." Of course I agreed. You would walk into such a meeting without hesitation, yes? But not I: I dreaded the "oh sure" look. And it was with enormous relief that I met him—lighter skinned than I, lighter haired, and equally blue-eyed.

So even in Indian Country my acceptance is harder earned, borne more lightly, more timorously. It is a fragile thing—carried inside, almost never outside except with other Native people who know me.

Of course it is not up to you to make people who look like me feel better about it, or—something that happens in spite of both of us—lend me racial credibility. I am fully aware—we all are—that those of us who look "white" enjoy choices others—you—don't. But there are some times when I wish, just for an hour, that I looked what I am, that everyone could see what I saw looking at you that first time in my living room in New York: the same face, the same bones, the same hair (the same big "Indian ears"!) all different only because of color.

Another airport, this in our home country, out west. It was, in fact, Portland, where I found the whole terminal awash in Oregon Trail celebrations. In one gift shop, a video played, over and over, scenes of courage on the trail. A voice described the people—again, over and over: "Brave settlers carrying out the destiny of this great nation."

For sale were dozens of pan-Indian and more local artifacts. Behind the shop counter, a giddily cheery (or did she just seem that way after the aggressive nastiness of New York?) woman explained to an overdressed Yuppie couple that all the goods were "real," made by "real Indians." When they had finished buying their bagful of "authentics," the woman turned to me. I was standing next to a display of silver jewelry decorated with the Columbia River petroglyphs drowned forever by the Celilo Falls Dam.[7] She bragged about the project that resulted in electricity for Portland. She was *boasting* to me, child of the people whose ancient art these pictures were! Child of the people whose sacred places, whose fishing grounds, whose lives had been swept away by the white greed for electricity. . . .

This would not happen to you. (Or would it? Behind my blue eyes, I don't know.)

Of course there are still more intricate complications in this matter of Indian identity—some we meet in the same way.

No Turning Back. . . . our parents and grandparents chose the white road. . . . Turning Back—retrieving our tribal selves, rediscovering lost relations, learning language, learning tradition, learning the origins of the behavior we learned from the old people around us—is it fake? isn't it wannabe? Can it only be thought "authentic" if one accepts the essentialist view (that of the last century's racist scientists) that Indianness is carried just where they said all along: in the blood?

But *is* this journey into a private past necessarily artificial? Is it not Kamau Brathwaite's journey to find the (drum) ties between Barbardos and West Africa? Do we not share the feelings captured in his most recent dedication to his place and people?

I pause for them . . . for those who have gone before . . . *"once you were here . . . hoed the earth . . . and left it for me . . . green rich ready / with yam shoot, the . . . tuberous smooth of cassava . . ."* that I may attempt here . . . that may I have strength to attempt here . . . strength enough to attempt here . . . *trying to play like myself*—no matter how idiosyncratic . . . *"eat and be happy . . . drink / may you rest . . ."* that we may welcome you into the tonnelle.[8]

How can it be that we cannot make the same journey, finding our people, finding ourselves, together?

But still, we mixed bloods, we partially deracinated thousands, will never return all the way home. We have no home.

"To be Hopi is to be *at* Hopi," Angela wrote once. But you and I (and our friends) have never felt this connection, both of us growing up far, far from the tribal people from whom we both come. As I knew more about being Navajo— or Hopi—than about being Nez Perce, so you know more about being Modoc or Klamath than about being what you are. So what does the tribal community mean to you? Is it a pan-Indian world? where "traditions" are the ragged remnants of Gerald Vizenor's "survivance"? Is it a world defined—and limited—by the physical markers of race? Is it the most recent eliminator of outsiders, tribal enrollment?

You will forgive me if I "go academic"? (I can hear you laughing: "This letter is going to have *footnotes*." And it is.)

You have read and heard the enrollment attacks on certain well-known academics, writers, artists, filmmakers, political militants. In their haste to exclude, attackers get confused, muddling "real" fakes with those whose blood quantum is insufficient for particular tribal enrollment—or who did not get enrolled at some point when no one was counting red blood cells. Ward Churchill goes to war with Tim Giago: accusations fly back and forth. Accusations and counter-accusations grow increasingly ridiculous: Hair dye and sunglasses worn indoors. . . . Skin coloring, pancake makeup, braid ties, ponytails . . . whose are *real?* The latest twist: Ward Churchill, according to *News from Indian Country,* has applied for "an honorary/associate membership in the United Ketoowah Band of Cherokee located in Oklahoma." This kind of enrollment "does not require a show of descendancy records according to Ketoowah sources."[9]

Rational voices intervene: from the Navajo nation comes a letter deploring the self-destructiveness of these harsh identity politics: "From the front page of *Indian Country Today,*" writes Kelly Begay, "I have learned about new efforts directed toward describing and limiting the definition of 'Indian.' I can tell you that I'm truly alarmed at what seems to be a concerted drive to create an exclusionary class of people who by their own doing will undo themselves in the end (and destroy all Indian people in a few generations). . . . Any legal definition of any person, place, or concept also creates a concomitant drawing of parameters which not only protect, but exclude as well. If only the legally defined Indian can call him or herself Indian, then all the rest (who might be full-blood but unable to fulfill tribal blood-quantum requirements) are left out in the cold."

Begay suggests criteria for "Who is Indian?" Her first principle seems to me to be a good one—though it will inevitably drive some into a frenzy: "First and paramount, anybody who states that he or she is Indian or descended from Indian people should be considered to be socially identified as Indian. This is the same right and courtesy which is extended to Jews, Irish, French, Italians, Blacks, Hispanics, Asians and any other group." With the same wisdom, the writer also addresses the knotty problem of claims for benefits and privileges: "Any person who claims to be Indian and who wants federal services from the BIA should have to comply with BIA rules and be enrolled in a federally recognized tribe with the required blood quantum."

And, more important, "Any person not asking for services which require them to be enrolled should not be prosecuted or persecuted by any group whether that group be Indian or non-Indian. They should have the legal right to be just who they say they are."[10]

But alas, like most things, it is much more complicated than that. What about the young professor hired recently by the University of Alaska "to increase ethnic diversity on its faculty" whose vita suggested that he was an Alaska Native? A newspaper reports that although adopted by a man who is part Native, the professor is not. He had fooled university officials by writing that he was "tribally affiliated with Ahtna," the regional Native corporation based in Glennallen, and by referring to his "Native American Indian heritage." When challenged, the young man insisted that though he was white, his "entire life" was lived "surrounded by my Alaska Native family." This, then, might rest the case: non-Jewish children adopted by Jewish families and raised in that culture and religion would never be challenged as to their "authenticity" as Jews. But even this claim turns out to be fake. When the supposedly Alaska Native family was questioned, the father—the only member of the family who had Native blood—said that his adopted son had grown up the son of an army officer, "a middle class kid who grew up around a military environment, with cars and television and everything else. . . . If he's used my Native heritage for his personal or professional gain, then that's wrong."[11]

So Kelly Begay's efforts to define the limits of identity-claimants runs into yet another snag: the same non-BIA affirmative action programs that allowed the Michigan students and their parents to defraud the university, the state's taxpayers, and Native people who were genuinely eligible for such programs. And these are not isolated cases: every newspaper from anywhere in Indian Country is full of such efforts by wannabes to advance their careers by claiming blood and heritage they do not possess.[12]

Still, not everyone who falsely claims to be Indian receives the same scorn and derision, even from those most rabid in their pursuit of "wannabes." When two of the Kennedy children, Robert Kennedy, Jr., and Kerry Kennedy Cuomo visited South Dakota in May 1993, *Indian Country Today*, vociferous in its protests against "wouldbes," reported with approval Kerry Kennedy Cuomo's revelation that "As she was growing up and people asked her what she wanted to be, she would always reply, 'I want to be an Indian.'" The origins of her desire were the presents Robert Kennedy brought back to his children after trips West. "The gifts," the paper reported, "were ceremonial bonnets and other Indian artifacts and he would tell them the story behind the gifts." The Kennedys were welcomed with "A special spiritual ceremony . . . held for them at the home of Tim and Lynn Giago. . . . Oglala spiritual leader Rick Two Dog conducted a sweat lodge ceremony for the Kennedys and for Lynn Giago and was told by *Tunkasila* of the names they should be given." Robert, Jr., was given the name "Spotted Eagle, his son [it's Indians, bring the kids!] Bobby Kennedy III was named White Buffalo Boy, Kerry Kennedy was named Good Earth Woman, and Mrs. Giago was named She Holds Them in Her Heart."[13]

Of course there is nothing at all intrinsically wrong about any of this: Oglala Lakota people and their representatives have every right to share sacred ceremonies with outsiders, to name them, to honor them with eagle plumes and so on. But one doubts that any less prominent wannabes, ordinary folks who declared that various artifacts had made them "want to be Indian," would have received the kinds of welcome and acceptance from those who have been among the most vigorous in their pursuit of others much less "white" than the Kennedy children.

All this identity policing was, of course, prompted most recently by implementation of the Indian Arts and Crafts Act. In keeping with the long history of relations between Native people and the feds, this act had good intentions behind it. But instead of protecting Native arts from foreign imitations (particularly from the flood of silver "Indian-type" jewelry made in the Philippines), the act, according to Kelly Begay, "has caused much division and misery to both Indian artists and craftspersons and for non-Indian (or Indian) art dealers."[14]

There is another "identity" act (this one touching close to your home, I think) that similarly poses myriad problems for the would-be purists. It, too, was motivated by good intentions, in this case to stop the drain of tribal children "adopted out" to white families.

[The adoption rate was staggering: white would-be parents, it seems, lusted after Indian children as much as they desired to collect Indian grown-ups. In the year the act was passed, Native American children were being adopted at a rate "20 times higher than the national rate."[15] Not surprisingly, the phrase, "adopted out," is common to all Indian families, including mine from which several of my father's cousins disappeared, their existence noted only by those ominous, foreclosing words.]

But the effects of the 1978 Indian Child Welfare Act, while nowhere near as divisive in Indian Country as the Arts and Crafts Act has been, have been more mixed than most would have hoped. Month after month, cases which reflect every aspect of identity confusions surface in the courts. One recent story may be typical of these. It involves a child of a white mother who gave the boy up for adoption when the child was one day old. He was adopted by white people who took him home to their dairy farm in Idaho. The New York Times reported that although the boy's father, an "Oglala Sioux Indian," "has never seen the boy or sought custody," the tribe has brought suit to reclaim him for his Indian relatives and to bring him back to Pine Ridge.

This child is one-half Lakota. Other children in similar suits possess less blood quantum. In one Oregon case, a child who is one-eighth Cherokee is being taken from the people who have raised him from infancy because "he belongs with Indians." This is not a tribal claim: rather, the state of Oregon is making a decision based solely on its interpretation of the law. Another recent case is knottier still. An eleven-year-old Standing Rock child was informally "adopted" at infancy by her (Choctaw/white) aunt and Standing Rock uncle. This event was quite in keeping with Lakota tradition: the paternal uncle has first option on children whose parents cannot raise them themselves. The new family moved to Kentucky, where they lived for the first decade of the girl's life. Recently, the non-Lakota adoptive mother filed for divorce from her Standing Rock husband. This prompted the tribe to intervene, asking that the girl be sent home to Standing Rock, to grow up in an Indian community. Her mother, anxious to keep the child with her, has hired an attorney. Like other lawyers arguing the "white" side of such cases, he is trying to demonstrate that the child should remain where she is because it is the only life she has ever known. Her religion, her "culture," her "language" are all, the lawyer insists, "typical of a non-Indian child residing in Ashland, Ky."[16]

Who wins in such cases? Does the issue have to do with blood quantum? the half-white child, after all, has half-white blood while the Cherokee boy is only one-eighth Indian. Does white blood not matter then? Moreover, would the same people claiming a child with one-eighth Indian blood allow that same child to enroll if he/she were not an adoption case? And what about children with even less "pure" blood? Most tribal members, as everyone knows, are themselves possessors of highly mixed blood. If a man whose "blood" is primarily Mexican (though of course some of that blood is probably also "Indian") fathers a child with a woman with one-sixteenth Indian blood, what does that make the child? And where do looks matter? If the child "looks" Indian, will he/she be more accepted in the tribe than a child whose genes coughed up a "white-looking" child? We know what the "outside" world will do and say about it. But what about the blood-conscious Indian world? Is the "white-looking" child, raised with a white family but "returned" to tribal life on a reservation at age four or five or twelve, ever going to belong the way a child might who "looked" his/her Indian heritage?

These are not easy questions to answer. The world of identity politics is complicated and vexed. What Shari and I share are the credentials that signal entree to the "in-group." We knew it at once when we met the first time at The Violet. Her blue eyes looked into mine, then at the brown hair, the lightish skin . . . and we both thought "You, too?"

It is a peculiar tie, this mixed-blood tie, artifact of racism, of an identity-shattering American history. It has happened with others, most recently in Davis with a Chicano, friend of a friend. Introduced as having two things in common—Indian blood and Los Angeles—we looked each other over: light skins, blue eyes . . . you, too?

But it is a hiding place—a place where we belong, with you, but also (not more intensely) with each other.

And because it is to this self—hidden from most of the outside world—that we flee, we may protect it more vehemently. Are we "the freebooters of racism"? Do we tumble too heedlessly into a heavily romanticized "Indian Country"? Do we demand that "rez" people stay as we need them to be? our romantic, nostalgic past? untouched, unchanged, unchanging? Do we, who move freely in and out, educated and credentialed, desire a red road fixed in concrete, an alternate path we can take (drive down) when, from time to time, *our* "modernist" (or, for some, post-modernist) world overwhelms? Does our blood quantum distinguish our sentiments from those of our white wannabe colleagues? Or is it something else?

I think of a cartoon I saw recently in *The New Yorker.* It shows two cows and a pig standing in a field gazing into the sky watching a third cow jump over the moon. The pig turns a questioning face to one of her bovine companions who explains, "It's a cow thing. You wouldn't understand."

Whatever our blood, we are all cows, and we do understand that, if nothing else. To paraphrase a most untribal poet, "We *must* love one another or die!"

So you are right.

From our Native land in the west, I send you my grandfather's favorite nickel. I send you my book.

Love,

MORE BLOOD TROUBLES

Trickster wasn't finished with me, it seems. No sooner did we all begin to accept the transformation of the Pennsylvania Quaker Penns into Osages than another very old relative mailed *her* "documents in the case." (Dickens's victims caught in Victorian England's Chancery courts were never so muddled as this!) A marriage certificate shows quite clearly that Grandfather's father, John Swain Penn, was really what we had thought all along: distant (and undistinguished) descendant of William, born in Philadelphia (stories say of mixed-blood parents, but no one knows what the mix *was*), a migrant to Indian territory where he met his Indian wife. It was she whose Indian blood was mixed. Family narratives continued to assign the Blue half of her to the Nez Perce tribe, Wallowa Band. Her other half, the Liptrapp half, although "full-blodded [*sic*] Indian," according to official records, may or may not have been Osage. No one, in fact, knows. All the old people I have contacted—none younger than eighty—know nothing but "Nez Perce" and "something else." They are similarly vague about the Mexican tie: they all know it is there, but that's it. "Consuelo"'s children, all with Spanish names, have disappeared from sight.

Someday I may try to track the Liptrapps. But not now.

Now I must pack my books and bags and head back to New York.

NOTES

CHAPTER 1: GETTING OUT OF DODGE

1. Estelle Reel, U.S. Office of Indian Affairs, *Course of Study for the Indian Schools of the United States: Industrial and Literary* (Washington, D.C.: Government Printing Office, 1901), 264. This text was intended to standardize teaching throughout the National Indian School System, established in 1890.

2. Writing in 1939, another white reformer of Indian life put it succinctly: "Everyone in America or western Europe is eager to make money. The typical American success story is about a poor boy who 'makes good' and that means, in nine cases out of ten, he makes a fortune, becomes a 'captain of industry.'" See Edwin R. Embree, *Indians of the Americas,* with a new introduction by Vine Deloria, Jr. (New York: Macmillan, 1970 [1939]), 235.

3. Reel, *Course of Study for the Indian Schools,* 189. Pratt invented the system of "outing" at his Carlisle, Pennsylvania, boarding school. See a concise description of Pratt's attitudes toward Indians in Hazel W. Hertzberg, *The Search for an American Indian Identity: Modern Pan-Indian Movements* (Syracuse: Syracuse University Press, 1971), 15–18.

4. Reel, 190–91. Any money the children had left after buying their own clothing and "other necessaries" was taken from them and placed into individual savings accounts kept by the school. The purpose of these funds was to allow the boys to "build the home and fit out the farm" and the girls "to furnish the house."

5. Indeed, in a lecture to my class at New York University in spring 1994, Gary Kimble, then executive director of the Association on American Indian Affairs, described his own lifelong fascination and personal identification with the aliens of science fiction and film.

6. The undertaking was prompted by an invitation to give a lecture in a New York University colloquium series, sponsored by the Committee on Culture and Theory, which explored the creation of identities both within and without North America. The other papers given in that series, by Kamau Brathwaite, Ngũgĩ wa Thiong'o, Adrian Piper, and Patricia Williams formed the background against which I began to develop my own ideas about mixed-blood Native American identity, and I should like to acknowledge their contributions to this work.

7. Julia Kristeva, "Talking about Polylogue," in Toril Moi, ed., *French Feminist Thought: A Reader* (Oxford: Basil Blackwell, 1992), 113.

8. The best study of Native American autobiography is Arnold Krupat, *For Those Who*

Come After: A Study of Native American Autobiography (Berkeley: University of California Press, 1985). In addition, both he and Brian Swann have written an important introduction to a collection of autobiographical writings they have edited, *I Tell You Now: Autobiographical Essays by Native American Writers* (Lincoln: University of Nebraska Press, 1987).

9. Gerald Vizenor, "The Ruins of Representation: Shadow Survivance and the Literature of Dominance," *American Indian Quarterly* 17 (Winter 1993): 7–30. Apess's remarkable work is *On Our Own Ground: The Complete Writings of William Apess, a Pequot*, Barry O'Connell, ed. (Amherst: University of Massachusetts Press, 1992).

10. Mark Twain, writing in 1890, described United States imperialism thus: "Extending the Blessings of Civilization to our Brother who Sits in Darkness has been a good trade and has paid well, on the whole; and there is money in it yet, if carefully worked." See Frederick Anderson, ed., *Mark Twain, A Pen Warmed Up in Hell: Mark Twain in Protest* (New York: Harper and Row, 1970), 80. Sixties radicals produced a satirical version of a World War I recruitment poster featuring Uncle Sam looking sternly at passersby, pointing his finger at them and uttering his call to patriotism. The new version, usually printed on T-shirts, employs the same picture, but adds to the familiar portrait:

UNCLE SAM WANTS YOU!
Join the Army
Travel to Exotic, Distant Lands
Meet Exciting, Unusual People,
AND KILL THEM!

11. Longfellow is quoted in Michael Kammen, *Mystic Chords of Memory: The Transformation of Tradition in American Culture* (Ithaca: Cornell University Press, 1991), 82–83, where the author makes this observation about the "pseudo-authenticity" of the poem.

12. Joan Weibel-Orlando, *Indian Country, L.A.* (Urbana: University of Illinois Press, 1991), 202. This question of the extent of genetic influence on identity—considerably more vexed than this author assumes—will be taken up later in these notes. Pop psychologists, together with their New Age followers, would probably claim the left, intuitive, "anti-rational" and therefore "tribal" side was disputing with the European, right, linear, "rational" side, thus ensuring the perpetuation of the "primitive/civilized" dichotomy.

13. E. Jane Gay, *With the Nez Perces: Alice Fletcher in the Field, 1889–92*, Frederick E. Hoxie and Joan T. Mark, eds. (Lincoln: University of Nebraska Press, 1981), 90. That Gay limited her understanding of war to men—male soldiers killing Indian fathers—was altogether typical of the way Americans understood Indians. But, of course killed with males of the Wallowa band were dozens of women, and children of both sexes.

14. Conversations with Erica Harth and Luisa Passerini, both feminist autobiographers of my generation, prompted many of these thoughts, and I thank them.

15. Louise Erdrich, "Indian Boarding School: the Runaways," in *Jacklight* (London: Sphere Books, 1990), 11.

16. *Essay on Man* I, 99–102, in William K. Wimsatt, Jr., ed., *Alexander Pope: Selected Poetry and Prose* (New York: Holt, Rinehart & Winston, 1962), 132. Of course, the poet was not unequivocally scornful of this "anti-European" mind, nor was he uncritical of the Euro-

pean conquest. The lines continue (in the stereotypical veins already prevalent among European intellectuals of Pope's day): "His soul, proud Science never taught to stray / Far as the solar-walk, or milky-way; / Yet simple Nature to his hope has given, / Behind the cloud-topp'd hill, and humbler Heaven, / Some safer world in depth of woods embraced, / Some happier island in the watery waste, / Where slaves once more their native land behold / No fiends torment, no Christians thirst for gold. / To Be, contents his natural desire, / He asks no angel's wings, no seraph's fire; / But thinks, admitted to that equal sky, / His faithful dog shall bear him company" (101–13). The late Norman Rabkin, then a young professor from Harvard, terrorized much of English poetry into our frightened English 102 heads, even as he taught us the language, methods, and indeed, religion of the New Critics.

17. They also encountered a complex social system of "identity creation" *avant la lettre*. See, for example, A. Irving Hallowell's discussion of eighteenth-century Native practices of "Indianization"—of captives of both African and European background—in "American Indians, White and Black: The Phenomenon of Transculturalization," *Current Anthropology* 4, no. 5 (December 1963): 519–30. I am grateful to Shari Huhndorf for this reference.

18. Paula Gunn Allen, "The Autobiography of a Confluence," in Brian Swann and Arnold Krupat, eds., *I Tell You Now* (Lincoln: University of Nebraska Press, 1987), 151.

19. Morrow Mayo, quoted in Mike Davis, *City of Quartz: Excavating the Future in Los Angeles* (New York: Vintage Books, 1992), 17.

20. Our white grandparents, we learned, held views similar to those expressed by the famous western historian H. H. Bancroft. His history of Oregon, quoted by Janet Campbell Hale, who is a mixed-blood descendant of the "founder" of Oregon, John McLoughlin, reads: "It has always seemed to me that the heaviest penalty the servants of the Hudson's Bay Company were obliged to pay for the wealth and authority advancement gave them was the wives they were expected to marry and the progeny they should rear. . . . I never could understand how such men as John McLoughlin and James Douglas could endure the thought of having their name and honors descend to a degenerate posterity. Surely they were of sufficient intelligence to know that by giving their children Indian mothers, their own Scotch, Irish, or English blood would be greatly debased. . . . Perish all the Hudson's Bay Company thrice over, I would say, sooner than bring upon my offspring such foul corruption, sooner than bring into being offspring of such a curse." From *Bloodlines: Odyssey of a Native Daughter* (New York: Random House, 1993), 109.

21. The distrust between those Native people who resisted and those who did not, a distrust we learned as children, remains. According to a story by Timothy Egan in the *New York Times* (June 1, 1993, A12): "Every day, the consequences of those wars, the reduced reservations, the lingering distrust between tribes that sided with whites and those who fought, are felt along the old Oregon Trail." Egan quotes Antone Minthorn, council chairman of the Umatilla Reservation: "People talk about Vietnam veterans and post-traumatic stress syndrome—Indians were born with that. . . . *We* just got off the battle field. It takes time for these things to heal. But they are starting to turn around."

22. General Nelson A. Miles, *Personal Recollections and Observations*, intro. by Robert M. Utley (New York: Da Capo Press, 1969 [1896]), 259, 275, 277.

23. For the tribe's story of the band's collective resistance to the theft of their land, see Allen P Slickpoo, Sr., *Noon Nee-Me-Poo (We the Nez Perces): Culture and History of the Nez Perces*, vol. 1 (Lapwai, Idaho: Nez Perce Tribe of Idaho, 1973), 77–194.

24. Miles, *Personal Recollections*, 280. Dee Brown's 1970 polemic *Bury My Heart at Wounded Knee* (New York: Henry Holt, 1970) recounts tale after tale of starvation, malaria, and death, as tribe after tribe endured their exile. Miles, like every other government official concerned with Indian affairs, was aware of this sorry history long before the Nez Perce people were condemned to the same tragedy.

25. Jane Gay, recalling Joseph's refusal to accept allotted land on the Idaho reservation, described what was, in fact, the experience of my family as well as that of hundreds of other non-reservation Indians: "Joseph," she wrote, "cannot be persuaded to take his land upon the Reservation. He will have none but the Wallowa Valley, from which he was driven; he will remain landless and homeless if he cannot have his own again." In the manner by then typical of American "liberal" observers of Native people, she added, "It was good to see an unsubjugated Indian. One could not help respecting the man who still stood firmly for his rights, after having fought and suffered and been defeated in the struggle." In *With the Nez Perces*, 90.

26. See Weibel-Orlando, *Indian Country*, 13.

27. Weibel-Orlando, 60.

28. That my brother's semi-autobiographical novel *Absence of Angels* (Sag Harbor, N.Y.: Permanent Press, 1994) takes place in Hopiland and Los Angeles was partly determined by this fact of our childhood.

29. The fact that the Joseph legend was, in large measure, created by General Howard, and perpetuated by a variety of non-scholars, did not matter to us. However, our grandfather was always reluctant to speak in praise of Joseph, despite my mother's assiduous anthropological efforts. Janet Campbell Hale's memory of her childhood stories about Joseph suggests that Grandfather may have wanted to spare us a different version of the man. Campbell Hale recalled hearing that the Nez Perce leader was "a mean person, a wicked man who hated women and treated them very badly. . . . Chief Joseph beat women and worse. On one occasion he had one of his wives put to death because he believed she had brought him bad luck at stick games." See *Bloodlines*, 153. It should be noted, further, that much of the "high status" I recall may well have been due to my phenotypically "European" appearance. (Campbell Hale's interpretation is, needless to say, open to dispute. Her claim that Joseph had a wife put to death seems particularly dubious.)

30. In Haruo Aoki, *Nez Perce Texts* (Berkeley: University of California Press, 1979), 123. A great deal of rubbish has been written about Joseph—and, indeed, will probably continue to be written as his myth continues to expand. One of the most absurd and patronizing portraits is Robert Penn Warren's prizewinning epic poem *Chief Joseph of the Nez Perce* (New York: Random House, 1982). In the opening stanza the poet writes, "Boys, bareback, ride naked, / leap on, shout 'Ai-yah!' Shout 'Ai-yee!' / In unbridled glory" (3). It is a poem exclusively about males.

31. Vine Deloria, Jr., *God Is Red* (New York: Dell, 1973), 54.

32. David Wilson Parker, "A Descriptive Analysis of the Lone Ranger as a Form of Popular Art" (Ph.D. diss., Northwestern University, 1955), 278.

33. Louise Erdrich, *Love Medicine* (New York: Henry Holt, 1984), 91. I am grateful to Janet McAdams for reminding me of this observation.

34. With apologies for punning with a term from British colonial years in India.

35. Anne Marie Penn Hamilton, private correspondence, September 9, 1993.

36. The use of Eco in this context is that of Gerald Vizenor. See *Crossbloods: Bone Courts, Bingo, and Other Reports* (Minneapolis: University of Minnesota Press, 1990), 55.

37. Muschamp, "Who Should Define a City?" *New York Times*, August 15, 1993, 32–H.

38. Davis, *City of Quartz*, 26–27.

39. Luis J. Rodriguez. *Always Running: La Vida Loca: Gang Days in L.A.* (Willimantic, Conn.: Curbstone Press, 1993), 87–88.

40. From *Shadows in Paradise*, quoted in Davis, *City of Quartz*, 50.

41. Sherman Alexie remarks, "I could spend my whole life on the reservation and never once would I see a friend of mine and think how Indian he looked. But as soon as I get off the reservation, among all the white people, every Indian gets exaggerated." See *The Lone Ranger and Tonto Fist-fight in Heaven* (New York: Atlantic Monthly Press, 1993), 219.

42. Here again, the language of social science reveals more than it intends. Weibel-Orlando's remark about a mixed-blood man suggests that race is read not only by physical appearance, but also by superficial signs of culture: Indian jewelry, feathers, moccasins, etc. Speaking of one leader of the L.A. Indian community, Weibel-Orlando writes, "He does not embody obvious markers of ethnic group membership. He is not phenotypically Indian. . . . He does not announce his ethnicity through easily recognized emblems such as Indian jewelry, clothing, or public displays of himself in stereotypical Indian activities." In *Indian Country, L.A.*, 203.

43. This is the formulation used by Diana Fane in "The Language of Things: Stewart Culin as Collector," in Fane, Ira Jacknis, Lise M. Breen, eds., *Objects of Myth and Memory: American Indian Art at the Brooklyn Museum* (Brooklyn: Brooklyn Museum, 1991), 13–27. Culin, a collector who worked at the turn of the century, believed that Indians were "vanishing." "If our museums are ever to have good collections of Indian things they must waste no time in setting out after them, for none will be left ten years from now," he wrote in 1900. "There are no real Indians among the young." (*Objects*, 19)

44. Thomas King's "A Seat in the Garden," collected in Craig Lesley, ed., *Talking Leaves: Contemporary Native American Short Stories* (New York: Laurel, 1991), 184–94, cleverly satirizes movie Indians.

45. Checkerboarding resulted from many government practices that allowed outsiders to move into land supposedly "reserved" for Indians as compensation for the land they "gave up." Today, many reservations are literally owned by non-Indians. The Nez Perce reservation in Idaho, for example, is 90 percent outsider-owned.

46. The importance of a positive image of the West to the collective imagination of the United States ruling classes was underscored by the outcry occasioned by a recent exhibit at the Smithsonian Institution that was critical of westward expansion. Ivan Karp told me

that criticism of that exhibit was immediately reflected by the cutting of federal funds for the museum.

47. As Alice Walker puts it in *Temple of My Familiar,* "Blue eyes are like money; they buy your way in."

48. Vine Deloria, Jr., writing of traditional versions of the Battle of the Little Big Horn in *Custer Died for Your Sins: An Indian Manifesto* (New York: Avon, 1970 [1969]), points out that Indian numbers are always increased so that "Custer stands out as a man fighting against insurmountable odds." But while non-Natives may accept the notion that Indians multiply whenever a battle looms, Indians wonder "how what they saw were twenty thousand Indians could be fed when gathered into one camp. What a tremendous pony herd must have been gathered there, what a fantastic herd of buffalo must have been nearby to feed that amount of Indians, what an incredible source of drinking water must have been available for fifty thousand animals and some twenty thousand Indians! . . . Just figuring water-needs to keep that many people and animals alive for a number of days must have been incredible. If you have estimated correctly, you will see that the Little Big Horn was the last great *naval* engagement of the Indian wars" (151–52).

49. A process similar to that employed by colonial powers in Africa—and detailed in Ngũgĩ wa Thiong'o's *De-Colonizing the Mind: The Politics of Language in African Literature* (London/Nairobi: Heinemann, 1986).

50. Anne Marie Penn Hamilton, private correspondence, September 9, 1993.

51. The term is that of M. Annette Jaimes, who titled a recent collection of essays *The State of Native America: Genocide, Colonization, and Resistance* (Boston: South End Press, 1992).

52. What assimilation there was was further promoted by my grandmother, the daughter of European immigrants. Her father had worked in a meat-packing plant in St. Louis, rising to the rank of foreman. She was the oldest of seven children and as such was unable to go beyond high school before going to work, as a secretary, an occupation she kept until retirement. Her drive to join the American middle class left little room for children attempting to retain their tribal lives. It is a tribute to her and my grandfather's efforts that both their sons "succeeded," my father getting degrees from UCLA and USC, and my uncle a degree from Stanford.

53. Quoted in Davis, *City of Quartz,* 56. Despite his dreams, however, my father had to refuse the scholarship because it was not enough to allow him to continue to help support his parents and younger brother. This is a dilemma still faced by Native American and other poor students, whose pleas to most university scholarship committees fall on ears deafened by privilege.

54. Davis, 162–63.

55. The film was made by Kent MacKenzie in 1961. An interesting commentary on these observations is provided by Jack D. Forbes's recently republished (and revised) *Africans and Native Americans: The Language of Race and the Evolution of Red-Black Peoples* (Urbana: University of Illinois Press, 1993 [1988]). The book argues that cultural and biological exchanges occurred between Native America and Africa, as well as with people from those continents and Europe, in the course of the period known as "European discovery," roughly

from the late fifteenth century on. People of the Americas, in Forbes's view, were taken to Africa in the slave trade, where they mixed with indigenous populations. Many "mixed bloods" then became victims of further slaving, sometimes ending up in the Caribbean, sometimes in North America, and so on.

56. Jack Forbes, growing up in L.A. in the 1950s, discovered much of his Indian identity in the library of the museum. See "Shouting Back to the Geese," in Swann and Krupat, eds., *I Tell You Now,* 111–25.

57. The struggle was to be a long one. That particular child, I recall, *was* reburied. But dozens of "scalps, human bones, sacred ceremonial articles, etc." remained when the Indians of All Tribes organized against the museum's retention of these things. See "The Southwest Museum: Museum Policy: The Only Good Indian Is a Dead Indian," *La Raza* 1, no. 4: 64–67. The author points out that the museum also held "a display of Chicano bones. Morbidly," the writer continued, "they are recognizing our anthropological similarities with the Indians" (64).

58. Charles Lummis, *Letters from the Southwest, Sept. 20, 1884, to March 14, 1885,* James W. Byrkit, ed. (Tucson: University of Arizona Press, 1989), xxii. Lummis's romanticization of Native people was common to his generation, but the usual attitude was not always as positive as Lummis's.

59. Luna has "exhibited" himself in various museums, lying still on a table, dressed in "Indian clothing." Films of his efforts show gallery visitors looking him over carefully and discussing him as a work of art, unable to consider that a live Indian can hear their words. I am grateful to Lloyd Oxendine for introducing me to this artist's work.

60. Lummis, *Letters from the Southwest,* xxxv.

61. Rose, "Excavation at Santa Barbara Mission," *Going to War with All My Relations* (Flagstaff, Ariz.: Northland, 1993), 7–8.

CHAPTER 2: ANCESTRAL BURDENS

1. Harriett Skye, "The Long Journey to the North," *Indian Affairs: Newsletter of the Association on American Indian Affairs, Inc.* 129 (Winter 1993): 1. Skye's report concerns the repatriation of remains that had long been the object of scientific investigation at the Smithsonian Institution and the Peabody Museum. The reburial took place in October 1993.

2. Thanks to Alfred Arteaga for this quote.

3. For details, see Francis Jennings, *The Invasion of America: Indians, Colonialism, and the Cant of Conquest* (New York: Norton, 1976), 166–68.

4. Russell, *The American Indian Digest* (Phoenix: Thunderbird Enterprises, 1993), 11.

5. On the subject of genocide, see Ward Churchill, *Indians Are Us? Culture and Genocide in Native North America* (Monroe, Me.: Common Courage Press, 1994), especially 11–63.

6. Quoted in Robert F. Heizer, ed., *The Destruction of California Indians: A Collection of Documents from the Period 1847 to 1865 in Which Are Described Some of the Things That Happened to Some of the Indians of California* (Santa Barbara and Salt Lake City: Peregrine Smith, 1974), 268, 269.

7. From Robert E. Beider, *Science Encounters the Indian, 1820–1880: The Early Years of American Ethnology* (Norman: University of Oklahoma Press, 1986), 63.

8. Miles, *Personal Recollections and Observations* (New York: Da Capo Press 1969 [1896]), 74.

9. Although I cannot claim to have read every physical anthropologist's work, I did explore New York University's admittedly sparse library shelves, looking for *any* mention of the questionable provenance of bones used by physical anthropologists. I found none.

10. Miles, 66. Linda Hogan's *Mean Spirit* (New York: Atheneum, 1990) features a group of "hill Indians" who act as "watchers" over Osage people and their graves, both made vulnerable to white greed by the oil found on Osage land. "Collectors," in Hogan's novel as in life, dug up bodies, cut off heads—and other body parts—and boiled them to obtain "clean" skulls or bones.

11. Tony Hillerman, *Talking God* (New York: Harper and Row, 1989).

12. Recent texts from that discipline are also much less open about the provenance of their objects of study. See, e.g., Frank Spencer, ed., *A History of American Physical Anthropology, 1930–1980* (New York: Academic Press, 1982), especially articles by Albert B. Harper and William S. Laughlin ("Inquiries into the Peopling of the New World: Development of Ideas and Recent Advances," 281–301) and George J. Armelagos, David S. Carlson, and Dennis P. Van Gerven ("The Theoretical Foundations and Development of Skeletal Biology," 305–21). None of the authors so much as nods in the direction of acknowledging the problems inherent in the Indian evidence they use for their "research."

13. It has been estimated that there are skeletal remains and burial objects of about two million Native people currently held in United States museums, state historical societies, universities, and National Park Service offices. Their actual nature is cloaked by the language of "techno-science," which refers to them as "resources," or even more abstractly, as "the data base." (Those funerary objects that have aesthetic merit disappear into the category of "art.") Maintaining these resources for scientific study has at least two consequences for tribal people: first, grieving cannot begin, and second, the spirits of the dead continue to wander, disturbing the living in their quest for proper burial rites.

14. It should be noted that thousands of pots coveted by collectors once held the ceremonially buried remains of Native people. Like their provenance, their purpose is carefully disguised, lest owners bear a taint.

15. The picture shows a disreputable-looking, unidentified man, grinning toothlessly at his friend with the camera, holding an Indian skull in his left hand. It illustrates a critical article by Aaron Sugerman, "The Treasures of America . . . Looted!" In typical fashion, however, the author is most outraged not by the desecration of Native burial sites but rather by the destruction of countryside. See *Condé Nast Traveler* (July 1992): 80–85, 121–24. (My thanks to Grant Besser for the citation.)

16. Vizenor, *Earthdivers: Tribal Narratives on Mixed Descent* (Minneapolis: University of Minnesota Press, 1981), 166.

17. See Pieter Hovens, "Native North American Studies in the Netherlands," in *European Review of Native American Studies* 7, no. 2 (1993): 1–4, and citation, "G. van Steenhoven De Hope, deur van verleden en toekomst, *De Kiva* 30(2): 57–66, illus. Amsterdam 1993." (ibid., 50) There are similar Indian groups, with journals, all over Europe. Turin's group, for example, publishes a journal called *Teepee.*

18. See Walter Benjamin, *Charles Baudelaire: A Lyric Poet in the Age of High Capitalism*, trans. Harry Zohn (London: New Left Books, 1973), 166.

19. The ad is found in *American Indian Art* (Autumn 1991): 12.

20. Price, *Primitive Art in Civilized Places* (Chicago: University of Chicago Press, 1989). The advertisement's efforts to stimulate the collection of Navajo blankets contains a second, unacknowledged, discourse: that involved with the European invaders' genocidal distribution among Indian people of blankets collected from the corpses of smallpox victims. This "recycling" effort resulted in the deaths of many thousands of Indian people.

21. Despite my mother's considerable efforts to counter the barrage of misinformation, I discovered that the influence of scurrilous images of California's hapless "Digger Indians" persisted somewhere below the surface of my mind when I first met people from several of the tribes represented in the museums of my childhood in the 1970s. The complexity of their pre-Spanish invasion cultures amazed me as they retaught me California history—a process accompanied by my profound embarrassment.

22. One general study of the period is Stan Steiner, *The New Indians* (New York: Harper and Row, 1967). A collection of essays describing those years is Alvin M. Josephy, Jr., ed., *Red Power: The American Indians' Fight for Freedom* (Lincoln: University of Nebraska Press, 1971).

23. See Vine Deloria's *God Is Red*, 29–38, for a moving discussion of grave-robbing. Stanford University's decision to return bones and religious artifacts for repatriation is described in Rosemary Cambra, "Restoring Life to the Dead," in Peter Nabokov, ed., *Native American Testimony* (New York: Viking, 1991), 424–27. For much of the information discussed here I am indebted to Grant Besser, who collaborated with me on a talk, "Bone Courts," given at Emory University's Multi-Cultural Center Speakers' Series, March 21, 1991.

24. See "Illinois to Shut an Exhibit of Indian Skeletons," *New York Times*, November 29, 1991, A30.

25. John Harmon, "Controversy Unearthed in Georgia Hills," *Atlanta Journal/Atlanta Constitution*, August 16, 1993, B1, B4. My source for these clippings and for those from the paper that follow, was, once again, Rainier Spencer.

26. "Proper Respect for the Dead," *Atlanta Constitution*, August 17, 1993, A18.

27. See "Letters," *Atlanta Constitution*, August 21, 1993, n.p.

28. In Arizona, too, a controversy involving business people, archaeologists, and Indians has erupted because of the state's efforts to comply locally with federal laws. See David Roberts, "Together, Scientists and Indians Explore the Conundrums of Casa Malpais," *Smithsonian* 22, no. 12 (March 1992): 28–37. This article was sent to me by Patricia White McClanahan.

29. *New York Times*, July 21, 1993.

30. Deloria, *God Is Red* (New York: Grosset and Dunlap, 1973), 32–33.

31. "Some Museums Complying with Return of Relics," *Indian Country Today*, November 17, 1993, B7.

32. Gerald Vizenor has proposed to assign legal rights to bones in order to address this problem. See *Crossbloods*, 62–82.

33. Wounded Knee seared the collective Native imagination. In addition to becoming

the title of Dee Brown's 1971 polemic (*Bury My Heart at Wounded Knee*), Buffy Sainte-Marie's recent record album includes a song with the same title. In the present decade, the events of Wounded Knee are meant to be put behind the Lakota—and other Native—people. This is because the present generation of young people is the "seventh generation," the generation when reconciliation becomes possible. Thus the motto of this year's Wounded Knee ride, "Wiping the Tears of Seven Generations," an event recorded in a documentary of the same title, produced by Gary Rhine and directed by Gary Rhine and Fidel Moreno for Kifaru Productions.

34. See *New York Times*, Section A, 12L.

35. Michael Kammen, *Mystic Chords of Memory: The Transformation of Tradition in American Culture* (Ithaca: Cornell University Press, 1991), 739, n.83.

36. See Deloria, *God Is Red*, chap. 2. Donna Haraway's work, in *Primate Visions: Gender, Race, and Nature in the World of Modern Science* (New York: Routledge, 1989), and *Simians, Cyborgs, and Women: The Reinvention of Nature* (New York: Routledge, 1991), thoroughly dismantles any pretensions "science" or "scientists" might have continued to entertain about "objectivity," especially when confronting the non-Euro-American world.

37. Ishi was a member of the Yahi tribe of the once three-tribe strong Yana people.

38. Quoted in Vizenor, *Crossbloods*, 62.

39. Rainier Spencer sent me a story from the *Atlanta Journal and Constitution*, "America's Discovery: How the Indians Arrived," by Mike Toner (February 13, 1993, E-1). It describes the work of an Emory University geneticist, Douglas Wallace, who has studied the DNA of bones in the Emory collection to demonstrate that Native people inhabited the continent as much as 34,000 years ago, a "fact" which justifies Emory's continued ownership of Native bones, but which, ironically, is already "known" to Native people themselves.

40. This story sounds like something Vine Deloria, Jr., would recount, but I am relying on memory.

41. In Deloria, *Custer Died*, 83, 85.

42. In M. Annette Jaimes, ed., *The State of Native America: Genocide, Colonization, and Resistance* (Boston: South End Press, 1992), 403–22.

43. An apparent inability to understand this inseparability of one's acts from one's moral life has complicated many commentators' judgments of notable men whose pasts include some flirtation (or more) with fascism. These include Paul De Man, Martin Heidegger, and Mircea Eliade. The question of whether or not their youthful fascism should influence historians' judgment of them might benefit from a reading of Primo Levi's *The Drowned and the Saved*, which explores such ethical and moral questions with great subtlety and wisdom.

44. Donna Haraway suggests that the group of linguistic anthropologists might have been even more exclusive than these more general categories might suggest. See her "Remodeling the Human Way of Life: Sherwood Washburn and the New Physical Anthropology, 1950–1980," in George W. Stocking, Jr., *Bones, Bodies, Behavior: Essays on Biological Anthropology* (Madison: University of Wisconsin Press, 1988), 206–59, which discusses the tiny circle of men—and a few women—who inhabit one sub-specialty of the discipline.

45. The phrase is used over and over since the publication of the essential text by Ngũgĩ wa Thiong'o, *De-Colonizing the Mind*.

46. I am grateful to Miryam Yataco for this insight, as well as many, many others.

47. The event took place in November, in conjunction with the Margaret Mead Film Festival. I was moderating the discussion of Ava Hamilton's film and that of an Australian aboriginal filmmaker, Frances Peters. I might add that none of the several Native Americans attending disagreed with Ava Hamilton's position.

48. See James H. Howard and Victoria Lindsay Levine, *Choctaw Music and Dance* (Norman: University of Oklahoma Press, 1990), as well as several articles.

49. From private correspondence, August 5, 1994.

50. Unfortunately for this feminist, many of those most enamored of themselves seem to be women scholars. Perhaps the nadir of self-voyeurism was reached when Jane Gallop decided to publish a photograph of herself giving birth for the cover of her aptly titled *Thinking Through the Body* (New York: Columbia University Press, 1988).

51. Price, *Primitive Art*, 5.

52. The metaphor is from David Lodge, review of David Bromwich, *Politics by Other Means: Higher Education and Group Thinking* (New Haven: Yale University Press, 1992), in the *New York Times Book Review* (October 4, 1992): 7.

53. Price, *Primitive Art*, 56.

54. Price, 58.

55. Price, 59.

56. Price, 70.

57. Price, 77.

58. Price, 78, 79.

59. Price, 77.

60. Price, 43.

61. Price, 93.

62. Price, 105.

63. In Stan Steiner, *New Indians*, 130.

64. Mel Thom's and Robert Thomas's statements come from Steiner, *New Indians*, 185, 154.

65. Barbara Tedlock, *The Beautiful and the Dangerous: Dialogues with the Zuni Indians* (New York: Penguin, 1992).

66. Tedlock, xi, xii, xiii.

67. Tedlock, xiii–xiv.

68. Joy Harjo, *In Mad Love and War* (Middletown, Conn.: Wesleyan University Press, 1990), 7–8.

69. Louis, *Among the Dog Eaters* (Albuquerque: West End Press, 1992), 13–15; Rose, *The Half Breed Chronicles and Other Poems* (Albuquerque: West End Press, 1985), 56–57. There are dozens more examples, in both prose and poetry.

70. Vitali Vitaliev, "Corners of Tasmania," *Élan, The European* (March 4–10, 1994): 16–17.

71. See Hardacre, "The Lone Woman of San Nicolas Island," in R. F. Heizer and M. A. Whipple, eds., *The California Indians: A Source Book* (Berkeley: University of California Press, 1971 [1951]), 282. The editors point out (272) that this woman was "the stimulus for the children's book, *Island of the Blue Dolphins*" by Scott O'Dell (1960).

72. Hardacre, 283.

73. Hardacre, 281.

74. Hardacre, 284.

75. Quoted in Ronald Wright, *Stolen Continents: The "New World" through Indian Eyes* (Boston: Houghton Mifflin, 1992), 332.

CHAPTER 3: BUFFALO BILL'S DEFUNCT

1. The title is taken from e. e. cummings's poem of the same name.

2. From J. J. Warner, Benjamin Hayes, and J. P. Widney, *Historical Sketch of Los Angeles County, California* (1987), quoted in John and Laree Caughey, *Los Angeles: Biography of a City* (Berkeley: University of California Press, 1976), 161, 165.

3. Durham, *Columbus Day* (Albuquerque: West End Press, 1993), 4. It is interesting to note that many African-Americans share the apparent white longing to be Indian. See Peter Noel, "Cutting on the Bias: Readers Sound Off on the Racism Quotient Test," *Village Voice* (March 9, 1993): 24, 26–27, which reports that among Blacks who wished to change race, some 35 percent wished to change into Native Americans (compared to only 20 percent of whites).

4. Indeed, the creators of the Lone Ranger radio show used such language to indicate that Tonto was Indian. When the television serials were made, a reluctant Jay Silverheels was forced to continue this "'Tonto-talk."

5. In *Atlas* (New York: Alfred A. Knopf, 1983), unpaged.

6. Quoted in Walter D. Mignolo, "When Speaking Was Not Good Enough: Illiterates, Barbarians, Savages, and Cannibals," in René Jara and Nicholas Spadaccini, eds., *Amerindian Images and the Legacy of Columbus* (Minneapolis: University of Minnesota Press, 1992), 315.

7. Quoted in Mignolo, 316.

8. Quoted in David E. Johnson, "The Place of the Translator in the Discourses of Conquest: Hernán Cortés's *Cartas de relación* and Roland Joffe's *The Mission*," in Jara and Spadaccini, eds., 403.

9. Pagden, *European Encounters with the New World: From Renaissance to Romanticism* (New Haven: Yale University Press, 1993), 119.

10. Pagden, 120.

11. This is a very French view of matters linguistic, in which "uselessness" is a positive thing. It would not be so in the more pragmatic Anglo-Saxon tongues. The Baron de Lahontan, author of *Dialogues curieux entre l'auteur et un sauvage de bon sens qui a voyagé*, 1703, is quoted in Pagden, 127.

12. Pagden, 132. It is interesting to note here the emergence of stereotypes that would soon be universally familiar: absence of *physical* signs (at least those recognized by European "universals") of curiosity became "stoicism" and" "emotionlessness."

13. Deloria, *Custer Died for Your Sins: An Indian Manifesto* (New York: Avon, 1970 [1969]), 119–20.

14. Cooper, *The Last of the Mohicans: A Narrative of 1757* (New York: Charles Scribner's Sons, 1991 [1826]), 346–47. Arnold Krupat reminds me that Leslie Fiedler's *Love and Death in the American Novel* (New York: Stein and Day, 1966) discusses Cooper's work at some length. Although the work's sexism and racism combined to erase it from my memory

shortly after I read it in the 1970s, I may have recalled some of his insights when rethinking Cooper. See Fiedler, 179 ff.

15. From *Fenimore Cooper's Literary Offenses* (1895), collected in Bernard De Voto, ed., *The Portable Mark Twain* (New York: Penguin, 1979), 544, 545–46, 548, 549.

16. Henry Wadsworth Longfellow, "The Song of Hiawatha," lines 108–111.

17. Melville, *Moby-Dick* (New York: Modern Library, 1950), 172, 175, 285, 504. *Moby-Dick* is infused with "Indians." Not only is the ship, the *Pequod*, named after "an extinct" tribe, and Nantucket an Indian island, but Queequeg, a South Pacific islander, employs a "tomahawk" pipe, Indian clothing, hair styles, and so on. Indians also provide metaphors for much of what Ishmael observes during the voyage.

18. *Tom Sawyer*, 77. Nineteenth-century literature was full of "evil" half-bloods such as "Injun Joe."

19. Laura Ingalls Wilder, *Little House on the Prairie* (New York: HarperCollins, 1991 [1935]), 46–47.

20. Wilder, 134.

21. Wilder, 139–40.

22. Wilder, 140–41.

23. Wilder, 235, 236. The Juniata is a river in Pennsylvania. The Indians referred to in this song are, of course, "safe" Indians, long "vanished" from their homes.

24. Wilder, 290–91.

25. Ibid.

26. Quotes from Carol Ryrie Brink, *Caddie Woodlawn* (New York: Macmillan, 1973 [1935]), 304–5. Chapter 14 is titled (oh capitalism), "A Dollar's Worth." The title refers to Caddie's explanation to her brother Tom as to why she had to spend the whole dollar, and not just part of it: "No, Tom, it had to be all of it. I wanted to drive that awful lonesome look out of their eyes, and it did, Tom. It did!"

27. Brink, 272.

28. Brink, 272–75.

29. See, for example, a work by an author who, like *Caddie Woodlawn*'s author, Carol Ryrie Brink, lived in Idaho and who purported to tell the story of *her* pioneering forebears' trip west, *Lucretia Ann in the Golden West* by Ruth Gipson Plowhead (Caldwell, Idaho: Caxton Printers, 1935). In this story, the Indians—males, speaking in grunts—are *never* close to being "civilized," though there are "good" Indians who repeatedly rescue the golden-haired, blue-eyed Lucretia Ann. Their barbarism is signaled repeatedly through the book by their nakedness, their terrifying cries, their dirt, their terrible eating manners. The irony of this work is—among other things—that it purports to tell of "Oregon" Indians, none of whom bore any resemblance at all to their portrait in this work.

30. See, inter alia, *Winnetou: A Novel*, trans. Michael Shaw (New York: Seabury Press, 1977 [1890]).

31. *The Indian in the Cupboard* (New York: Avon—"a division of the Hearst Corporation"—1980), 9, 10. It must be said, however, that despite the best efforts of many anthropologists, a quick examination of recent American children's books suggests that U.S. writers, at least, seem to have gotten the point at last. See, for example, a recent work by

"Carolyn Keene," *Nancy Drew: The Kachina Doll Mystery* (New York: Pocket Books, 1981). In this work, the Hopis involved manage to speak the same English as everyone else, and, indeed, to behave in a "normal" manner.

32. General Nelson A. Miles, *Personal Recollections and Observations* (New York: Da Capo Press, 1969 [1896]), 75.

33. Cass, writing in *North American Review*, 1826, is quoted in William Clements, "'Tokens of Literary Faculty': Native American Literature and Euroamerican Translation in the Early Nineteenth Century," in Brian Swann ed., *On the Translation of Native American Literatures* (Washington, D.C.: Smithsonian Institution Press, 1992), 35. James Fenimore Cooper includes a Wyandot character speaking in "a deep and guttural voice" in *Last of the Mohicans*, 320.

34. Mrs. C. M. Kirkland, quoted in Clements, 40.

35. Quoted in Jenni Calder, *There Must Be a Lone Ranger: The American West in Film and Reality* (New York: McGraw-Hill, 1974), 57.

36. But also "lone," as Arnold Krupat reminds me, because he is the last of a group of Texas Rangers, ambushed by a gang he resolves to capture.

37. I should never have guessed that he had thought about this at all, but when my sister and I were joking about having rewatched Tonto and the Lone Ranger on video, my father suddenly intervened to say, "Of course you realize what the name 'Tonto' means? it means 'fool' or 'idiot.'" Had he sat there silently musing about this as we listened to our radio show? He says he doesn't remember how he made this connection, he just "always knew it."

38. The creators of the Lone Ranger, in fact, made a great point of keeping the Ranger's language "pure." According to one agency publication, "correctly spoken English and proper grammar are taught through imitation. When the child hears the type of language used by the Lone Ranger he imitates that language." Amid other instructions, the creator of the series, George Trendle, instructed his chief writer, Fran Striker, to keep "pure English, good grammar when the Lone Ranger speaks." See David Wilson Parker, "A Descriptive Analysis of the Lone Ranger as a Form of Popular Art" (Ph.D. diss., Northwestern University, 1955), 197, 137.

39. Quoted in Parker, 178.

40. This is a paraphrase of the version recounted in Ariel Dorfman, *The Empire's Old Clothes: What the Lone Ranger, Babar, and Other Innocent Heroes Do to Our Minds* (New York: Pantheon, 1983), 211.

41. As for "Silver," his past was venerable. Here is Herman Melville: "Most famous in our Western annals and Indian traditions is that of the White Steed of the Prairies; a magnificent milk-white charger, large-eyed, small-headed, bluff-chested, and with the dignity of a thousand monarchs in his lofty, overscorning carriage. He was the elected Xerxes of vast herds of wild horses, whose pastures in those days were only fenced by the Rocky Mountains and the Alleghanies. . . . The flashing cascade of his mane, the curving comet of his tail, invested him with housings more resplendent than gold and silver beaters could have furnished him. . . . In whatever aspect he presented himself, always to the bravest Indians he was the object of trembling reverence and awe." *Moby-Dick*, 189–90.

42. Oh, those ungrateful minorities! Both remarks quoted in Parker, "A Descriptive Analysis," 202, 207.

43. In truth, however, it would not have been our favorite had our parents allowed us to listen to "Dial M for Murder." But that was forbidden.

44. Miles, *Personal Recollections*, 252.

45. Trendle is quoted by Dorfman, *The Empire's Old Clothes*, 130. The disease of "graphomania" is described by Milan Kundera in *The Book of Laughter and Forgetting*, trans. by Michael Henry Heim (New York: Alfred A. Knopf, 1980).

46. Dorfman, 128–29. This anti-macho character was a considerable part of "Tonto's" appeal to us. The term "double consciousness" is, of course, that of W. E. B. Du Bois.

47. See Marc Swetlitz, "The Minds of Beavers and the Minds of Humans: National Suggestion, National Selection, and Experience in the Work of Lewis Henry Morgan," in George W. Stocking, Jr., ed., *Bones, Bodies, Behavior: Essays on Biological Anthropology* (Madison: University of Wisconsin Press, 1988), 63.

48. David Zinman, *Saturday Afternoon at the Bijou* (New York: Castle Books, 1973), 114.

49. Parker, "Descriptive Analysis," 208, 166. Interestingly, it was claimed that American soldiers, going "over the top" in the Battle of the Bulge, were heard crying out "Heigh-yo Silver." See 211.

50. Parker, 213.

51. Parker, 172.

52. Quoted in Parker, 224.

53. Parker, 277.

54. Ariel Dorfman recounts one adventure, "The Buffalo Herd," which is about a Sioux chief who decides to help defend white ownership of what was rightfully—by treaty— Sioux land. "The one who's been plundered becomes a retroactive guardian of the laws that gave rise to the plunder. Whoever attempts to go against those laws, whether they're Indian or white, will receive their exemplary sanction." Thus, "Neither in reality nor in the script will the Indians ever again recover Wild Horse Valley" (80).

55. D'Arcy McNickle, *The Surrounded* (Albuquerque, University of New Mexico Press, 1976 [1936]), 182.

56. Ideology-carrying cereal brings e. e. cummings to mind: "as freedom is a breakfast-food / or truth can live with right and wrong." See "25," in *Poems: 1923–1954* (New York: Harcourt, Brace & World, 1968), 366.

57. Perhaps needless to say, Straight Arrow will "save" the tribes by making peace with whites—at the latter's terms.

58. Henry William Elson, *History of the United States of America* (New York: Macmillan, 1904), 30. The author insists that he has been as fair as possible. Not for this writer any accusation of bias! "My aim has been to present an accurate narrative of the origin and growth of our country and its institutions" (v). This professor got his "unbiased" information about Indians from "Mr. Stewart Culing," [probably Culin], "former curator and Indian specialist at the U. of Pennsylvania, who kindly read and criticized the chapter dealing with the Indian character" (vii). Culin was also the curator of the Brooklyn Museum's Indian collection, much of which he collected during several trips to the West. Although this

work was written nearly a hundred years ago, a student told me that one of my colleagues described Indian religious beliefs in much the same terms of constant fear.

59. Lummis, *Letters from the Southwest, September 20, 1884, to March 14, 1885*, James W. Byrkit, ed. (Tucson: University of Arizona Press, 1989), 19–20.

60. It should be noted, however, that Native people have more recently turned the insult on its head, "re-appropriating" these names with pride. Forcing white people to say and write the Indian names assigned by translators has a salutarily stunning effect, especially in political confrontations. In fact, so desired are such names that a rash of "self-naming" has broken out among "wannabes," some of whom insult Native people by assuming the names of great leaders, such as Cochise. Of course, naming ceremonies, which differ throughout Native America, have other kinds of importance than those understood by this practice of self-naming or of "translation." An important discussion of these issues is Paul Smith's "Challenging the Non-Indian Community" in *Indigenous Woman* 1, no. 1 (Spring 1991): 52–53.

61. I am grateful to the Pow Wow Club's president, Mr. Bill Harper, who kindly sent me several items from his collection of Straight Arrow memorabilia, including copies of comics, the newsletter of this collectors' club, some 'Injun-uity' cards, and so on. The group is dedicated to ensuring that the public remember that Nabisco's Straight Arrow—played by a white actor—was a positive, "authentic" portrayal of Indian life as it was once lived in the West.

62. Lummis, *Letters*, 71. The use of the term "dialect" to describe Indian languages was part of the universal denigration of Native culture—a practice that continues, as we shall see. Later, in a fit of turn-of-the-century political correctness, Lummis attacked the settlers' use of "Manitou" to name their town: "these folks would never think of naming a town God in plain English, but it's all right in Choctaw" (71–72).

63. Here, again, I am grateful to Mr. Bill Harper for the material quoted.

64. Quoted in John and Laree Caughey, *Los Angeles: Biography of a City* (Berkeley: University of California Press, 1976), 180.

65. Oliver Howard, *My Life and Experiences Among Our Hostile Indians: A Record of Personal Observations, Adventures, and Campaigns Among the Indians of the Great West, with Some Account of Their Life, Habits, Traits, Religion, Ceremonies, Dress, Savage Instincts, and Customs in Peace and War* (New York: Da Capo Press, 1972), 116.

66. Durham, "Those Dead Guys for a Hundred Years," in Arnold Krupat and Brian Swann, eds., *I Tell You Now: Autobiographical Essays by Native American Writers* (Lincoln: University of Nebraska Press, 1987), 163. Emory University is not entirely staffed by an upper administration of flicking tongues, though it has an unfair share. New York University, on the other hand, could corner the market.

67. Wendy Rose offered this description in an interview in Laura Coltelli, *Winged Words: American Indian Writers Speak* (Lincoln: University of Nebraska Press, 1990), 124. "Very often in a confrontational or in an uncomfortable situation, an Indian will turn into a potted plant." A preference for silence over words is also reflected in Indians' reputation for laconic replies to questions. So, for example, when an anthropologist asked what the Indians called

America before the Europeans came, "an Indian said, simply, 'Ours' " (from Deloria, *Custer Died*, 167).

68. The phrase is Milan Kundera's, from *The Book of Laughter and Forgetting.*

69. Quoted in Jimmie Durham, "Cowboys and . . . notes on art, literature, and American Indians in the modern American mind," in Annette Jaimes, ed., *The State of Native America: Genocide, Colonization, and Resistance* (Boston: South End Press, 1992), 423.

70. Miles, *Personal Recollections,* 241. Note the characteristic hypocrisy of the soldiers' reactions!

71. Robert J. Havighurst and Bernice L. Neugarten, *American Indian and White Children: A Socio-Psychological Investigation,* (Chicago: University of Chicago Press, 1955), 44. It should be noted, perhaps, that the Sioux children were mostly "mixed bloods," a fact noted by the researchers to explain other differences with the "pure bloods."

72. In a recent discussion about anthropology, students in a graduate seminar at Emory University argued heatedly over whether any group had a "right" to retain secrets, preventing access to outsiders, including anthropologists. One American student, angered by the suggestion that any person had such a "right" to secrecy, insisted that in all those cases, American scholars had an "equal right" to locate an informer within the closed group who would, for some consideration, tell the secrets to the outsider. This, in his mind, was a good thing: the accumulation of knowledge, he argued, demanded the use of such informers. Two African students, as well as most of the rest of the class, were enraged by his argument, accusing him of displaying "typical American arrogance." One American student compared such informers to Vichy collaborators. Two days later, a visiting folklorist joined the discussion, she, too, claiming that the use of informants (or those anthropologists have taken to naming "consultants") willing to violate the traditions of their group was justified in the name of "pure scholarship."

73. See Wendy Rose's discussion of Hopi secrets in, "The Great Pretenders: Further Reflections on White-shamanism," in Jaimes, ed., *State of Native America,* 403–22.

74. Deems Taylor, ed., *A Treasury of Stephen Foster* (New York: Random House, 1946), 135–36.

75. Hogan, in Swann and Krupat, *I Tell You Now,* 248.

76. The link between popular fiction and Indians is a venerable one, of course. In the recent past, there are two typical examples. In the 1920s and '30s, a series of historical romances was written by Robert W. Chambers. The books were advertised as shown in *The Mentor* (August 1928): 65. Tony Hillerman is the most popular of a number of writers producing detective novels in the present era. The gold spray, sold in bodegas across New York, probably stems from the plaster bust of an "Indian Chief" used in Santería ceremonies. (This is from an advertisement from the *New York Times Magazine.*) Michael Taussig showed me one such improbably pink plaster bust which he had found in Colombia. Miryam Yataco was the source of the information on Santería, and I am grateful.

77. Henry Wadsworth Longfellow, "The Song of Hiawatha," lines 133–39.

78. "Navaho" is, ironically, the choice of a Japanese car manufacturer. For a satirical attack on such car names see Randy Redroad, "Custer's Last Burger," *Native Nations* 1, no. 4

(June/July 1991): 20–22. The dispute over national sports teams' Indian names continues. Among the many essays written on the subject is Ward Churchill's recent "Crimes against Humanity," *Z Magazine* (March 1993): 43–47.

79. From the dust jacket of *Ramona*, published by Little, Brown & Co. (Boston, 1949). Jackson was motivated to write the novel by her earlier study of the Indian-White problem, *A Century of Dishonor*, published immediately before.

80. Vine Deloria recounts a joke about two men, one black, one Indian, sitting in a bar talking about the problems of their respective groups. The black man reviewed all of the progress his people had made over the past decade and tried to get the Indian inspired to start a similar movement of activism among the tribes. Finally the black man concluded, "Well, I guess you can't do much, there are so few of you." "Yes," said the Indian, "and there won't be very many of you if they decide to play cowboys and blacks." *Custer Died*, 163.

81. Thomas Jefferson would have opposed removal of the Creeks and others from the South. Indeed, in 1803 he wrote to the Creek agent, "In truth the ultimate point of rest and happiness for them is to let our settlements and theirs meet and blend together, to intermix, and become one people. Incorporating themselves with us as citizens of the United States, this is what the natural progress of things will, of course, bring on, and it will be better to promote than to retard it." Quoted in Julie Schimmel, "Inventing 'the Indian,' " in William H. Treuttner, ed., *The West as America: Reinterpreting Images of the Frontier, 1820–1920* (Washington, D.C.: Smithsonian Institution Press, 1991), 174.

82. This was far from the case with our peers, however. See Jane Thompkins's *West of Everything: The Inner Life of Westerns* (Oxford: Oxford University Press, 1992), which begins, in the startlingly self-confessional mode fashionable among one prominent school of literary scholars, "I make no secret of the fact: I love Westerns" (3). She makes what seems to me to be an overly simplified argument about males and westerns, but remains uninterested in the perpetuation and exacerbation of the problem of American racism.

83. Jenni Calder, *There Must Be a Lone Ranger*, 54, 48.

84. Jim Hitt, *The American West: From Fiction (1823–1976) into Film (1909–1986)* (Jefferson, N.C.: McFarland, 1990), 77, 78, 79.

85. Parks, *The Western Hero in Film and Television: Mass Media Mythology* (Ann Arbor: UMI Research Press, 1982), 99–100.

CHAPTER 4: DISLOCATIONS

1. *Borderlands/Frontera: The New Mestiza* (San Francisco: Aunt Lute Books, 1987).

2. Needless to say, perhaps, this theory or origins contradicts most Native American traditional beliefs regarding the origins of indigenous people, including that of traditional Nez Perce people, whose origins lie in Idaho where a hill marks the burial place of the heart of the monster tricked by coyote, and whose body and blood provided the matter from which many tribal people sprang. It should be noted, here, too, that for many Native people, this "land bridge" theory not only contradicts their own origin stories, but also provides European-Americans with the comforting myth that they were only the "last" in a series of waves of "outsiders" who "peopled" the "empty" continent. Thus Indian people were only "America's First Settlers," as one *National Geographic* article headlined. See Matthew W. Stir-

ling, "America's First Settlers, the Indians," in Stirling, ed., *National Geographic on Indians of the Americas* (Washington, D.C.: National Geographic Society, 1955), 13.

3. This is not to say, however, that Chinese-Americans had an easy time of it during the war. My grandmother used to tell a horror story about watching from her kitchen window in Los Angeles while a Chinese-American man was hit over the head by a milk-bottle-wielding white man hollering "You Japs don't belong here!" She had rushed outside to help the bleeding dazed passerby and noted that he was wearing a note pinned to his suit lapel: "I AM CHINESE." It had not sufficed to spare him the propaganda-induced rage of some California bigot.

4. How painstakingly Chinese immigrants had guarded themselves against white vigilantes only became clear when a Chinese-American friend offered to show a group of us "the real Chinatown." We saw for the first time "underground" Chinatown, where thousands of new immigrants lived in cellars dug beneath Chinatown streets, sleeping in eight-hour shifts in beds built one on top of another, sometimes four beds high. During this journey into an unexpected world, we encountered reinforcement for my father's Chinese-American friend's story of prejudice. Our mixed-race group included a girl visiting Palo Alto from a tiny, poverty-stricken rural town in California's Central Valley. Her parents were European-American tenant farmers, eking a precarious living out of an absentee owner's land. From the moment we set out in a car for San Francisco, this girl made it clear that she was terrified. Why? She was utterly convinced that Chinatown's streets were full of "yellow-eyed, cleaver-wielding murderers," each of whom longed to bury a blade in the pure neck of a white female. Hers was a stunning ignorance, an idiotic bigotry, horrifying to all us correct-thinking Palo Alto kids. However, we still did not understand that our attitudes were exceptional in racist California. A few years later, when I was working as a long-distance telephone operator, I met a Chinese-American woman who told me that in her early days as an operator in Chinatown, the local citizenry, justifiably fearful, refused to allow individual telephone numbers. Thus not only did each telephone require its own hole in the vast, room-sized switchboard, but every operator also had to be local and sufficiently knowledgeable about the community to be able to connect callers with the desired party, described only as "Mrs. Chin" or "Mr. Wang." Given the relatively few surnames shared by most descendants of Cantonese immigrants, operators were veritable encyclopedias of Chinatown's inhabitants. Numbering and the publication of numbers only began in the late 1950s.

5. And no wonder: the textbooks that raved a triumphalist history of European-Americans' manifest destiny had even less room for Asian-Americans than they did for the continent's indigenous peoples. The bleak and ugly history that was hidden from school children, however, included many many massacres of Chinese and Chinese-Americans in southern as well as northern California, events that continued through the "lynching" years of the 1950s and early '60s.

6. The house's previous owner, a member of Palo Alto's city council, had known that the fatal germs remained in her garden. She did not tell us this—or that she knew our house was scheduled to be demolished by the city to make way for an "expressway."

7. I was very lucky to be assigned a counselor, Frank Ratliff, who helped counter my

ignorance by choosing classes and arranging a schedule that allowed me to begin to catch up with my classmates who had been in Palo Alto's superb schools all their lives. Mr. Ratliff looked after me with painstaking and unusual care for two years. I have wondered since if the fact that he, too, led a closeted existence as a gay man made him particularly sensitive to my "closet"? Cultural displacement was both our lots in that town in those years. (I am grateful to discussions with John Howard, Jarrod Hayes, and Marvin Taylor for this comparison of America's various "closets.")

8. I shall never forget either the occasion or its cause. I had written a sugary account of a day spent dreaming of a cattle drive on the old Wrigley Ranch which had once comprised most of Catalina Island. Our summer Girl Scout Camp was on Catalina, and I had spent many hours wandering alone amid the wreckage of the ranch, sometimes sitting and writing my execrably romanticized free verse.

9. I owe the re-memory of these events and those days to Alfred Arteaga, a fellow native of Los Angeles who later participated in the Chicano politics that overwhelmed East Los Angeles long after we had moved north. What I remember that he doesn't, however, is how to dance the pachuco.

10. We found this poem in Ferlinghetti's paperback *A Coney Island of the Mind*, originally published by San Francisco's City Lights in 1958.

11. Stephen Bayne, "A Non-Answer to a Request for a Teacher's Guide to Indian Children," *Journal of American Indian Education* 10, no. 2 (January 1971): 32–33.

12. Vulgar psychoanalysis was in the process of becoming extremely trendy. Soon almost everyone believed in the unequivocal value of "telling everything" to a perfect stranger. Wendy Rose is not the only Indian commentator who has discussed the extent to which this European belief in the efficacy of "openness" and the unstinting collection of "information" is utterly antithetical to most Native American tradition. In addition to psychoanalytical explanations for my behavior, other friends offered European heritage theories, including that I was very "English" or even "Dutch" in my emotional restraint. Why I might be more "English" or "Dutch" than Indian I don't know—especially because I did not grow up in either country or with either culture.

13. The awful difficulty of writing this—a document that seems to me to be deeply self-aggrandizing, self-revealing—stems from this Indian tradition. To do it, one has to try to stay "white" throughout. At the same time, it seems a rare opportunity to try to explain—albeit once again—one of the reasons why so much misunderstanding exists between European and Native American.

14. In fact, it is likely that much more cultural crossing would have to occur before the Navajo young people began to articulate differences. A recent article about Dr. Lori Cupp, the Navajo nation's first woman surgeon, described the differences she experienced when working as a doctor in both the Anglo world (hyper-Anglo, as she did her training at Stanford) and that of her Navajo nation. The reporter notes that, among other things, Dr. Cupp "never did get used to looking directly at someone while conversing. 'It's still not comfortable, but I have to do it.'" See "The Navajo Nation's First Woman Surgeon: Parallel Realities and the Quest for Harmony," *TQS News* (March 1992): 5.

15. *New York Times,* June 1, 1994, B8.

16. At least as interpreted for us by the gurus of the period, Vance Packard, Nelson Algren, and the Beats.

17. This event produced a song we sang proudly, accompanied by our new guitars: Malvina Reynolds's "Did They Wash You Down the Stairs, Billy Boy, Billy Boy?"

18. I had a terrible argument with my mother when I informed her that I had no intention of joining a sorority at Berkeley, despite her family's "sorority-fraternity" credentials. In her defense, however, I should say that she soon came round to my way of thinking, acknowledging the horrors of such class- and race-determined living. Her father, on the other hand, a lifelong and determined bigot, refused to speak to me again after I informed him— during one of his very rare visits to us—that I scorned his absurd insistence that life in a sorority would protect me from "Jews and Negroes." On the other hand, I became much more acquainted with the idiocy of sorority life than I had intended when several of my closest friends from high school joined the same sorority and regularly invited the other rebel in our group and me to dinner at the sorority house. The girls of "Tri-Delt" were awed by us "politicals," not only by our demonstrating but also by the fact that we "got good grades" and cared about our minds. We found them—their pretensions, their ignorance, their utter preoccupation with their social lives, with clothes, with hair and makeup—hilarious.

19. In those pre–blue-jean days, when girls were forced to wear skirts to school, I owned two skirts and a few blouses and sweaters; my sister owned more because she could sew. We traded and shared—often with acrimony—through those Palo Alto months. But our clothes were never the objects of envy, even from our most modestly outfitted friends.

20. See Winerup, "In School," B8. Note the author's exoticization of the students' longing for home, here: "Navajos say . . ."

21. Our younger brother's experience suggests that this was the case. He moved to Palo Alto while still a vulnerable nine or ten. During his years there, our parents had an increasing income—not least because we sisters moved away from home—and he was thus the recipient of many more material objects than we had ever enjoyed. He regularly drove Mother's car (we had not even had driver's licenses in high school), wore expensive sheepskin jackets and correctly labeled shirts, trousers, and shoes, and indeed marked his assimilation by becoming senior class president at Palo Alto's second "rich kids high school," built after Anne and I had left town.

22. Ortiz, "American Indian Philosophy: Its Relation to the Modern World," in *Indian Voices: The First Convocation of American Indian Scholars* (San Francisco: Indian Historian Press, 1970), 13.

23. This turn of phrase comes from the Dutch term for those who "go underground" which is—not surprisingly, given the geography of the Netherlands—"onderduiver," or "diver under."

24. Lord Berkeley's poem was written in 1726 to celebrate the founding of a college in Bermuda meant to "convert and educate American Indians." Berkeley thought that indigenous people had the capacity to be "enlightened" by European teachers.

25. The book was a catalog accompanying, according to the title page, "the greatest photographic exhibition of all time," created by Steichen and held at the Museum of Modern Art in New York in 1955.

26. The prologue is unpaged. As I attack Carl Sandburg's inability to think beyond the mundane and banal, I cannot help but feel guilty. Richard Eberhardt once told me about an incident at a Library of Congress dinner when Robert Frost, assuredly the superior poet, cruelly made sport of Sandburg's versifying until the latter began to weep.

27. Needless to add, I hope, I do not find any plausibility in Rosenblatt's "explanation," or in the essentialist convictions of some that women's behavior is similarly outside history and therefore biologically different (usually better) than men's. Both letter and article are in the magazine on June 5, 1994, 16, 41. Rosenblatt's essay is titled "The Killer in the Next Tent: The Surreal Horror of the Rwanda Refugees." For a far more intelligent and sophisticated account of the events in Rwanda, see Alex De Waal's "The Genocidal State: Hutu Extremism and the Origins of the 'Final Solution' in Rwanda," *Times Literary Supplement* (July 1, 1994): 3–4.

28. The Middle Eastern world is strikingly absent from this text—and this in the same era when Kahlil Gibran's prophecies (though shunned by the higher of aesthetic brow) lay on every student desk, along with Fitzgerald's translation of Omar Khayam. . . . Or, in another dimension, when Israel was replicating another "universal," pushing Palestinians out of their homeland and sending them into exile.

29. Hobson, "The Rise of the White Shaman as a New Version of Cultural Imperialism," in Hobson, ed., *The Remembered Earth: An Anthology of Contemporary Native American Literature* (Albuquerque: University of New Mexico Press, 1979), 103.

30. From Duane Niatum, "Preface," in Niatum, ed., *Harper's Anthology of 20th Century Native American Poetry* (San Francisco: HarperSanFrancisco, 1988), xi. The European invaders had, of course, used the criterion of "land use," by which they meant agricultural use, to determine what land was "wilderness," available for seizure by those a European god had sent forth. Needless to add, perhaps, the clear evidence of extensive farming by indigenous people did not prevent either land theft or its justification by this "wilderness" designation.

31. This belief of the inhabitants of imperialist nations was, of course, not new. Adam Lively, in "Fisticuffs" (a review of Paul Gilroy's *The Black Atlantic* and *Small Acts*), quotes Richard Crashaw's 1646 poem, "On the Baptised Aethiopian," which described Christianization as washing "an Ethiopian white," or, better, discovering that beneath the black skin lay a "white soule." William Blake's "Little Black Boy" of 1789 was similar. (Although he does not mention it, Lively might have added Rudyard Kipling's "and despite his dusky hide / He was white, pure white inside / When he went to tend the wounded under fire"— Gunga Din of course.) Lively concludes that these various British writers agreed that "we are all equal under the skin, meaning we are all white under the skin." *London Review of Books* (March 10, 1994): 16.

32. Scholder, "Native Arts in America," *Indian Voices*, 221.

33. The two poems are found in Niatum, *Harper's Anthology*, 103–5, 270–75. There are dozens of such examples; these are merely the first I encountered consciously. Once again,

I owe thanks to Janet McAdams for her help with the Ray Young Bear reference. She has traced Emily Dickinson's influence on Young Bear's other work. See her review of *The Invisible Musician* in *American Indian Quarterly* (Winter 1994): 87–89.

34. How young we were, how callow, how innocent! But however precious all this sounds today, I think it is a fair representation of what most of us felt then.

35. *The Plague*, trans. by Stuart Gilbert (New York: Modern Library College Edition, 1948), 278.

36. Brandon, in a discussion with Mary Byler, Alfonso Ortiz, and D'Arcy McNickle, is quoted in *Indian Voices*, 40. His analysis, he said, was prompted by reading McNickle's much earlier analysis of *The Tempest*, in which he explored how freedom came to dominate Western thinking about "rights."

37. Ortiz, "American Indian Philosophy," *Indian Voices*, 12.

38. Ortiz, 71.

39. Quoted in Helen Addison Howard and Dan L. McGrath, *Chief Joseph of the Nez Perces* (Lincoln: University of Nebraska Press, 1941), 311. The speech is, needless to say as it must be abundantly obvious, a translation.

40. *Indian Voices*, 17–47. The exchanges quoted are on 44, 45.

41. Sheila Rowbotham, *Woman's Consciousness, Man's World* (Harmondsworth, England: Penguin, 1979 [1976]).

42. C. Robinson, Superintendent of Haskell in 1888, remarked that his charges returned home "like the swine return to their wallowing filth and barbarism." This telling statement is quoted in Michael C. Coleman, *American Indian Children at School, 1850–1930* (Jackson: University Press of Mississippi, 1993), 43.

43. Discussion of "Innovations in Education," *Indian Voices*, 145–46.

44. There were many figures important in this revision of the history of slavery, including John W. Blassingame, and Eugene Genovese. What allowed me to undertake to develop a new curriculum was the fact that I had taken my only U.S. history course from Lawrence Levine, then, and now, an important figure in the development and growth of the new history. At the same time, I graduated from Berkeley, with a minor in history, without ever having read W. E. B. Du Bois or C. L. R. James, not to mention hundreds of others. (Nor had I heard a single word about American Indians.)

45. It should be remembered that this was still the era when women—students or teachers—did not wear trousers to school. Dresses, and indeed rather stiff, professional dresses, were the standard to which we all conformed. That no teacher would even have considered wearing blue jeans to school suggests the extent of the horror effected by the leotard.

46. Quoted in *Self-Determination: A Program of Commitment*, Arizona Affiliated Tribes, Inc., Indian Community Action Project (May 1971), 116. As will become clear shortly, there were Native American leaders who had already begun to find solutions and to act without the confusion or hopelessness reflected here and that Jesse and I certainly both expressed. But we didn't know about their efforts until later.

47. Both views, together with those of others, are found in the very interesting report of the discussion "Native American Studies Programs," chaired by Roger Buffalohead, at the *Indian Voices* conference. Buffalohead's remark is on 171–72; Medicine's on 179.

48. See *Indian Voices*, 70–71.

49. Quoted in discussion, "American Indian Philosophy," *Indian Voices*, 31.

50. My friend Harriett Skye was there; I hope she one day tells her own, much more knowledgeable, story of these days.

51. See Beatrice Medicine's excellent discussion of the emergence of the Red Power movement in "Red Power: Real or Potential?" *Indian Voices*, 299–307. See also the very interesting discussion of the subject which is reported on 307–31. Wilson's remarks are on 313, 308, 317. Joe Sando's remark is on 318. See also the story of the FBI's war against youthful radicals in Ward Churchill and Jim Vander Wall, *Agents of Repression: The FBI's Secret Wars against the Black Panther Party and the American Indian Movement* (Boston: South End Press, 1990).

52. Kenneth R. Philp, ed., *Indian Self-Rule: First-Hand Accounts of Indian-White Relations from Roosevelt to Reagan* (Salt Lake City: Howe Brothers, 1986), 238.

53. Momaday, "The Man Made of Words," *Indian Voices*, 70–71.

54. See a recent account of these days, Adam Fortunate Eagle, *Alcatraz! Alcatraz! The Indian Occupation of 1969–1971* (Berkeley: Heyday Books, 1992).

55. See Kenneth R. Philp, ed., *Indian Self-Rule*. This is a particularly rich work because it quotes a variety of Native people's varied reactions to government policy shifts and new legislation.

56. There were, of course, dozens of other groups and efforts, including the American Indian Historical Society which brought together the first national meeting of Indian scholars at Princeton in 1970. The text of these meetings is found in *Indian Voices*.

57. Mander, *In the Absence of the Sacred* (San Francisco: Sierra Club Books, 1991), 4.

58. Brown, *Bury My Heart at Wounded Knee* (New York: Holt, Rinehart & Winston, 1970), 446.

59. See Shari Huhndorf, "Who Speaks? Black Elk, John Neihardt, and the Problem of Authorship in Native American Autobiography" (master's thesis, New York University, 1991). She is not the first to note Neihardt's use of Black Elk, as Arnold Krupat reminds me. See also Sallie McCluskey's "*Black Elk Speaks* and So Does John Neihardt," *Western American Literature* 4 (Winter 1972): 231–42, and Raymond J. DeMallie's "Introduction," *The Sixth Grandfather: Black Elk's Teachings Given to John G. Neihardt* (Lincoln: University of Nebraska Press, 1985). I had not been aware of these explorations of the work, however, until I first read Shari Huhndorf's thesis. The historian Dan Carter, a distant relation of Asa Carter, has exposed the *Little Tree* fraud in "The Transformation of a Klansman" in the *New York Times* (October 4, 1991). I am grateful to him for sending me this clipping and further information. Despite his efforts, however, the publisher of the book continues to promote the work as "autobiography." Bookstores, too, display the book in sections labeled "Native America."

60. Not everyone agrees that AIM's arrival was positive, or that Dick Wilson was a corrupt or bad tribal chairman. See varying and contradictory views of several Lakota people who were living at Pine Ridge at the time published in *Indian Country Today* (February 25, 1993).

61. Peltier remains in the federal penitentiary at Leavenworth, serving two consecutive life sentences. See the discussion of his corrupt arrest, trial, and imprisonment in

Matthiessen's *In the Spirit of Crazy Horse* (New York: Viking), originally published in 1983 and reissued in 1991 following a successful court battle against plaintiffs alleging libel, who had halted its distribution.

62. Floyd A. O'Neil, June K. Lyman, and Susan McKay, eds., *Wounded Knee 1973: A Personal Account* (Lincoln: University of Nebraska Press, 1991).

63. This information comes from Alvin Josephy's unjudgmental introduction to the book, primarily from xx and xxi.

64. O'Neil et al., 5.

65. O'Neil et al., 32, 47. He was very proud of this "bootlegging," as he called it in a fit of Eliot Ness worship, and remarked it over and over again as though he had risked something by stealing from the government to support the BIA side of the affair!

66. O'Neil et al., 92. Interestingly, such a view would be less common among "middle Americans" following the illegal assault on the Branch Davidian complex in Waco, Texas, in 1993. But in those days, everything the FBI—or, for that matter, the CIA—did was viewed by most of Richard Nixon's "silent majority" as both exciting and necessary for the protection of suburbia from creeping, "red" (!) hordes. Later in his narrative, after Clearwater has died, Lyman attempts to "excuse" his death by declaring him a "non-Indian" because he was "not enrolled in any tribe." This is ostensibly the reason that Dick Wilson's tribal government refuses to let him be buried at Pine Ridge. 124–25. (He was finally buried at Rosebud, in a "white man's cemetery.")

67. O'Neil et al., 106–7.

68. O'Neil et al., 42, 82.

69. O'Neil et al., 31. His sexism had its racist analogue: "There was the minister himself, a big, good-looking Lakota boy," 39. There are other infantilizations and objectifications of both Lakota men and women.

70. O'Neil et al., 102.

71. See, e.g., 127, where Ethel Merrival is described as a mixed-blood tribal activist, who is "definitely an AIM supporter and admits to being one."

72. O'Neil et al., xx. Josephy admits here that this is oversimplified, but Lyman never questions what must have been the standard BIA interpretation of militant activities.

73. O'Neil et al., 21.

74. O'Neil et al., 32.

75. O'Neil et al., 30. I know of one Canadian plane chartered by a friend of mine to take some occupiers out of Wounded Knee.

76. See "Review and Evaluation: Native American Studies Programs," *Indian Voices*, 164.

77. Discussion, *Indian Voices*, 316.

78. This was directed by Phil Perez, who made Davis's Upward Bound one of the most successful in the country. I still hear now and then from some of the students who graduated from the summer program and who then went on to complete university.

CHAPTER 5: BLOOD WARS

1. It should be noted that Frank La Peña was then in the process of creating a highly successful rival program at what was then Sacramento State College (now California State

University at Sacramento). Many Upward Bound students attended Davis in the summer, but then moved to Sacramento State for their university career.

2. David Risling was responsible for founding and developing a Native American Studies Program at the university. In 1974 his courses and programs were already extremely successful. Students had also founded the Tecumseh Center, a place where Native and some non-Native students could gather.

3. The prevalence of lies in this world goes almost completely unremarked. Those who believe what they are told are often viewed as fools or hopeless innocents. But the Native American students' dismay was not merely a result of their youth or inexperience. Adult Native American academics found themselves equally unable to accept that people's words did not reflect the truth in their hearts. During a 1970 discussion of Native American Studies programs, one anonymous speaker summarized the Indian experience of academia: "Write down everything the administration tells you, because we have had this problem too. A white person in certain cases will say something. Then, a month later, will say, well, 'I didn't really say that.' You have to write it down so they can't renege on you." *Indian Voices: the First Convocation of American Indian Scholars* (San Francisco: Indian Historian Press, 1970), 186. It is a lesson administrators at Emory University, and even more strikingly at New York University, have certainly taught me. But their behavior is even more complex than many Indians have understood. They don't think they've "lied"; rather, they tell and retell stories of various situations until they find the one that they need. This, then, becomes the one they believe. Native people, on the whole, find this even more bizarre and incomprehensible.

4. Indian students are not the only victims of this kind of political "over-preparation." A few years ago, a young African-American woman at Emory University found herself utterly baffled by the differences between what some militant African-American youth had predicted would be her experiences and her actual experiences of Emory. The result was that this young woman from rural Georgia set up horrifying racist incidents purportedly aimed at herself. It was several weeks, during which the campus overflowed with liberal breast-beating, before the real problems surfaced. Racism. . . .

5. The tutors in this program were all U.C. Davis students and all members of minority groups. There were a few Native American tutors, but most were African-American, Asian-American, or Latino(a). They were assigned by subject, not by race.

6. This was not her name, of course.

7. Polingaysi Qoyawayma (Elizabeth Q. White) described a similar antipathy to traditional Hopi rituals and ceremonies she learned from Mennonite missionaries. And unlike Maria, she was reared in Hopi, with her large family all around her. Her book, "as told to Vada F. Carlson," is suggestively titled *No Turning Back: A Hopi Indian Woman's Struggle to Live in Two Worlds* (Albuquerque: University of New Mexico Press, 1964).

8. "Maria" was at considerable risk for suicide. As the painful statistics make clear, Indian children adopted or fostered by non-Indian families have a suicide rate of 70 per 100,000, six times the rate for the general youth population of the United States. See Troy Johnson, "Depression, Despair, and Death: Indian Youth Suicide," in *Fiction International 20* [special focus: American Indian writers] (Fall 1991): 91–104.

9. She lived in a room that reminded me of mine in the Berkeley student hospital. It was very far from resembling a classic "psychiatric" hospital ward. For one thing, there were no psychotic, drugged patients wandering around in bathrobes. Everyone in the center was a student with one or another illness.

10. Maria's dilemma has a filmic echo in Arlene Bowman's highly controversial film *Navajo Talking Picture*. Bowman, too, was deliberately separated from her nation, though, unlike Maria, she was not separated from her Navajo parents.

11. The Native American students' program at Davis has developed procedures for coping with Native students' need to return home from time to time. The program, founded by David Risling and currently directed by Jack Forbes, has been so successful, in fact, that it graduates more of its matriculated Native students than any program in the United States. See a description of their efforts in Teri R. Bachman, "One Man's Promise," *UC Davis Magazine* 9, no. 1 (Fall 1991): 24–27.

12. Here, too, I am indebted to Harriett Skye for her comments.

13. Vizenor, *Crossbloods: Bone Courts, Bingo, and Other Reports* (Minneapolis: University of Minnesota Press, 1976), 159.

14. In McNickle, *Surrounded* (Albuquerque: University of New Mexico Press, 1976 [1936]), 192–93.

15. See Henry, "The American Indian in American History," *Indian Voices*, 155–56.

16. Henry, 245–46.

17. Henry, 245. It is striking to note that most of those who constantly remark—with dismay—their "white" appearance are women. Here again, it seems likely that the constant preoccupation with their looks that helps define females in western cultures gives "white-looking" Native women a greater self-consciousness than is articulated by their male counterparts.

18. Henry, 152.

19. Rose and Vizenor are cited above. Niatum's remark comes from his "Autobiographical Sketch," and Hogan's comment from her "The Two Lives," both in Brian Swann and Arnold Krupat, eds., *I Tell You Now*, 137, 243.

20. Momaday's views are found in *Indian Voices*, 70–71.

21. Betty Louise Bell has created a hilarious comedy of this situation in her novel, *Faces in the Moon* (Norman: University of Oklahoma Press, 1994). See 57–58.

22. Adrian Piper has outlined some problems of African-American "passing" in "Passing for White, Passing for Black," in *Transitions*, no. 58, 4–32.

23. Owens, *Wolfsong* (Albuquerque: West End Press, 1991), 127.

24. Sainte-Marie's song is published by Gypsy Boy Music. Floyd Westerman's, recorded by Red Crow Productions, was written by Westerman and Jimmy Curtis.

25. See M. Annette Jaimes, "Federal Indian Identification Policy: A Usurpation of Indigenous Sovereignty in North America," in Jaimes, ed., *State of Native America*, 123–38. As Jaimes points out, identifying Indians solely by blood means that soon either the "one drop" rule will have to be applied (as it is for African-Americans, whose experience of racism is the negative mirror image of that of Native people) or there will be few "real" Indians left in North America. In this sense, in other words, Indians *are* "vanishing"—despite the rise in self-identified "Native Americans" in recent U.S. censuses.

26. Quoted in Julie Schimmel, "Inventing 'The Indian,'" in William H. Truettner, ed., *The West as America: Reinterpreting Images of the Frontier, 1820–1920* (Washington, D.C.: Smithsonian Institution Press, 1991), 174.

27. Nott is quoted in Robert F. Berkhofer, Jr., *The White Man's Indian: Images of the American Indian from Columbus to the Present* (New York: Vintage Books, 1979), 58–59. Choctaws and Cherokees posed a problem for such racists. Both were part of the group known as the "Five Civilized Tribes" of the Southeastern United States. Note, here, the reference to Indians' ability to die stoically—and thus heroically.

28. Is there another academic discipline with such disgusting founding fathers? One wonders. Morgan is quoted in Robert E. Beider, *Science Encounters the Indian, 1820–1880: The Early Years of American Ethnology* (Norman: University of Oklahoma Press, 1986), 219, 220. Morgan was an important influence on the ideas of both Karl Marx and Friedrich Engels. The latter depended on Morgan's theories for his historical argument in *The Origins of the Family, Private Property, and the State*, a text much quoted by socialist-feminists of his era as well as those of the contemporary movement.

29. Beider, 223.

30. Quoted in Marc Swetlitz, "The Minds of Beavers and The Minds of Humans: National Suggestion, Natural Selection, and Experiment in the Work of Lewis Henry Morgan," in George W. Stocking, Jr., ed., *Bones, Bodies, Behavior: Essays on Biological Anthropology* (Madison: University of Wisconsin Press, 1988), 71.

31. These remarks come from *Systems of Consanguinity and Affinity*, published in 1871 by the Smithsonian Institution. Morgan is quoted by Beider, 230. It should be noted that there was *no* discussion of mixing African with Indian blood, although intermarriages between Native and African Americans was common. *Whiteness* was the desired result of all blood mixing.

32. See Karl May, *Winnetou*, trans. Michael Shaw (New York: Seabury, 1977 [1891]), 274, 275.

33. It is interesting to note here that other bourgeois societies, most openly Belgium, were similarly enamored of the notion that giving potentially rebellious "outs" some stake in owning property would quickly transform them into solid, bourgeois citizens. In Belgium's case, of course, the "outs" were industrial workers. This "Age of High Capitalism" was far more open about its ruling ideology than most capitalist societies are today.

34. Many have written about the tragic results of the Dawes Act, including Patricia Nelson Limerick, in *The Legacy of Conquest: The Unbroken Past of the American West* (New York: Norton, 1987), 195–99. Two books that recount the "allotting" work of the government-appointed anthropologist Alice Fletcher are E. Jane Gay, *With the Nez Perce: Alice Fletcher in the Field, 1889–92* (Lincoln: University of Nebraska Press, 1981), and Sheila Marks, *A Stranger in Her Native Land: Alice Fletcher and the American Indians* (Lincoln: University of Nebraska Press, 1988). As the title of the latter suggests, Fletcher was yet another in a long line of discontented easterners who found a "home" among western tribal people—whose land she helped other Americans steal!

35. The picture of this field is from the cover of a catalog selling shoes. The company is called "Foot-prints: The Birkenstock Store," and the catalog is from winter 1992. Interest-

ingly, the story of Lawrence told inside the front cover, "Kansas," by Jon Bell, recounts the town's historic relations to the Oregon Trail and the Underground Railroad but makes no mention of Haskell! The "before and after" Carlisle picture is reproduced in Hazel W. Hertzberg, *The Search for an American Indian Identity: Modern Pan-Indian Movements* (Syracuse: Syracuse University Press, 1971), 11. I should note here that Haskell has been transformed into one of the country's best Native-run colleges.

36. Erdrich, *Jacklight* (New York: Holt, Rinehart & Winston, 1984), 11.

37. Hogan, *Mean Spirit* (New York: Atheneum, 1990), 215.

38. J. E. Jenkins's report was written in 1906. He is quoted in Louis Owens, *Other Destinies: Understanding the American Indian Novel* (Norman: University of Oklahoma Press, 1992), 55.

39. Deloria, *Custer Died*, 83, 96–97.

40. See Retamar's rewriting of *The Tempest* from the point of view of Latin America in *Caliban and Other Essays*, trans. Edward Baker (Minneapolis: University of Minnesota Press, 1989). See also the work of Kamau Brathwaite, especially *Islands* (London: Oxford University Press, 1969), which Retamar cites.

41. See accounts of the effects of the IRA told by participants in Kenneth R. Philp, ed., *Indian Self-Rule*, 21–110. See also D'Arcy McNickle's reassessment of the effects of the act in "The Surfacing of Native Leadership," in Marc-Adelard Tremblay, ed., *Les Facettes de l'Identité Amérindienne* (Québec: Presses de l'Université Laval, 1976), 7–15.

42. Hogan, *Mean Spirit*, 238.

43. Quoted in Jenni Calder, *There Must Be a Lone Ranger: The American West in Film* (New York: McGraw-Hill, 1974), 54.

44. See Andrea Smith, "For All Those . . . ," an unpublished paper sent to me by Angela Gonzales. In a slightly altered form, it appears as "Opinion: The New Age Movement and Native Spirituality," *Indigenous Woman* 1, no. 1 (Spring 1991): 27–28.

45. Smith's "For All Those" is highly critical of the Lynn Andrews industry: *Jaguar Woman and the Wisdom of the Butterfly Tree* (San Francisco: Harper and Row, 1989). Estés's book, *Women Who Run With the Wolves: Myths and Stories of the Wild Woman Archetype* comes from New York (Ballantine Books) in 1991. Both cry out for satire.

CHAPTER 6: DE-COLONIZING THE [WOMEN'S] MIND

1. In "Introduction: Cartographies of Struggle," in Chandra Talpade Mohanty, Ann Russo, and Lourdes Torres, eds., *Third World Women and the Politics of Feminism* (Bloomington: Indiana University Press, 1991), 15. The author notes that feminist scholars have recently begun exploring the ways in which "the project of western colonialism" has utilized "this imperial [white] masculine self" as an "instrument of rule" as the "military, judiciary, and administrative service" are overwhelmingly masculine (16).

2. Such attitudes have a long history. As D'Arcy McNickle, who was a member of John Collier's staff, recalled, when Collier decided to transform governmental attitudes toward Indians in the course of the New Deal, one of his first acts was to hire anthropologists who could tell the objects of Collier's attentions all about themselves! See McNickle, "The Sur-

facing of Native Leadership," in Marc-Adelard Tremblay, ed., *Les Facettes de l'Identité Amerindienne* (Québec: Presses de l'Université Laval, 1976), 13. A few years later, when I first met Njeeri wa Ngũgĩ, I wished heartily that this Rosi Braidotti had been available to hear Njeeri's reaction to Alice Walker's lectures to Kenyan women about female infibulation.

3. From M. Annette Jaimes, ed., *State of Native America: Genocide, Colonization, and Resistance* (Boston: South End Press, 1992), 314. The remark was made at the University of Colorado during International Women's Week in April 1985.

4. Quoted in Ronnie Farley, "Women of the Native Struggle," *Native Peoples: The Arts and Lifeways* (Summer 1993): 28. The troupe, which now includes three sisters, Gloria and Muriel Miguel, and Lisa Mayo, continues their pioneering theatrical exploration of feminist politics, always from their unique and powerful point of view.

5. Again, much of my understanding of the complex difficulties facing indigenous women in Latin America comes from discussions with my friend Miryam Yataco.

6. "Seeking the Balance" in *Akwe:kon: A Journal of Indigenous Issues* 10, no. 2 (Summer 1993): 22.

7. White women in the East, when they did ride, sat—idiotically and uncomfortably— "sidesaddle." This riding position—like the corsets and high-heeled shoes dictated for "respectable women"—prevented them from all those physical feats of horsemanship that helped define manhood. Indian women, I should add, rode astride their horses. Where there were "women's saddles," as among Nez Perce people, they were quite similar to men's and in no way restricted Nez Perce women from hunting buffalo or riding to war if they chose.

8. William H. Truettner describes the painting, "Baptism of Pocahontas" by John Gadsby Chapman, which was chosen in 1836 to hang in the Capitol Rotunda: "Pocahontas stands foremost in the train of those wandering children of the forest who have at different times . . . been snatched from the fangs of a barbarous idolatry, to become lambs in the fold of the Divine Shepherd. She therefore appeals to our religious as well as our patriotic sympathies and is equally associated with the rise and progress of the Christian Church." In Truettner, ed., *The West as America: Reinterpreting Images of the Frontier, 1820–1920* (Washington D.C.: Smithsonian Institution Press, 1991), 71.

9. Quoted in Michael Kammen, *Mystic Chords of Memory: The Transformation of Tradition in American Culture* (Ithaca: Cornell University Press, 1991), 86. Kammen approves what he sees as "the genuine concern to preserve Native American traditions" shared by Morgan with others of his ilk.

10. Hobson, "The Rise of the White Shaman as a New Version of Cultural Imperialism," in *The Remembered Earth: An Anthology of Contemporary Native American Literature* (Albuquerque: University of New Mexico Press, 1979), 105.

11. David Banks Rogers, *Pre-Historic Man of the Santa Barbara Coast* (Santa Barbara: Santa Barbara Museum of Natural History, 1929), 12.

12. Quoted in an important article by Castillo, "Gender Status Decline, Resistance, and Accommodation among Female Neophytes in the Missions of California: A San Gabriel Case Study," in *American Indian Culture and Research Journal* 181 (1994): 71. This essay was published after I had nearly completed this book. But its information—as well as its skill-

ful use of feminist concepts and techniques—is sufficiently important to cite here, however briefly.

13. Rogers, *Pre-Historic Man*, 13.

14. Rogers, 21.

15. Betty Louise Bell, *Faces in the Moon* (Norman: University of Oklahoma Press, 1994).

16. Pattie's eyewitness account of the desperate servitude of California's Native people, whose every movement was controlled by priests, "matrons," or *alcaldes* (a group whose functions were similar to those of the kapos in Nazi concentration camps and included vicious beatings meted out to anyone not working at their assignments at a rate fast enough to suit the overseers), is in John and Laree Caughey, *Los Angeles: Biography of a City* (Berkeley: University of California Press, 1976), 87–88.

17. In Bell, "Slave Mart," 125.

18. Quoted in Bell, 127. See also John O. Pohlmann, "The Mission Romanticized," 240: "Shadows cast by the old missions have given California one of its oldest and most durable legends. The essence of the nostalgic tale is that the missions, founded by one of California's greatest heroes, Junipero Serra, were spectacularly successful in Christianizing and civilizing a mass of stupid, ignorant, and savage Indians. In the words of John Steven McGroarty . . . the Franciscan padres 'took an idle race and put it to work—a useless race that they made useful in the world, a naked race and they clothed it, a hungry race and they lifted it up into the great white glory of God.' "

19. Bell, 165.

20. Eyewitness, quoted in Bell, 165.

21. Bell, 22.

22. Nelson A. Miles, *Personal Recollections and Observations* (New York: Da Capo Press, 1969 [1896]), 72, 88, 213–14, 217.

23. Henry William Elson, *History of the United States of America* (New York: Macmillan, 1904), 30.

24. Elson, 31. It might be noted that some observers felt considerable admiration for Indian women *because* they seemed to do "all the work." George Catlin made such observations. When his claims spread through Europe—both through his published work and his visits—many working women boasted of the fact that America's Indian women were proof positive that women were equal at manual labor.

25. This same work includes an even more amazing flight of fancy in the chapter entitled "Explorations," where Elson describes a character he names "the Indian Queen," who "as a young and beautiful girl of eighteen years" led a "powerful Indian nation known as Cafachiqui, or Cofitachiqui," encountered by De Soto in what is now Georgia, in a scene reminiscent of those imagined by Cooper. She was, of course, "dressed with the highest art known to the red children of the forest." The Spaniards were "greatly impressed with her dignity, her modest, graceful manner, and her rare beauty." They exchanged gifts, the queen giving De Soto a "rich and costly" string of pearls! This is the same De Soto whom Elson insists "was not at heart a cruel man. He had no desire to wantonly slay the natives, he fully intended, however, to give battle whenever the Indians opposed his march." Just so we'll know he's a reasonable man, Elson adds the following in a footnote: "One con-

temporary writer, Oviedo, states that De Soto was fond of the sport of killing Indians." See Elson, 47–48, 43, 43 n.1.

26. See Estelle Reel, *Course of Study for the Indian Schools of the United States: Industrial and Literary* (Washington, D.C.: Government Printing Office, 1901).

27. My memories here *in no way* describe gender relations within exclusively Native politics, where women's activities were prominent and respected. Not only were contemporary women's roles quite different from those that shaped daily life outside exclusively Indian communities, but the traditional roles of women and men were very different within land-based Indian nations. Such roles, of course, as well as community attitudes toward both women and men, varied from nation to nation. Generalizations here concern only attitudes and behaviors I observed in these years of urban, mixed-blood politics. For a useful overview of Native American women's lives, see Rayna Green's *Women in American Indian Society* (New York: Chelsea House, 1992). See also *Indian* accounts of *Indian* politics in these years such as Adam Fortunate Eagle's *Alcatraz! Alcatraz! The Indian Occupation of 1969–1971* (Berkeley: Heyday Books, 1992), or the discussions of many issues in *Indian Voices*. This is not to romanticize gender relations in Indian America, either in the pre-conquest period or after. In some traditional societies, females were heavily oppressed. In others, they inhabited a more egalitarian world. In the contemporary world, many of the exploitative and oppressive behaviors—including wife beating—of "mainstream" American society occur on reservations. There are women-run efforts to counter these imports from European-American society as well. But it is important to distinguish between imported—and then imposed—European systems of gender relations and those which existed in indigenous societies through the period of the invasion(s).

28. These rather patronizing remarks are from Joan Weibel-Orlando, *Indian Country, L.A.* (Urbana: University of Illinois Press, 1991), 60.

29. See Beatrice Medicine, review of *Choteau Creek: A Sioux Remembrance*, by Joseph Iron Eyes Dudley (Lincoln: University of Nebraska Press, 1992) in *American Indian Culture and Research Journal* 17, no. 2 (1993): 199–201, which asserts, "Increasing numbers of Lakota/Dakota persons reading these latter books [*Lakota Woman* and *Madonna Swan*] are questioning their authenticity."

30. Crow Dog with Erdoes, *Lakota Woman* (New York: Grove Press, 1990), 174–76.

31. A friend who is a poet told me that in some Chicano circles, "piercing" is believed by many to be a rite of initiation into full manhood—despite the fact that he, like his "piercing" movement friends, does not come from a culture where Sun Dancing is practiced. I have had two unpleasant confrontations with non-Plains Indian men when I suggested that some Indian nations had other kinds of initiations, often non-gender specific. It is certainly the case, too, that young Native American men of all tribal heritages encounter considerable pressure to undertake this ritual before they are welcomed fully into pan-Indian political life.

32. Crow Dog, 244–45. Actually, although there is a widespread problem with wife battering all over Indian Country, the Lakota women I know would not accept such things passively. Still, this phenomenon of wife, and women, abuse is symptomatic of the results of cultural conquest. Communities that once controlled the antisocial behavior of individu-

als have broken down, and the mores and actions of the mainstream society, where masculinity (conveyed in a thousand different popular culture media) is measured primarily by violence, have taken over.

33. Recently, a sequel appeared, *Ohitika Woman*, by Mary Brave Bird with Richard Erdoes (New York: Grove Press, 1993). It will doubtless prove as controversial among Native Americans as the first book, which won the 1991 American Book Award.

34. See the story in *Indian Country Today*, August 25, 1993, 1, A2.

35. See note 29 above.

36. Gutiérrez has elsewhere published "Marriage and Seduction in Colonial New Mexico." In this scholarly article, his imagination seems to have gotten away from him. At one point he writes, "Sitting there in the pews at Santa Fe's San Miguel Church on Sunday, 17 April 1702, the visibly pregnant Juana Lujan heard the news. The announcement took her totally by surprise. How could Bentura be contracting marriage with Bernardina, she wondered?" See Antonio Rios-Bustamante, ed., *Regions of La Raza: Changing Interpretations of Mexican American Regional History and Culture* (Encino, Calif.: Floricanto Press, 1993), 143.

37. "When Jesus Came . . . Rewriting Pueblo History," *The Circle* (March 1994): 10. Evidence that previously ignored, oppressed people "resisted" those who oppressed them is *de rigueur* for left-wing labor historians—at least ever since Eric Hobsbawm showed us all how to do it. It is interesting to see how such methods and assumptions can be stood on their heads, however, in work such as this.

38. Quoted in "Let Us Now Combine Mythologies: The Theatrical Art of Tomson Highway," an interview with Robert Enright in *Border Crossings* (December 1992): 24. See also Scott Ellis's analysis of gender—and other things—in "Phantom Indians: Some Observations on Recent Cinema," in ibid., 42–45.

39. In *Indian Country Today*, July 21, 1993, A5.

40. See Avis Little Eagle, "Zimiga Works to Erase 'Squaw' Names from Maps," in *Indian Country Today*, n.d., 1994, B1, B3. This issue of the widespread use of the derogatory word "squaw" remains important in Indian Country.

41. I recall my surprise when a blue-eyed, light-skinned man in his thirties, clothed in blankets and fringed leather, his long blond hair tied in a ponytail, arrived at U.C. Davis's Tecumseh Center and was *immediately* welcomed as an Indian (tribeless), even by the Lakota bully who made my life so difficult. Had he been female, I am certain, his welcome would have been much more equivocal, his claim of Indian identity much more open to question.

42. See Jack D. Forbes, *Native Americans and Nixon: Presidential Politics and Minority Self-Determination, 1969–1972* (Native American Studies Center, University of California at Los Angeles, 1981).

43. I like to think this is sold as *"pain gras."*

CHAPTER 7: INDIAN FASHION

1. "Foreign Children," by Robert Louis Stevenson, appeared in his *A Child's Garden of Verses* (New York: Current Literature Publishing Co., 1909), 38. Its penultimate stanza reads: "You have curious things to eat / I am fed on proper meat; / You must dwell beyond the

foam, / But I am safe and live at home." Such sentiments, especially concerning food, strike any foreigner who has lived in England as hilarious.

2. See Peter C. T. Elsworth, "Tintin Searches for a U.S. Audience," *New York Times*, December 24, 1991, C16–C17, and "European 'Greens' Give Blackfeet Leader Clout with Oil Giant," *Indian Country Today* 12, no. 37 (March 10, 1993): 37.

3. *Indian Country Today*, August 18, 1993, A7.

4. The advertisement for this Steinbach nutcracker comes from a page torn out of a merchandise catalog by a student and given to me without reference except for the page number, 74. It is accompanied by three other "Indian" items: a "southwest watch," a "Plains Indian Mandella [*sic*] Wall Shield" (bringing "luck and happiness"), and "Sioux Sandals" of "Indian design." Oddly, the "mandella" claims that "no animal or bird has been killed for the fur or feathers in mandella."

5. "Business Hopes to Reunite Families with World War II Lakota Warriors Buried Overseas," *Indian Country Today*, January 5, 1994, A7.

6. When we first met, he began by announcing that his family was "Blank hundreds of years old." I had been in Cambridge long enough to know what I was being told, though his words were unnecessary. He had been an officer in the Grenadier Guards. He wore the seal ring on the little finger of his right hand that both amused this Californian and announced his status to the world. His accent, moreover, was pure "U," as were his various usages—"laughing like drains" was one. From our first meeting, it was absolutely clear that he came from Britain's upper classes and felt very lucky about it indeed.

7. It is really frustrating. When I pointed out the idiocy of women's roles in the film, numbers of people, including white feminists, insisted that Costner was only being accurate in depicting silent and utterly subservient Lakota women. Such is the power of the false history told of Native women!

8. David Lodge, review of David Bromwich, *Politics by Other Means: Higher Education and Group Thinking* (New Haven: Yale University Press, 1992) in *New York Times Book Review* (October 4, 1992): 7.

9. See Arnold Krupat's elegant and reasoned effort to sort out the hype from its deeply problematic roots in *Ethnocriticism: Ethnography, History, Literature* (Berkeley: University of California Press, 1992), 101–26.

10. Clifford, *Predicament* (Cambridge: Harvard University Press, 1988), 13.

11. Clifford, 213.

12. Victor Masayesva, a culture hero to most Native Americans, was asked to take part in such a "transformation" of the American Museum of the American Indian. Leaders from tribes whose artifacts—and bones—are held by the museum were invited to inspect the collections with an eye to identifying and assessing correctly materials long without proper identification. According to a friend who was then working at the Museum, Masayesva stalked the corridors following the curators who showed him, room by room, case by case all the Hopi materials. Unlike all the other Native American leaders who obligingly commented on what they were shown, Masayesva remained silent. At the end of the tour, the perplexed curator asked him why he had agreed to participate if he didn't intend to take

part in the exercise. He replied: "Oh, I came just to look—and to take note of all the things we are going to have to get back."

13. "I really love this Tlingit pin," one well-known anthropologist told me one day, pointing to a large, elaborately carved silver brooch pinned on her suit. "My husband bought it for me because I used them in my most recent work."

14. Clifford, "Objects and Selves—An Afterword," in George W. Stocking, Jr., *Objects and Others: Essays on Museums and Material Culture*, vol. 3, *History of Anthropology* (Madison: University of Wisconsin Press, 1985), 236, 238.

15. Deloria, *Custer Died*, 83.

16. Harold von Kursk, "On the Sun King's Wild Frontier," *The European* (March 18–21, 1993): 22.

17. This film, based on a novel of the same name by Brian Moore (New York, 1985) was much touted as being one of the first films to portray Indians "as they really were"—cruel, mysterious, dirty, and so on. But Moore writes in the introduction to his novel that his source of information was a collection of letters written by Jesuit missionaries to their superiors in France. Here is what he learned from reading these letters: "To succeed, they had to learn the 'Savages'' often scatological tongues and study their religious and tribal customs. These letters, the only real [*sic*] record of the early Indians of North America, introduce us to a people who bear little relationship to the 'Red Indians' of fiction and folklore. The Huron, Iroquois, and Algonkin were a [*sic*] handsome, brave, incredibly cruel people who, at that early stage [*sic*] were in no way dependent on the white man, and, in fact, judged him to be their physical and mental inferior. They were warlike; they practiced ritual cannibalism and, for reasons of religion, subjected their enemies to prolonged and unbearable tortures" (viii–ix). This information, of course, comes from the pens of men whose compatriots were busily slaughtering each other—in "unspeakably cruel ways"—also "for reasons of religion." "Ethnocentrism" was not born in the nineteenth century!

18. "The Arts," *New York Times*, March 18, 1993.

19. Gerald Vizenor, *Crossbloods*, 246.

20. The title of an essay by Sherman Alexie in the *New York Times Magazine* (October 4, 1992): 30–31.

21. From *The Realist*, sent by a student in the summer of 1992.

22. One critique of men's movement efforts to "seize the warrior inside" which details many of the behaviors of this group is by Philomena Mariani, " 'God Is a Man,' " in Mariani, ed., *Critical Fictions: The Politics of Imaginative Writing* (Seattle: Bay Press, 1991), 3–12.

23. Alexie, "White Men," 30.

24. Thomas is quoted in Stan Steiner, *The New Indians*, 154. He continues, "This difference between living in nature and the conquest of nature is the difference between enjoying life and consuming life."

25. From Swann and Krupat, *I Tell You Now*, 165–66.

26. Allin is quoted in Michael Kammen, *Mystic Chords of Memory: The Transformation of Tradition in American Culture* (Ithaca: Cornell University Press, 1991), 187. Clinton's Oval

Office decor is described in Maureen Dowd, "The 'New' Oval Office: Slight Changes, But Tidier," in the *New York Times*, September 3, 1993, A15.

27. See Kammen, *Mystic Chords*, 87.

28. Ariel Dorfman, *The Empire's Old Clothes: What the Lone Ranger, Babar, and Other Innocent Heroes Do to Our Minds* (New York: Pantheon, 1983), 29–30.

29. See the *New Yorker* 19, no. 27 (August 23, 1993): 166.

30. This ad appeared in the *New York Times* on October 31, 1993.

31. This clipping was given to me by a student without attribution. It looks as though it might have come from the *Atlanta Constitution*, perhaps during the winter of 1991–92.

32. The doll is, or was, available from the Danbury Mint in Norwalk, Connecticut.

33. Both toys are described in *Indian Country Today*, August 25, 1993, 1, A2. One article is by Carol Mellor, "Exhibit Exposes Stereotypes," and describes a collection of stereotype-perpetuating artifacts made by Tom Huff. The Ninja Turtle is his. The second story is by Anne-Marie Clifford and is titled, "Newly Released Native American Barbie Wears Mixed Tribal Regalia."

34. See Lora J. Finnegan, "Making History Again on the Oregon Trail," *Sunset Magazine* (June 1993): 84–85.

35. Niatum, "Autobiographical Sketch," in Swann and Krupat, *I Tell You Now*, 137.

36. Just to underscore how problematic all this is, Stephen Wall argues, in "Grandpa Was One-Tenth Cherokee," IV:VIII (August 1992): 16–17, that the three requirements are membership in a tribe, federal recognition of one-fourth blood, and "self-identification." There are numerous other examples—and a wide variety of records certifying that those not enrolled in any tribe do, indeed, possess "Indian blood."

37. Smith, *Indigenous Woman*, 53. He continues: "I'm sometimes asked . . . 'Are you a full blood?' From people who've never asked Black people, lightskinned or otherwise, 'How much Black are you?' or 'Are you a fullblood Black?' "

38. See a fuller discussion of this and related issues in Robin Cembalest, "Native America Art: Pride and Prejudice," *ArtNews* 91, no. 2 (February 1992): 86–91. See also Ward Churchill, "I'm Nobody's Pet Poodle," *Z Magazine* (February 1992): 68–72. This is the position shared by everyone published in Jaimes, ed., *State of Native America*, for example, and might be said to characterize the political left wing among Native people.

39. See Paige St. John, "American Indians Hurt by College Admissions Abuses," *Detroit News*, April 12, 1992, 1. I am grateful to Angela Gonzales for sending me these articles and for discussing the problem of identity among American college students of her generation.

40. Examples in St. John, "American Indians Hurt," *Detroit News*, 13A. Recently, interviewing prospective Native American graduate students for a program at New York University, I encountered a young woman from southern California who had checked "Native American" in the racial identity box on her application. Meeting me in my capacity as advisor to the Native American students' group, she immediately confessed, "My father says I should tell you that my Indian identity comes from a great-great grandmother we think was Cherokee, so I don't really have much connection with Indians except I am really interested in exploring that part of my background. We also think there may have been some Indian on the other side of the family. He told me I should tell you this because I don't look

Indian and he didn't want me to have any problems." I was nonplussed, never having encountered this phenomenon of students claiming this identity on university application forms in the early years of my work in Native American education programs. Would such a student check "African-American," and then confess to a startled faculty advisor to African-American students that the family thought there "might be" an African-American great-great grandmother? Would such a young women blather on about her interest in exploring her black identity?

41. I am grateful to several people for discussions of race and the African-American community. They include Rainier Spencer, Akinyele Umoja, Makungu Akinyela, Patricia J. Williams (who explores this and many other facets of American life in *The Alchemy of Race and Rights: Diary of a Law Professor* [Cambridge: Harvard University Press, 1991]), and Adrian Piper, some of whose work is cited above.

42. Waukena Cuyjet-Kapsch has written a very interesting master's essay on this topic. She was exploring her own ancestry, which mixes Delaware Indian with African and European. This "mix" kept her family isolated from all other racial groups—at least until Waukena joined our talking circle.

43. In addition to Adrian Piper's "Passing," see Peter Noel, "Cutting on the Bias," *Village Voice*, cited above.

44. Quoted in *Detroit News*, 2. But what is "the Native American voice"? This issue, like all the others, is also complicated. Much hostility exists, for example, between Native Americans from reservations—or at least from fairly cohesive rural Indian communities—and those whose lives have been spent in cities. Further complications arise from conflicts between those of various tribal descent: some Anishnaabeg refer to members of the eastern band of Cherokees (where one-thirty-second blood qualifies people for membership) as "white Indians." Those of mixed African-American and Indian blood encounter other variations on this theme of race. Then, too, there are many figures prominent in Indian affairs in some cities whose Native American background is of Latin American origin. They may or may not come from what North American Native people recognize as "Indian" communities; some, moreover, speak Native languages and some do not.

CHAPTER 8: 'TIL INDIAN VOICES WAKE US . . .

1. Quoted in Lewis Nkosi, "Ironies of Exile: Post-Colonial Homelessness and the Anti-Climax of Return," *Times Literary Supplement* (April 1, 1994).

2. Quoted in Nkosi.

3. From the oral qualifying exams of Shari Huhndorf, Department of Comparative Literature, New York University, April 10, 1994.

4. Quoted in Lucy Lippard, ed., *Partial Recall* (New York: New Press, 1992), 26.

5. Lippard, 27.

6. Richard Sieburth claimed his authority to speak about Native America from an acquaintance with one of Arnold Krupat's critical studies of Native American writing. He admitted, however, that he had never known that "real Native Americans" wrote criticism. Indeed, it came as a surprise to him to learn that "real Indians" wrote at all; he evidently

believed that those few who had not vanished when everyone said they did were likely only to produce oral works—"told-tos," with the "real" author an (alienated) anthropologist.

7. Woody Guthrie's celebration of this dam was sung by that important troubador of our time, Country Joe. "Roll on, Columbia roll on . . ." My friends sang along . . . then.

8. *Barabajan Poems 1492–1992* (New York: Savacou North, 1993), 19.

9. *News from Indian Country* 8, no. 12 (June 1994): 9.

10. Letter in *Indian Country Today*, September 15, 1993, A6.

11. *News from Indian Country* 8, no. 12 (June 1994): 4.

12. Of course this is only one kind of fraud. This generation of young people, the "post-60s" group, is renowned for dubious resumes and invented *curricula vitae*. When universities take the time to check claims for degrees, for publications, for honors, officials are often startled to discover the extent of the lying. But usually no one checks.

13. *Indian Country Today*, May 19, 1993, A1, A2.

14. *Indian Country Today*, September 15, 1993.

15. Rita J. Simon and Howard Altstein, *Transracial Adoption: A Follow-Up* (Lexington, Mass.: Lexington Books, 1981), 68.

16. See *News from Indian Country* 8, no. 12 (June 1994): 2.

INDEX

Abnaki, 193
Acoma Pueblo, 45
Acosta, José de, 54
Acquash, Anna Mae Pictou, 46–47
Adventures of Tom Sawyer, The (Twain), 58–59
Advertising and Indians, 82, 194–95, 200, 223n20, 248n4
Affirmative action, 115, 155, 174–75, 210
Africa, 106, 122, 158
African-Americans, 109, 117, 121–22, 123, 199, 240n4; and Indian identity, 226n3, 251nn42, 44; and race 251n41
Alcatraz Island, 126, 130, 205
Alexie, Sherman, 189, 190, 219n41
Allen, Paula Gunn, 7, 173
Allitt, Patrick, 56
Allotment, 5, 126, 242n34. *See also* Dawes Severalty Act (1887)
American Historical Association, 172, 238n56
American Indian Movement (AIM), 121, 131–35, 168–71, 174, 180, 205, 238n60
American Indian Studies programs, 126–27, 239n1, 240n2, 241n11
Andean peoples, 107, 205
Andrews, Lynn, 156, 243n45
Anishnaabeg, 185
Anthropologists, 37–40, 41, 45–46, 99, 102, 123, 149, 167, 186–87, 230n67, 243n2, 249n13
Anthropology, 16, 27, 28, 32, 35, 36, 37, 39, 175–76, 187, 204–5, 231n72; and bone collections, 222nn9, 12, 242n28
Anzaldúa, Gloria, 91
Apaches, 9, 10, 14, 22, 47, 159–60, 206; Winnetou as, 28, 150
Apess, William, 3–4, 129, 216n9
Arapahos, 39
Archaeologists, 24, 31, 32, 33
Arctic peoples, 107, 109
Arteaga, Alfred, 234n9
Artichoker, Karen, 172
Art historians, 42

Art market, 29, 30, 41–44, 196–97, 211. *See also* Price, Sally
Asian-Americans, 109, 117, 199; racism against, 233n3n4
Asians, 106, 117
Assimilation, 1, 10, 17–18, 19, 53–54, 79–80, 154, 197
Association on American Indian Affairs, 34, 215n5
Authenticity, 48–49, 177, 187–89, 196–201, 208; of art objects, 43; of *Black Elk Speaks*, 131; of *Lakota Woman*, 171
Autobiography, 2–4
Autry, Gene, 71

Babbitt (Lewis), 101–2
Badger Two-Medicine, 178–79
Bahr, Don, 40
Bancroft, H. H., 217n20
Banks, Lynn Reid, 66
Baudelaire, Charles, 203
Bear Claw, Dean Curtis, 205, 206
Beautiful and the Dangerous, The (Tedlock), 46, 186
Begay, Kelly, 209–210, 211
Beider, Robert E., 150
Belgium, 176, 178–79, 242n33
Bell, Betty Louise, 164, 241n21
Bell, Horace, 164
Benedict, Ruth, 102
Benjamin, Walter, 29, 40, 105
Berkeley, Calif., 102, 116–17, 135, 142
Billington, Ray Allen, 99
Birch, John, Society, 123
Bison, Doug, 14, 15, 84
Black Elk Speaks, 130–31, 238n59
Blackfeet, 120, 154, 178
Black Hawk, 67–68
Black Panther Party, 128, 133, 181
Black Robe, 188, 249n17
Blatchford, Herb, 116

Stone, Oliver, 170
Straight Arrow, 74–81, 167, 230n61
Striker, Fran, 69, 71
Sun Dance, 169–70; and masculinity, 246n31
Sunset Magazine, 196
Surrounded, The (McNickle), 145
Swann, Brian, 216n8

Talking God (Hillerman), 28
Tallchief, Maria, 82
Tashtego *(Moby-Dick)*, 58
Tasmania, 47
Taussig, Michael, 231n76
Tedlock, Barbara, 46, 186
Tedlock, Dennis, 46
Television, Indians in, 188–89
Termination of tribal status, 155
Thom, Mel, 45
Thomas, Robert, 45, 190
Thunderheart, 188
Tintin, 178–79
Tonto, 10, 68–72, 73, 74, 167, 228n37; "Tonto-talk," 52, 55, 56, 57, 64, 67, 68, 69, 73, 76, 108, 226n4. *See also* Lone Ranger
Torquemada, Juan de, 53
Trail of Broken Treaties (1972), 121, 205
Trail of Tears (1838), 86, 185
Trendle, George, 70, 71
Tribal colleges, 174, 189
Trinity Hall, Cambridge, 183
Trudell, John, 172
Truettner, William H., 244n8
"'Truganinny" (Rose), 47
Tubman, Harriet, 121
Tule River Reservation (Calif.), 77
Turner, John, 95, 96, 97, 103
Turner Television Network, 171
Tuscaroras, 185
Twain, Mark, 57, 58–59, 155, 216n10
Two Rode Together, 87–88

Umatilla Indian Reservation (Ore.), 196, 217n21
Unforgiven, The, 88–90
Universals, 44, 103–10; and race, 236n31
University of California, Berkeley, 35, 57, 100, 103, 110, 111, 117; anthropology museum, 175

University of California, Davis, 135, 137–46, 240n5
Upward Bound, 135, 136, 175, 205, 239n78

Valens, Ritchie, 96
Vietnam, 34, 110–11, 116
Vizenor, Gerald, 3–4, 28, 44, 145, 147, 189, 198, 209, 216n9, 219n36, 223n32

Wallowa band, 8, 10, 112, 214, 218n25
Wanatee, Don, 127
"Wannabes," 147–48, 156, 174, 179–80, 198–200, 210–11, 250n40; Cherokee ancestors of, 147, 156; and Indian names, 230n60
War on Poverty, 31, 120–22, 127, 135–36, 144
Watt, James, 174
Westerman, Floyd, 148
Westerns, 85, 232n82, 248n7
When Jesus Came, the Corn Mothers Went Away (Gutiérrez), 171–72
"White Shamanism," 162, 179–81
Widmark, Richard, 87–88
Wilder, Laura Ingalls, 59–63
Wilkinson, Gerald, 129
Williams, Patricia, 215n6, 251n41
Wilson, Billie, 143
Wilson, Dick, 128
Winnetou, 28–29, 150–51
Wolfsong (Owens), 148
Women of All Red Nations, 128, 167
Wounded Knee (1890), 34, 161; Black Elk and, 131
Wounded Knee (1973), 46, 131–35, 168, 205, 223n33, 238n60
Wright, Robin K., 41
Wyandots, 67

Yakimas, 10
Yataco, Miryam, 39, 205, 206, 244n5
Yellowbank, James, 31
Young Bear, Ray, 236n33
Yumans, 40

Zimiga, Arthur, 173, 247n40
Zunigha, Curtis, 34
Zunis, 46, 79–80, 186